This edition is reprinted by arrangement with
Alfred A. Knopf, Inc.

A portion of this book appeared in the June 1970
issue of *Natural History Magazine*. © *Natural
History Magazine*, June 1970.

The University of Chicago Press, Chicago 60637

Library of Congress Cataloging in Publication Data

Schaller, George B.
  Golden shadows, flying hooves.

  Reprint. Originally published: New York: Knopf,
1973.
    1. Lions — Behavior. 2. Natural history —
Tanzania — Serengeti Plain. 3. Serengeti Plain
(Tanzania) 4. Mammals — Behavior.
5. Mammals — Tanzania — Serengeti Plain —
Behavior.   I. Title.
[QL737.C23S29   1983]   599.74'428   82-23731
ISBN 0-226-73650-4

GOLDEN SHADOWS,
FLYING HOOVES

GOLDEN SHADOWS, FLYING HOOVES

With a new Afterword

George B. Schaller

The University of Chicago Press

TO

Bernhard Grzimek

Acknowledgments

My study depended on the generous assistance of several institutions and many individuals. The National Science Foundation and New York Zoological Society provided the funds for the project, and the Institute for Research in Animal Behavior of the New York Zoological Society and Rockefeller University sponsored it. The National Geographic Society assisted with photography. The trustees of the Tanzania National Parks permitted me to do research in the Serengeti, where I received the cooperation of the Serengeti Research Institute. Many of the persons who helped me in East Africa are mentioned in the text, but I would like to extend my special gratitude to John Owen, former director of the Tanzania National Parks, who invited me to study lions, and to Myles Turner, Alan and Joan Root, Hans Kruuk, Stephen Makacha, Rüdiger Sachs, Tony Sinclair, Howard and Dorothy Baldwin, Hugh Lamprey, William Holz, Hubert and Anneke Braun, and Charles Guggisberg for help in various ways. At my home institutions the late Fairfield Osborn, William Conway, Donald Griffin, and Peter Marler provided assistance. Richard Keane made the excellent lion sketches. Gordon Lowther was a stimulating field companion during our week of living the life of early hominids.

My wife, Kay, not only helped with the field work, spending many hours watching predators, but also schooled our sons, managed our home, and provided the stability and love without which the project would have lacked some of its essential ingredients.

The University of Chicago Press kindly permitted me to quote from and reproduce illustrative material from my scientific report *The Serengeti Lion*. Permission to excerpt some paragraphs from an article on the cheetah was granted by *Natural History* magazine.

Gordon Lowther and John Pfeiffer read and commented on the last chapter.

Assistance from the New York Zoological Society and a fellowship from the John Simon Guggenheim Memorial Foundation enabled me to spend time in writing this book.

Contents

Illustrations

xi

Introduction

The day after we arrived at Seronera, headquarters of the
Serengeti National Park, I found two lionesses at the edge of
the plains. They sat in the golden grass, their eyes fixed on a
herd of Thomson's gazelle, their bodies straining toward the
advancing animals as if willing them to come closer. As the
herd continued its approach along a well-worn trail, oblivious
to danger, the lionesses parted, one to the right, the other to
the left. Their tawny bodies became but wisps of wind in the
grass as they stalked into position to attack. Closer, closer
came the gazelle until they were between the lionesses. Suddenly a breeze stirred, the gazelle scented the lions and
scattered with wild leaps and twists, each racing blindly
through the grass ignorant as to where the enemy lurked.
One gazelle rushed toward a concealed lioness, and, spotting
the motionless form too late, it leaped high in a desperate
attempt to escape. But with exquisite timing the lioness
reached up and with gleaming agate claws plucked the
animal from the air. I took notes throughout the incident—
the size of the gazelle herd, wind direction, height of vegeta-

tion, the movement patterns of the lionesses, the age and sex of the victim and many of the other small facts that I hoped would ultimately contribute to an understanding of lion predation. The long, slow task of collecting information had begun.

When John Owen asked me to study the lions of the Serengeti, I was delighted to take on the task for several reasons. One was the lion itself—its beauty, its aura of barely contained power. Man feels an emotional kinship to these predators even though he is filled with primordial apprehension by their presence. When visiting a national park, he spends his time not with the giraffe, impala, or zebra but with the lion and leopard, vicariously exulting in the strength of these animals from the safety of a vehicle. This contagion probably reflects man's past as a hunter. Though a primate by inheritance, man has been a predator for several million years, and his whole outlook on life has been influenced by this. I knew that I would enjoy my months and years with the great cats, an important consideration, for even science may become tedious if the subject of the study does not provide both sensual pleasure and a touch of the mysterious.

There was also the challenge of studying the lion's life, of unraveling the intricacies of its social system and of clarifying the effects of natural forces on its population. Little was known about lions when I began to study them. In the past, contacts between man and lion were largely based on enmity, resulting in the extermination of the cat over much of its former range. Within historic times this range stretched from Greece through the Middle East to India, as well as over most of Africa. In the ninth century B.C. an Assyrian king boasted: "By my stretched-out arm and through my furious courage, 15 mighty lions from the mountains and the woods in my hand I captured, and 50 lion cubs I carried away." The last lions in that part of the world vanished in about 1935. When Xerxes, King of Persia, marched through Greece in 480 B.C. his baggage camels were attacked by lions; by 300 B.C. Aristotle thought them rare, and by 100 A.D. they were gone from that country. Today only about 150 Asiatic lions survive in the wild, all in the Gir Sanctuary of Gujarat State in India. The lions of North Africa fared no better, being first pushed toward extinction by the Romans, who imported thousands for slaughter in their arenas. Julius Caesar once consecrated his forum with the killing of four hundred lions. By the 1920's the North African lion had vanished. But the species survived in the vast savannas south of the Sahara, in part because Europeans and other foreigners with their mania for killing that which is neither good to eat nor otherwise useful did not penetrate many areas until the turn of this century. The first European visited the Serengeti in 1892, and in 1920 the first motorized tourist reached Seronera. Soon after that date, in 1925, Stewart Edward White arrived there with several friends to annihilate fifty-one lions. Fortunately some nine hundred square miles around Seronera were designated as a game reserve in 1929 and all lion hunting within that area was stopped in 1937.

The many early accounts of the lion's habits are superficial and often erroneous, which is not surprising when it is remembered that studies at that time were generally carried out along the sights of a rifle. A few books, such as those by James Stevenson-Hamilton and by George and Joy Adamson, contain interesting anecdotes and life history notes but none provide a comprehensive picture of lion biology. The first scientist to devote himself to lions was Charles Guggisberg, who has watched these cats intermittently in Nairobi National Park since 1953, and his book *Simba*, published in 1961, is a very valuable summary not only of his own work, but also of the early literature. A few short accounts on food habits, play, and territorial behavior were also available, but I had an opportunity as no one before to enter into the lion's world.

Information about lions and other cats is essential if

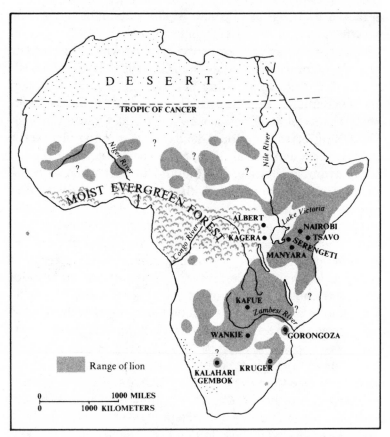

The approximate present distribution of the lion in
Africa. The locations of important wildlife reserves are
also indicated. (Prepared with the assistance of
C. A. W. Guggisberg.)

these magnificent animals are to be preserved. Shot for sport
or merely because man has a deep-seated fear of them,
trapped and poisoned for the fur trade or because they kill
wild and domestic animals, all big cats have declined drastically in recent years. Man and these large predators seem
unable to coexist. As the human population continues to increase, only national parks and reserves will ultimately re-

main as samples of wilderness where we can relive our past by meeting the predators that were once our competitors and where we can feel the timelessness and richness of experience that only a natural environment can provide. To preserve a species, especially one that lives confined in a relatively small park, requires detailed knowledge about its extent of travel, its rate of reproduction, its food habits, and so forth. Answers to these problems are particularly important with respect to predators, for their habit of killing prey has engendered much revulsion and false sentiment on the part of man. Several visitors to the Serengeti were so outraged at seeing lions capture a wildebeest and pull it down that they drove the cats away. Unfortunately the predator's role in the natural community is still widely misunderstood. Mountain lions and wolves were systematically destroyed in Yellowstone National Park until the 1930's and even today these predators are harassed on state and federal lands in the United States; lions and cheetah, among others, were shot in the Kruger National Park of South Africa until the 1960's on the assumption that this would benefit the wildlife.

When a predator kills, there is obviously one less animal. But the loss of an individual may not influence a prey population adversely. Was the killed animal sick, old, or in other ways a surplus individual, soon doomed to die anyway, whose loss actually had little effect on the population as a whole? Our sympathies lie with the individual, yet nature is concerned with the population, working on the democratic principle of the greatest good for the greatest number. To find out how lions affected the prey in the Serengeti was my main task. No creature stands alone, and the scope of the study soon broadened to include not only the lion's predatory associates such as the hunting dog, but also the array of prey species on which the carnivores depend for survival.

To keep the animal and plant communities balanced and fit, some form of management may ultimately be necessary in all national parks. Only by having available a substantial body of facts will it be possible to do so intelligently. There is also the unspoken assumption that only through knowledge can we argue for the rights of predators, pointing out the economic, scientific, and aesthetic reasons for preserving them. We should not have to place a value on animals to whom values are unknown; we should be able to guarantee their freedom solely for their own sake, but man's thinking has only just begun to approach such a level of morality. These, then, were among the justifications for my study. However, in an age when man is so intent on modifying his environment that he is in danger of losing the last remnants of wilderness, I feel that work devoted to the preservation of animals and plants requires no justification. Indeed, to watch animals satisfies an urge to explore past the limits of knowledge and to contemplate life in all its diversity; it teaches sympathy and humility; and it strengthens man's feeling of belonging to the natural world.

I find it difficult to separate scientific reasons for the study from personal ones. Many people seem content with the anonymity of modern life, subverting themselves by restlessly searching for ever more powerful stimuli—louder noises, faster cars—until their inner selves shrivel, their existence loses awareness, while their bodies race on. Others abhor life in the city. They strive to return to the elemental complexity of the wilderness; they seek the touch of earth and wind and rock. I am of the latter type, and throughout my life I have tried to heed the ancient call that demands contact with nature, foregoing security for pleasure. I prefer a life of quiet, of consciousness with beauty around me, a life where my scientific endeavors are enriched by a sense of unity with the animals I study. A Buddhist poet in India wrote:

> The fowl in the coop has food but will soon
> be boiled in the pot.
> No provisions are given to the wild crane but
> the heavens and the earth are his.

Watching animals alone, without fear of interruption, for hour after hour, one feels the senses take on a new dimension—they become more acute in discerning small nuances of behavior. Such intimacy adds immeasurably to an understanding of animals. These animals then become individuals, and with that awareness a study moves to its most satisfying and sensitive pitch. For having become acquaintances, the animals evolve into discrete memories on which I can draw long after I have moved on to other tasks. Solitude provokes reflection and a study becomes a quest for meaning, not just of the animals but also of myself. To me, field work is a form of self-indulgence that I hope does not detract from its scientific validity and usefulness. I believe, as did Joseph Wood Krutch, that no scientist "can realize full human potentials if he is without wonder, or love, or a sense of beauty . . . ," and in this book I hope to convey both the scientific aspects of the study and my personal involvement with the animals and their realm.

Kay and I first drove through the Serengeti in 1960. We entered the park along the northwestern boundary, where the terrain is gently rolling and covered with a sparse woodland, a subdued land gray-green in hue. After an hour of driving over rutted roads the view suddenly widened. Scattered here and there were flat-topped umbrella acacia, their feathery leaves diffusing the vertical rays of the sun. Fever trees with lemon-colored bark traced the banks of streams, and kopjes, jumbled islands of granite, with boulders worn smooth by wind and rain, jutted above the level of the plain. To us this area represented the quintessence of Africa, and quietly within a matter of hours we surrendered our hearts to it. It was Seronera. We remained but one night, and then headed eastward across the open plains, our vehicle seemingly lost between earth and sky as it moved toward the horizon, trailing a thick cloud of dust. The views were wide, alien in their immensity, and our eyes searched restlessly ahead for a landmark, but the plains rolled on until it seemed that the world was enlarging before us. Finally, the Ngoron-goro Crater highlands appeared ahead, featureless in the dry-season haze, and winding up their burned flanks we left the Serengeti. But with us we carried a yearning to return, and this we did in June 1966.

The study lasted until September 1969, and this book describes some of the things we did, some of the sights that pleased me, and some of the facts and conclusions I derived from my research. I do not know how typical the behavior of the lion, cheetah, and other predators around Seronera and on the plains is of these species as a whole because at the time of writing this book in 1971 little comparative information was available. Social systems, food habits, and other aspects of behavior are strongly influenced by ecological conditions, and only further studies can show to what extent the animals I observed were affected by droughts, migratory prey, and other factors. Fortunately Brian Bertram continued the predator studies in the Serengeti, concentrating his efforts in the woodlands, where I did relatively little work.

This book, then, is about animals, not about the many people who touched on our lives in the Serengeti. Somehow in that harsh land, with its many herds ever on the move in their search for forage, the presence of man seems unimportant. To species that in their racial history have witnessed the evolutionary rise and passing of the earliest pre-men and men, we represent just a moment in time, a trivial intrusion. However, on the good intentions of modern man rests the fate of the Serengeti and its wildlife. Several years ago Bernhard Grzimek, in collaboration with his son Michael, wrote eloquently about the area in the book *Serengeti Shall Not Die*, a work that focused our consciousness on that priceless heritage hidden in the vastness of Tanzania. Because of my admiration for Bernhard Grzimek's efforts to preserve the Serengeti and other remnants of wilderness, this book is dedicated to him. By describing the beauty of the Serengeti, the measureless waves of grass stems that no plough has ever touched, by describing the predators and prey, each intricately dependent on the other, I also hope to contribute to the interest and understanding the area needs to survive in perpetuity. The more detailed substance of the research can be found in my scientific report, *The Serengeti Lion*, and a popularly written summary, in effect a condensation of this work but with numerous photographs, appeared under the title *Serengeti: A Kingdom of Predators*.

GOLDEN SHADOWS, FLYING HOOVES

THE SEASONS

WE HAD A HOUSE AT SERONERA, A PREFABRICATED WOODEN
one painted yellow with a galvanized iron roof. It had a living
room, three small bedrooms, one of which I used as a study,
a bathroom, and a kitchen. Bottled gas supplied fuel for the
stove, refrigerator, and water heater, and a generator gave
electricity in the evening until about eleven p.m. An Artesian
well provided water and we augmented this supply with
rain collected in a huge barrel. Never before on an expedition
had we had such a modern home. Although I find tech-
nological complexity and possessions meaningless past a
certain point, I must admit that electricity and refrigeration
are pleasant to have. A lovely umbrella acacia shaded one
side of the house, giving it a feeling of intimacy in this seemingly harsh land. Next to the house was a kopje crowned by
a candelabra euphorbia, its austere limbs pointing skyward.
Out of sight, on the other side of the kopje, lived our closest
neighbors, Warden Joe Fourie and his family. Unfortunately
the kopje had been desecrated at its base with a guest house
of cement blocks and a tin shed, both hideous in appearance,

built like so much of Seronera without concern for beauty. From the back of our house we could see the tourist lodge and several other buildings. Luckily for us, the garage and shacks of the African staff quarters were hidden behind distant trees. There was litter here and there. No scavenger has as yet evolved that consumes broken bottles and scrap metal. Lavatory buckets from the lodge were for a period merely emptied into warthog burrows. I remember stepping from the house one dawn and listening to the sounds. Lions roared far away and a zebra brayed, then a rooster crowed and a radio blared, an incompatible mixture of two worlds. The rot of civilization had come to Seronera, even though the community lies two hundred miles from Arusha, the nearest town.

But from our veranda we looked into the past, into a time when the heavy hand of man was not yet evident. Neither fence nor building interrupted the parkland of acacia trees that stretched to the rocky slopes of Nyaraswiga Hill rising a thousand feet above the level of the plain. Our eyes invariably sought its brooding ruggedness, for it changed its aspect throughout the day, sometimes standing stark and rigid, only the occasional cloud shadow adding life to its contours, at other times floating ephemerally and trembling in the midday heat. And beyond the hill, the trees continued for over sixty miles westward. The mere thought of all this space was a gift to the spirit. Here was the same view seen by the early expeditions that had camped at Seronera. Carl Akeley, for example, came here in 1926 to collect specimens for the American Museum of Natural History, and Martin and Osa Johnson photographed the wildlife in 1928. Recorded history is young in this corner of Africa.

Some 5,600 square miles were established as a park in 1940, a huge area stretching from Lake Victoria in the west to the Crater Highlands in the east. The boundaries were somewhat realigned in 1951, but increasing conflict between the demands of the Masai tribe for grazing lands to satisfy their growing herds of cattle and goats and the needs of wildlife led to drastic changes in 1959. The highlands and eastern plains were excised from the park and a block of woodlands that extended north to the Kenya border was added instead. This Northern Extension, as it is still called, brought the size of the park to about five thousand square miles, an area the size of Connecticut. The wildlife wanders in and out of the park, heeding not political boundaries but ecological ones. The ancient needs of wildebeest, zebra, and others dictate the use of some ten thousand square miles, and this area is known as the Serengeti Ecological Unit.

The whole region is a high plateau that slopes from an altitude of about 6,300 feet in the eastern part to 3,800 feet near Lake Victoria. Drainage, too, is westward, but the Grumeti, Orangi, Mbalageti, and Duma, to name only some of the important rivers, dry up for part of the year, except for some pools; only the Bologonja and Mara rivers in the north of the park are perennial. The eastern two thousand square miles of the unit comprise a rolling plain, broken mainly by the Oldoinyo Gol, desolate mountains whose slopes of quartzite and gneiss are covered with scrubby acacia and other trees. Olduvai Gorge, which has revealed more of man's history than any other site on earth, cuts the plains south of these mountains. In the eastern plains the grass is short, but farther west, where the soil is rich and deep, it reaches a height of three feet. "And all this a sea of grass, grass, grass, grass and grass. One looks around and sees only grass and sky," wrote Fritz Jaeger, one of the first Europeans to cross these plains, in 1907. Seeing them now, unchanged, still spreading boundlessly to the horizon, one knows the reason for his exultation. Seronera lies at the western edge of the plains, and beyond, to the north and west, are the woodlands—or more properly, wooded grasslands—broken here and there by small plains. The northern part has few prominent landmarks, except for the Kuka and Lobo hills along the eastern edge of the ecological unit, but the Cor-

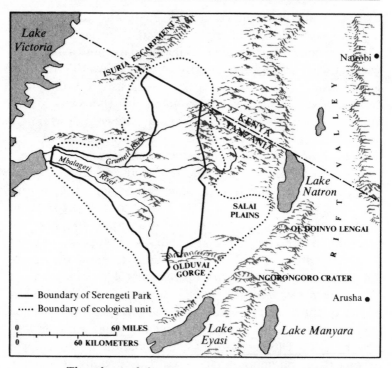

The physical features of the Serengeti ecological unit
and surrounding areas.

ridor, as the western portion is called, features several
ranges, among them the Itonjo, Nyaraboro, and Nyamuma
hills. This, in brief, was my study area, but dry words do little
to convey my first impressions. It is a hard land, without the
gentle charm and intimate views that give a person confidence and linger in his memory; instead, one feels that man
is barely permitted to exist. It does not have scenic grandeur,
but it has an austere beauty and the timelessness of great
solitudes, and I longed to explore the hills and plains, the
distant horizon.

It was clearly impossible for me to study lions throughout the ecological unit, and one of my first tasks was to choose
a limited area where I could observe the cats throughout the

year. The region outside of the park was unsuitable for my purpose because of human disturbance—Masai and their livestock in the east, cultivators and poachers north and south of the Corridor. For the first few days I cruised in my Land Rover near home, tracing the wooded courses of the Seronera River and its tributaries and investigating the Masai kopjes, which stand like sentinels high on a ridge at the edge of the plains. I followed various rough tracks, not knowing where they led, and cut cross-country to places that intrigued me. Having found lions and other predators quite readily, I decided to make the one hundred square miles around Seronera my main study area. In it I would for the next three years record the history of every lion, births and deaths, social interactions, and the many other aspects that would help me to understand the dynamics of lion society. A few days after our arrival, I got up as usual with the first light to look for lions. Hearing water running from the tap outside our house, I walked over to turn it off. Three lions rose from the shadows and ambled off, their play with the tap interrupted by my precipitous appearance and even more precipitous retreat. With lions visiting me at home, I had obviously chosen a good locality for the study.

I also needed a research area larger than the one around Seronera so that the distribution and movements of prides could be plotted. Other scientists helped me become acquainted with the sites they knew best. Research on wildlife in the Serengeti began during the 1950's and included the work of Bernhard and Michael Grzimek in 1957 and 1958. When in the early 1960's John Owen took over as director of the Tanzania National Parks, he realized that conservation and management practices in the parks could only be based on detailed ecological studies. With characteristic initiative and vigor he established the Serengeti Research Project, which on July 1, 1966, became the Serengeti Research Institute. Fritz Walther was working on Thomson's gazelle behavior when we arrived in the Serengeti. He lived at

Banagi, eleven miles north of Seronera, the old game reserve headquarters during the 1930's and the site of a small
laboratory built by Bernhard Grzimek. Fritz showed me his
study area in the Northern Extension. Although at first Fritz
seems curt and loath to be distracted from his work, he becomes voluble and his enthusiasm infectious when the
conversation turns to gazelle, for he has studied one kind or
another for nearly two decades. He refers to Thomson's
gazelle as "my people," not as an affectation but from a
genuine love for these animals which he to some extent resembles in his lithe frame and nervous vitality.

Hans Kruuk introduced me to the plains where he had
been studying spotted hyenas since 1964. He is a tall, blond
Dutchman whose outward conviviality hides a very determined character. For the past few years he has been fighting
a moral battle to rehabilitate the hyena in the mind of the
public. With the excuse that hyenas were mere scavengers and
killers of defenseless young, man had been shooting them,
even in the Serengeti Park, until the early 1960's. I remembered a passage in Ernest Hemingway's *Green Hills of Africa*:

> Highly humorous was the hyena obscenely
> loping, full belly dragging, at daylight on the plain,
> who, shot from the stern, skittered on into speed to
> tumble end over end. Mirth provoking was the
> hyena that stopped out of range by an alkali lake
> to look back and, hit in the chest, went over on his
> back, his four feet and his full belly in the air.
> Nothing could be more jolly than the hyena coming
> suddenly wedge-headed and stinking out of high
> grass by a *donga* hit at ten yards, who raced his
> tail in three narrowing, scampering circles until he
> died.

Hans is justifiably furious at such wanton killing, for, other
considerations aside, he knew the hyena not only as a
courageous and powerful hunter but also as a fascinating

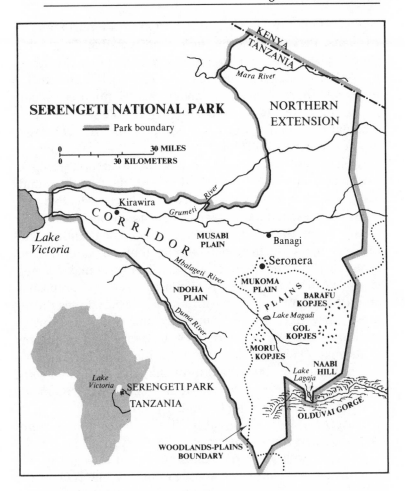

SERENGETI NATIONAL PARK
— Park boundary

NORTHERN EXTENSION

KENYA
TANZANIA

Mara River

0 30 MILES
0 30 KILOMETERS

Kirawira

CORRIDOR

Grumeti River

MUSABI PLAIN

Banagi

Lake Victoria

Seronera

Mbalageti River

NDOHA PLAIN

MUKOMA PLAIN

PLAINS

BARAFU KOPJES

Lake Magadi

Duma River

GOL KOPJES

MORU KOPJES

NAABI HILL

Lake Lagaja

Lake Victoria

SERENGETI PARK
TANZANIA

OLDUVAI GORGE

WOODLANDS-PLAINS BOUNDARY

and utterly delightful animal. However, public opinion changes slowly. The hyena's sloping back and harried look fail to inspire admiration as does the majestic appearance of the lion, and to the Africans the animal is a buffon who in their fables is the butt of all jests. Among the African staff at the park each scientist was simply known by the animal he was studying. Hans was Bwana Fizi. Introduced as Mr.

Hyena, Hans always elicited a paroxysm of mirth among Africans. Perhaps if admiration is not possible, laughter is the next best thing, for who would want to kill a clown?

After looking over various parts of the park, I decided to limit my investigations to about fifteen hundred square miles, to a rectangle stretching from the eastern park boundary across the plains past Seronera into the woodlands of the Corridor. With that decision I began the study in earnest. These days science aspires to treat everything in mathematical terms. This, together with the fact that funds are given only for a short period, puts a considerable constraint on research. One tends to focus on one narrow objective. Animals are treated as mere statistical entities and the search for broad understanding that comes only from sympathetic observation of the environment may be neglected. With such an outlook one loses a sense of proportion and a feeling of intimacy with animals. Many times during those early days I saw something that interested me, a warthog enlarging its burrow, a secretary bird displaying to its mate, yet I did not tarry, for the lions beckoned insistently. But the calm rhythm of the days dissipated some of my urgency and as time went on I spent many moments in trivial pursuits, my life the richer for it.

An area does not reveal itself all at once and not until one has spent much time in it, viewing it in all its moods, by night as well as by day, does one begin to see it with a heightened consciousness. With familiarity one notices the intimate aspects, and everyday things acquire a new perspective. Most animals do not roam at will but cling to a familiar plot of land, and I encountered the same ones again and again on my daily rounds. They gave the area a feeling of stability that was somehow reassuring. Of course, driving around in a Land Rover, engulfed by the noise and stench of its engine, is a poor way to derive the ultimate in pleasure, and I often cursed my metal prison, vowing that never again would I do a project that deprived me of the joys of smelling and hearing. But work from a car was essential. Not only are distances vast but also animals have learned to accept a vehicle, whereas they flee from a person on foot, as if heeding that awful prophesy:

> God told Noah after the Flood: "And the fear of you and the dread of you shall be upon every beast of the earth, and upon every fowl of the air, upon all that moveth upon the earth, and upon all the fishes of the sea; into your hand are they delivered."

Still, I looked forward to meeting certain acquaintances each day and I derived a quiet delight in nodding to them as I passed.

There was George the bull giraffe, a long-time Seronera resident, who led a misanthropic existence, browsing alone over about twenty-five square miles of terrain. He was often in his preferred corner of woodland and there he looked haughtily down on the car as I drove by. His wanderings sometimes brought him to our house and we would watch as with his blue prehensile tongue he plucked acacia pods from the branches overhanging our roof. The first time we heard the branches swish and thump on the house at night, Kay and I leaped from bed to look out the window. George stood so close that we could have stroked his creamy belly. He would sometimes amble through and break the clothesline that we had stretched between two trees, but there is something spiritually satisfying in having a giraffe do so.

In Seronera, too, lived a male waterbuck who claimed about a square mile of woodlands as his territory. Usually he was alone, living a precarious existence in the favorite haunts of a lion pride. Occasionally several females drifted into his area to remain with him for a few days or a few months. It pleased me to see his faithful vigil rewarded. Waterbuck have a long, coarse coat of hair, one that seems best adapted to a northern clime. I have no idea what advantage they derive from it, but such points are interesting to ponder.

In the waterbuck's territory stood a kopje, which was the center of the universe for a pair of dik-dik, diminutive antelope weighing a mere ten pounds. The two sometimes stood at the edge of a bush and watched me pass, the tuft of hair on their heads raised in excitement, but they vanished as soon as I stopped, only shrill snorting whistles revealing the direction of their retreat in the dense under-growth. As Ursula Hendrichs found out, each pair per-manently inhabits a territory of a few acres in extent. The male defends the territory against the intrusion of other dik-dik and both demarcate it by depositing their feces at definite lavatories along its boundaries. The female gives birth twice a year, but each youngster is evicted by his parents at the age of seven months.

The dry season had begun in May. No clouds marred the sky. Heat waves raced over the ground driven by a wind that blew incessantly from the east. The grass stalks were yellow and brittle, rustling softly as they swayed. When I looked into the rising sun the expanse of ripe grass heads took on a leaden sheen, so polished and smooth that one wanted to reach out and stroke them. With the scattered pools drying out, animals began to concentrate along the Seronera River, and I, too, spent more and more time there. Here the dappled shade of fever trees and the intense green of the *Phoenix* palms brought relief from the glare and sun-burned hues of the open country. I particularly liked to drive the winding stretch between Ker's Dam and Downey's Dam, a distance of about five miles. Lions favored this area, and I knew many of the other creatures that lived there. A crocodile, some eleven feet long, called an algae-covered pool its own. It had lost a hindfoot, perhaps in some saurian battle. A little farther on was the favorite perch of a pied kingfisher, overhanging the stream. Once, within a period of an hour, this bird hurled itself thirty times into the murky water before catching one small fish. Among my favorite acquaintances were the buff-colored Egyptian geese, of which there were five pairs along this stretch of river, each pair pugnaciously gracing one pool. When a goose saw its mate approach, it would call a raucous greeting, ka-ka-ka, and the other would raise its head and spread its wings while emitting an ecstatic krrraa. These geese may nest at any time of the year, but most do so at the onset of the dry season. Some choose abandoned vulture nests in which to lay their eggs. Hammerkop storks build bulky nests of sticks and reeds in the low forks of trees near water and then raise their young in a darkened chamber that is accessible only through one small entrance hole. Geese often become tenants, using the top of the nest to lay their clutch of up to fourteen eggs. Many dangers face the newly hatched goslings, for most broods I watched grew smaller as the days passed. But some young survive and these leave the parental home toward the end of the year.

Occasionally I drove to the eastern plains to look for predators but few of them were there. As the grasses shriveled in the sun and the water in the alkali pools evaporated, most hoofed animals trekked to greener pastures in the west, and the majority of predators followed. The plains in the dry season presented a desolate scene. As I walked, the dry stubble crackled under my feet and wind whipped over the rises, stinging my face with dust. There were few animals to be seen. An occasional zebra family plodded westward along the horizon, a few ostriches swayed along until swallowed by the haze, a lone jackal nosed under desiccated wildebeest droppings in search of beetles. Only the Grant's gazelle seemed truly at home on these sun-drenched plains. Unlike most other antelope, they can survive without drinking. Physiological experiments by Richard Taylor have shown that the body temperature of Grant's gazelle may rise as high as 107° during the heat of the day. Yet the animals do not pant or sweat and this reduces their use of water for evaporative cooling. Some plants absorb moisture when humidity rises at night and by foraging on them at that time the gazelle can apparently satisfy their daily water requirements. Overhead winged an occasional small compact flock of yellow-throated sand grouse, pigeonlike birds that herald their passing with a ringing staccato o-a-a-a-a, a wild and seemingly forlorn call in this land of remote skylines. They are on their way to water. A pair incubates its three eggs on the bare ground on the plains during the dry season. But sand grouse chicks need drinking water, and to supply it to them the male has evolved a unique system. As described by T. Cade and G. Maclean, a male soaks his belly and chest feathers in a pool and then hurries to his nest. There the youngsters cluster around him and strip the water from his wet feathers with their beaks.

Like islands, numerous kopjes jut from the plains, some standing alone, others clustered in archipelagos. These kopjes are worlds of their own and I delighted in exploring them. First, however, I clapped my hands to alert any lion or leopard that might be slumbering in a shady retreat. Fleshy-leafed aloes grow between the rocks, and sometimes *Gloriosa* lilies blaze in a moist niche, their crimson blossoms incongruous in this landscape of modest hues. Watching me pass were beady-eyed *Agama* lizards, their six-inch bodies a striking blue and orange in color. Though pastoralists have denuded the kopjes of woody vegetation for firewood and for fencing livestock, an occasional tree remains. Sitting in its shade, eyes squinting against the harsh light, I scanned the horizon. The rises and swales vibrated in the heat, distorting my vision. Plump gazelle turned into lean viscous creatures and flocks of ostrich floated by silently and legless on aerial waves.

Once an Egyptian vulture landed on a rock nearby. It was a handsome bird dressed in black and white with a yellow face and jaunty tufts of feathers sticking from its head. We eyed each other speculatively, it probably wondering if my motionless form represented a possible meal. I was intrigued by one of its habits, that of opening ostrich eggs with stones. In 1903, William Sclater reported an incident involving Egyptian vultures in South Africa: "Mr. Gurney states in the country about the Orange river they prey on the eggs of the Ostrich, which they break by dropping upon them a stone carried up into the air for the purpose." James Stevenson-Hamilton related in 1912 a similar incident from the Athi Plains in Kenya. A different technique was first described by A. Meyers from the Sudan in a book entitled *Life with the Hamran Arabs,* published in 1876. Meyers and a friend had concealed themselves by an ostrich nest in order to shoot the adult bird when it returned:

> After an hour of this very monotonous amuse-ment, two visitors in the form of vultures pounced down upon the nest, and, apparently quite satisfied with the certainty of a quiet feast, commenced operations by a personal hunt amongst their own feathers; then a general survey was made of the white objects before them; and finally, having re-tired for a moment, each returned with a stone in its beak, and set to work to hammer a hole through the shell of an egg.

Unfortunately the ostrich chose this moment to return and a shot ended the incident. Such tool-using was also photo-graphed several years ago in the Serengeti area by Hugo van Lawick, Norman Myers, and others. Recently Leslie Brown and Emil Urban watched as Egyptian vultures picked up pelican eggs and hurled them onto rocks, just the reverse method from the one used to open ostrich eggs. This latter method probably evolved first, for small eggs are certainly readily available throughout the vulture's range, whereas ostrich eggs are not. This example illustrates how tool use could develop from a relatively simple existing behavior pattern without there being a need to postulate a high level of mental activity.

My beacon in the area was Naabi Hill, which rises alone from the plains. Even on moonlight nights I could orient myself by its dark shape. A few miles beyond the hill is Lake Lagaja, a shallow soda lake ringed by a fringe of woodland. Clouds of lesser flamingo often imparted a rosy hue to the shallows, but as the dry season advanced these birds sought the large lakes of the rift valley to the north and east. I often crisscrossed the plains for fifty or more miles in a day, searching for predators. Although this was an efficient way to gather information, I envied those explorers who had trudged across the area on foot, deriving, at least in retrospect, that satisfaction from their accomplishments which only a struggle can give. Oskar Baumann, a German, discovered Ngorongoro Crater on March 18, 1892. By March 27 he reached the vicinity of Lake Lagaja with his porters and a guide whom he had commandeered in Arusha. Looking at the huge herds of wild animals, a sight such as few had ever seen, Baumann noted laconically in his journal: "Animals . . . are here visible in great numbers." Two days later he wrote: "Around midday of March 29 the acacias disappeared and we moved through a wide, almost completely tree-less grass plains, a real prairie." After crossing the plains and reaching the vicinity of Oldoinyo Labal, a hill at the edge of the woodlands, he headed first northwest, then to Lake Victoria, the journey taking just over three weeks.

Soon after the study began I became interested in the Mbalageti River, which meanders westward from Lake Magadi, flanked along part of its way by rocky hills. It is a small river, often no more than twenty feet wide, shaded by fig trees, fever trees, and others that crowd its banks. The woodland animals come daily, filing apprehensively down some narrow trail to reach the scattered pools, ever conscious that a lion or leopard may be lurking in the brush. To find predators, I tried to follow each tortuous bend of the river.

My approach invariably startled the impala, zebra, and others that had come to drink and they fled, their pounding hooves churning up dense clouds of dust. Then, from a safe distance, they stood and watched me pass, muscles tensed for instant flight. In looking for predators, I soon learned to rely on the assistance of other animals. It is easy to miss a tawny lion asleep in a yellow sward of grass, but if a giraffe, for example, stands rigidly staring at a certain spot, even to the extent of ignoring the clanking and rattling that signals the approach of a car, then the chances are good that a predator is hidden nearby. One becomes an adept vulture watcher, too, learning to distinguish the difference between those birds roosting casually from those that crowd a trembling branch near a carcass. The fact that they are not eating can mean either that they are satiated, having perhaps found an animal dead of disease, or that the lion is still at its kill. If the kill was accessible, I collected the head for later identification of the age and sex of the victim. A couple of hand claps were usually enough to send lions scurrying, enabling me to check the carcass. Still, crawling under a bush in order to drag out the remains, never knowing if the lion might assert his claims, caused a certain apprehension. At times a lion refused to relinquish any part of its kill, even in the name of science, and I did not press my demands.

To follow the Mbalageti River was surprisingly hard work. The grass was high in places and I had to creep ahead, never knowing when a boulder, log, or hole would bring the car to an abrupt halt. Thickets of whistling thorn barred the way, the long whitish spines of the trees gleaming menacingly. I pushed through these thickets, knowing that the spines would break in the tires and slowly penetrate until, perhaps a week later, I would have one or more punctures. Grass seeds clogged the radiator, causing the engine to overheat. Narrow but deep ravines and rocky hillocks demanded long detours, either by heading away from the river or by fording it. But fords were scarce and at times I had to remove boulders and dig before the car could be taken down one bank and up the other. And always there were tsetse flies. In size and appearance tsetse flies somewhat resemble the horse flies of temperate climes. Their bite transmits the deadly protozoans that cause sleeping sickness in man and *nagana* in livestock. Wildlife is usually immune to these diseases and acts as a reservoir for them. Although I welcomed tsetse flies as a species because their presence has prevented human encroachment into some of the finest wildlife areas of Africa, I was emphatically not well disposed toward them as individuals when a searing pain advertised the presence of one somewhere on my body. Active mainly in daytime, the tsetse fly clings to a shady branch near a thicket waiting for a meal of blood, mainly from hoofed animals but also from lizards, lions, and other vertebrates. Tsetse flies are attracted by movement, which they can detect from a distance of at least three hundred feet. Sometimes as many as a hundred flies sat on my car and many of these found their way inside, more, I think, in search of shade than to bite. In any case, they zoomed around, not readily ignored, for an unlucky bite causing sleeping sickness may mean a month or more in the hospital. A slap seldom killed a fly: they had to be squashed until they popped with a satisfying snap. To pursue a dozen or more flies while trying to keep the car from ramming or falling into one of the many obstacles made me feel like the proverbial one-armed paperhanger. I could have kept the windows closed but that would have been like sitting in an oven.

To grant myself a respite, I stopped at intervals and sat on the bank of the river. The spreading shiny-leafed crowns of fig trees offered particularly inviting retreats, refuges from the sense of exposure in this wide, dusty land. Sitting there quietly, I ceased to be an obvious component of the environment and instead achieved a sense of intimacy with it. If I closed my eyes there came to me various sounds and odors, subdued yet each insistent. Around me the heavy sweetness of ripe figs pervaded the air and mingled with the musky odor of baboons, groups of which often sleep in these trees during the night. Fronds of a borassus palm may clatter dryly when a vulture lands on them, a sound so like a rhinoceros crashing through a thicket that at first I was always startled. I was fond of the borassus palms that lined the river. With their gray spindle-shaped boles and fan-shaped fronds clustered at the top they conferred a peculiar distinction, a primitive elegance, to the area. White-backed vultures often placed their nests in the crowns, an apt association, for both seemed dedicated to the past, survivors of an age when mammals had not yet achieved their dominance. Fisher's lovebirds may build their nests in the maze of sticks that form the vulture's nest. These trim birds with their bright green bodies were lovely indeed, as flocks of them wheeled against the sky. After a while I stepped from my shady retreat, momentarily shattered by the brilliance of the light, and continued my search along the river's edge.

At times the search for lion kills did not require a difficult journey. Horrible growls woke us one night. Investigating, I found several lionesses on a zebra kill within a hundred feet of the house. As I watched them, other lions squabbled over something near the lodge. Another zebra had been killed there in front of a row of tourist rooms. Around five a.m. a door opened and a drowsy woman headed for the restroom a few doors down the open hallway. A snarl at the kill made her scuttle back to her room with incredible speed and the slammed door stayed shut far into daylight. Many members of the Research Institute also reported kills to me, and these records helped me considerably. For instance, Tom Moore, the administrator of the Institute, might stop by at our house to tell me that a lion was feeding on a gazelle by the river; David Houston might relate how lions had chased away feeding vultures and scavenged a dead zebra much to his annoyance, for he was studying vultures, not lions; and Graham Dangerfield might rush up at midnight, deposit a bloody wildebeest head on our doorstep, and vanish again into the night in pursuit of some elusive sound he hoped to capture on his tape recorder.

As the dry season advances, fires begin to sweep through the park. Over two thirds of the woodlands and large portions of the long-grass plains are burned annually. Some of these fires are set by pastoralists outside of the park, for burning stimulates green grass to grow on the burn, a nutritious source of food for livestock at a time when otherwise only dry forage remains. Frequent heavy grazing of such green shoots may be detrimental to the grasses. By growing at a time when they should lie dormant, they use up the stored nutrients they need to survive the dry season, and the heavy grazing prevents them from depositing more food in their roots. On the other hand, dry stems may be grazed to the ground by hoofed animals with little effect on the grasses because they have their energy already stored. Other fires start through carelessness—a discarded cigarette, an untended campfire—or from a mere pyromaniacal impulse. As the fires burn, distant hills disappear in the smoke haze and at midday the sun is a pale disk that changes to a fiery, coppery orb as toward evening the earth leans slowly away from it. Fires that in daytime creep inconspicuously up some hill become visible at night as disembodied flames dancing in glowing lines inexorably into the sky. Yellowish smoke and ash permeate the air. On the plains, dust devils spin over the ground now bleak and bare except for a few scorched tufts of grass. In the woodlands flames have swept away the grass, assaulted thickets, and devoured dead trees. With the rocky bones of the hills exposed, the earth dry and cracked, the Serengeti now presents a bleak appearance, its bright colors leached away.

The large mammals almost ignore the advancing fires, casually detouring around flames or moving onto burned ground that is still warm. One male lion fed on a warthog, seemingly oblivious to the line of flames that crackled toward him through the grass. At last, with the fire only three feet from his paws, so close that I was afraid his mane might ignite, he reluctantly dragged his meal to a safer spot. Some birds benefit directly from fires. Marabou storks pace gravely around the edge, their preoccupied mien interrupted by occasional rapid thrusts of their bills, which may net them a mouse, snake, or other small vertebrate fleeing from the flames. Lilac-breasted rollers, spectacular in their iridescent blue plumage, plunge into the smoke to snag grasshoppers. Small animals may be harmed by the flames, and I particularly remember a leopard tortoise dragging its house along on scorched legs, moving even more slowly than usual.

The annual fires present ecologists with a dilemma, for they both benefit and harm the hoofed animals. Antelopes have had their major evolutionary development in African grasslands, and many are adapted to feeding on grass in their tooth structure, digestive system, and other ways. Without fires to depress the growth of woody vegetation, much of the Serengeti would in a few years become covered with brush. Only the eastern plains would remain as they are, for there the sandy loam is shallow and underlaid with a layer of rocky calcium carbonate that prevents the vegetation from reaching the water table. These eastern plains have probably remained relatively unchanged for several thousand years, but the western ones were most likely wooded until fires and perhaps also other causes pushed back the tree line. While the wildlife needs grasslands, too-frequent fires, particularly fires late in the dry season, when every desiccated stalk burns with a fierce heat, prevent the regeneration of trees and ultimately the whole park might consist of nothing but plains. Acacia saplings need at least three years of protection before they can tolerate even a mild blaze. And before that, so many factors conspire against seeds that it is surprising that any trees sprout at all. Rodents eat them and insects attack them. The seeds of some species germinate better after first passing whole through the digestive tract of an impala, giraffe, elephant or other animal, and they grow poorly or not at all if chance deposits them beneath the canopy of an existing tree. Consequently stands of saplings occur mainly in open areas that have accidentally escaped the fires. The flames also destroy any litter on the ground. Exposed to the elements, the soil surface dries and compacts, causing rain water to run off rather than seep in, thus leading to erosion. Some species cannot tolerate repeated burning, with the result that fire reduces the spectrum of plants in an area, leaving only those that are fire-resistant.

The fires also remove the dry grass, which represents the only available forage for many hoofed animals until the rains at the end of the dry season stimulate a new growth. Perhaps as little as one quarter of the annual grass production is eaten; most of the rest is burned. Dry grass is much less nutritious than green grass, but still it sustains animals at a time of year when malnutrition is always a threat. One year, late in the dry season, I visited the northern part of the park where wildebeest and zebra had massed in search of food. Many carcasses littered the hillsides, whole skeletons encased in shriveled hides that gave a hollow rattle when I kicked them. The animals had most likely died of malnutrition, perhaps coupled with disease, which often strikes when the body's resistance has been lowered. The carcasses were mute evidence of the struggle for life, the outcome of which is so easily influenced by man's unthinking interference.

The pleasing balance between woodlands and plains, as well as the huge herds for which the Serengeti is famous, are in part the product of, or at least maintained by, fire. Now, however, fire threatens the ecological variety of the area. It is the task of man to use fire as a management tool in such a way that the diversity of the community is maintained. For years the park had only a nebulous fire policy, which was poorly enforced, but it is now attempting to protect some areas from burning for several years. In other parts fires are set early in the dry season at a time when grasses are still damp, leaving a mosaic of small burns and patches of vegetation.

The whole matter of vegetation change is made even more complex by the presence of elephants. As the research of Iain Douglas-Hamilton has shown, elephants live in extended family units consisting of a mother and her offspring, who in turn may have youngsters of their own. One or more matriarchs lead the family and protect it in times of danger. Since a female does not have her first young until the age of at least fifteen years and the calving interval may be as long as six years, large families may have been together for several decades. Bulls reach their sociological maturity at the age of about twenty-five years, and such adults are often alone or in small bachelor groups, having been chased from their families by the cows at puberty. Bulls join families only casually and then mainly when a cow is in estrus. During the dry season, herds are generally small, averaging about twenty-five animals in size and consisting of one to several family units. However, many families and bulls may join during the rains to form large herds, and over five hundred animals are sometimes seen together in the Serengeti.

There are about 2,500 elephants divided into a northern and southern population that use the park for at least part of the year. As an elephant eats the equivalent of about five percent of its body weight per day, a herd of these beasts, with individuals scaling as much as ten thousand pounds, needs a considerable amount of forage. The animals rip the bark off trees and eat it, leaving the tree to die and later be devoured by fire; and they push over whole trees, carefully selecting but a few branches to eat before abandoning the rest untouched. After a visit from an elephant herd, an area may look as if it had been struck by a tornado.

Hubert Hendrichs studied the way bulls damage trees. Although the composition of bull herds changes constantly, certain individuals assume particular roles in herds. One may be dominant, a second the leader, a third the rear guard —and one or more push over trees. "Not every bull pushes over trees," wrote Hubert. "Some try it over and over again and do not succeed, others never try. Some bulls get very adept at pushing over trees. They make the tree swing by pushing with the base of the trunk from different sides and then choose one side for the final push with the lower or the upper base of the trunk. . . . Per bull about one tree is killed daily." By breaking down trees and shrubs, elephants open up thickets to penetration by fire. Because of this, the woodlands in parts of the Northern Extension are retreating at the rate of about five percent per year. Will the decline of the woodlands stop if fire is controlled, or will the natural increase, if any, of the elephant population negate any gains? Ecologists still know too little about the intricate relationships between vegetation, elephants, and fire to be able to predict accurately what may happen if conditions are slightly changed.

Seronera is a microcosm of this elephant problem. Every dry season a number of elephant bulls arrive at the Seronera River and with cheerful abandon knock down trees, usually doing so where the damage is most obvious. These visits began in the early 1960's, when the southern elephant population apparently extended its range northward. In fact, one night while I was away several elephants broke down some large trees in our front yard. Kay, who claims to be a light sleeper, didn't hear a thing. Some people, notably park warden Myles Turner, stated vehemently that these elephants should be removed, for the beauty of the river was being impaired, and that if present trends continued the whole area would be denuded in a few years. Just as vehemently, Harvey Croze, who was studying these elephants along the river, replied that only about a fifth of the trees were damaged and that regeneration was so adequate that the number of large trees in the area had actually increased in the past ten years. The argument was not yet resolved at the time I left the Serengeti.

As the dry season drags on, one begins anxiously scanning the horizon for those drifting white clouds that may herald a rain. But there is only the pallid sky and the seared soil. Fine dust and ash pervade everything, and after a drive one's body takes on an earthen hue. At the first light small flocks of guinea fowl flutter from their nightly retreats in the trees along the river and begin to scratch the soil in search of seeds and insects. Each nervous sweep of a foot raises a puff of dust until a cloud of it hovers over the feeding site. Hoofed animals stand listlessly in the shade of trees.

The ostrich, however, has chosen this season for its most vigorous activity, that of courting and nesting. In late May the male's neck and thighs turn red for the nuptial season, and his black and white plumage is then at its glossiest. Although he may begin displaying to hens in April, his courtship reaches its highest pitch of excitement in June and July. Squatting down, he spreads his quivering wings, all the while weaving his neck and head from side to side. One or more hens may then pirouette around him, tremulously inviting him with their wings fluttering and their heads lowered almost to the ground. Courting males also boom one or more times, a sound that at a distance resembles the roar of a lion. Hens are rather careless about their eggs, and from June to November one may find single eggs here and there on the ground. For some reason, hens often choose to lay such eggs in the ash of a burned tree. When I discovered one of these vagrant eggs, I took it home, drilled a small hole in one end, inserted a straw, and with much puffing blew out the contents. Kay would then make omelets, adding an exotic touch to our menu. Once I found three stray eggs in a week and she felt it was too much of a good thing—each ostrich egg being the equivalent of almost a dozen and a half chicken eggs.

An ostrich nest consists of a mere shallow scrape hidden

usually in brush or grass, though it may be placed in the open with only the incubating hen providing camouflage. The hen resembles a mound of earth, but when the black male sits on the eggs, as he often does in the morning and late afternoon, the nest is marked rather conspicuously. Since several hens may lay in the same nest, the daily increment of eggs is phenomenal. One nest I checked had six eggs on September 14, eighteen eggs on September 18, and thirty-seven eggs by September 27. But, like most others, this nest was destroyed. Fires ruin some nests, hyenas others, and one evening I watched several lions stalk a hen, which fled leaving behind one egg. This the lions bit open and then slurped up the contents. Surviving ostrich broods may join together, and on one occasion I met four hens accompanied by seventy-five chicks, all of them large enough to have a good chance of surviving into the coming seasons.

Among the charms of the Serengeti are the seasons, which, unlike those of northern latitudes, arrive and depart with a flourish. They are so erratic that one seldom experiences a typical year. The whole tempo of life is governed by the rains, but these come either earlier or later than usual, or are heavier or lighter than usual. I waited in vain for a "normal" season. When in late August 1966 it poured for a week, the rain was said to be unseasonably heavy. Be that as it may, rain lashed the woodlands in tremendous downpours that turned the ruts in the roads into torrents. Standing on the veranda of our home, the rain drumming on the roof and clouds roiling around the summit of Nyaraswiga Hill, I felt so exhilarated that it was as if some pressure within me had been released. Some animals may have had this feeling too, for various Thomson's gazelle herds raced in compact masses across the plains, with the animals exuberantly kicking up their heels. As the earth thirstily absorbed the moisture, life stirred beneath the surface. Worker termites frantically constructed turrets of moist soil on their mounds, and at dusk thousands of adults funneled upward into the sky in a nuptial exodus from the colony. If a female and male meet, they both land and immediately shed their fragile wings with a muscular action. Then the pair excavates a chamber and mates, the genesis of a new colony. But few manage to fulfill their destiny, for many birds and various mammals, including man, find these juicy termites appetizing. They are nourishing, too, one ounce of them providing 160 calories.

Within a day after a rain, shoots of grass emerge to impart a soft sheen of green to the somber terrain. These blades of grass, so fragile and modest, are the foundation of the Serengeti's character, for without them the vast aggregations of hoofed animals would not be able to exist. The Serengeti holds many pleasant memories: of silence on the plains at night, of the last streak of evening gold on a hill, but, most of all, memories of the immense herds. Standing on a rise and seeing this inexhaustible vigor of life—the wildebeest and zebra, the gazelle, wherever my eyes came to rest—made my heart leap with delight. In the words of Shakespeare: "O wonderful, wonderful, and most wonderful, wonderful! and yet again wonderful . . ." The sight released my thoughts to roam the past, back to a time when this land still lay waiting for the first human voice. It is a Pleistocene vision, which imparts a primordial feeling of well-being as if one's existence still depended on these animals.

The Serengeti has long been famous for its wildlife. In 1907, when Tanganyika was still a German colony, Fritz Jaeger noted that "it is probably the richest wildlife area in our whole colony." After a visit to what is now the Northern Extension, Stewart Edward White wrote: "Never have I seen anything like that game. It covered every hill, standing in the openings, strolling in and out among groves, feeding on the bottom lands, singly, or in little groups. It did not matter in what direction I looked, there it was; as abundant one place as another." Then in the 1920's, Martin and Osa Johnson reported that "at least 10 million head of zebra and wildebeest covered the veldt for miles in front of us." On the basis of what is now known about the carrying capacity of the area, this figure is greatly exaggerated, but it does convey not only the abundance of animals but also the difficulty in estimating numbers. Only in the past few years have counts of various species been made. Buffalo and wildebeest were censused quite accurately from airplanes while I was there, but the numbers of most other species were only vaguely known. To obtain some idea of what prey remained available to the lions in the woodlands during the rains when most migratory species were on the plains, I censused a number of large areas by air. With Chief Park Warden Sandy Field as my frequent pilot, we crisscrossed our selected plot in a definite pattern, counting all topi, impala, giraffe, and others, and later I extrapolated the results to the ecological unit as a whole. While crude, this method gave me at least a rough idea as to what the predators had to eat. Here are some numerical estimates of the most abundant species as of 1969, based on counts by others and on my own: at least 500,000 wildebeest, about 150,000 zebra, 50,000 buffalo, 65,000 impala, 25,000 topi, 18,000 kongoni, 8,000 giraffe. The small Thomson's gazelle had defied accurate censuses and at the time I completed my study estimates of their numbers ranged from 125,000 to 800,000.

The amount of grass and browse needed to support this many animals is huge, a fact most forcefully evident when a herd of wildebeest moves into an area of tall grass and shortly thereafter leaves it like a newly mown lawn, the grass both trimmed short by thousands of mouths and trampled by myriad hooves. Of course not all species depend on grass and those that do frequently harvest either different kinds of grass or different portions of the same kind. Thomson's gazelle eat mainly the tenderest blades and also some browse; wildebeest prefer the leaves of grass, ingesting few stems, whereas in zebra the pattern is reversed; buffalo may specialize in the tall coarse grasses along rivers; impala may browse low on shrubs and giraffe on the tops of trees. Competition is also decreased to some extent by habitat preferences. Buffalo prefer drainage lines, reedbuck confine themselves largely to riverine thickets, and Thomson's gazelle gravitate to open areas with short grass. In addition, various species use different areas at different seasons. Grazers prefer growing plants because the protein level is highest in short green grass. The length of the growing season and therefore the height of the grass are dependent on the amount of soil moisture. As Richard Bell found out in his study of grazing preferences of hoofed animals in the Corridor, the growing season is shortest in the leached sandy soils along the hilltops and longest in heavy clays of the valleys. Consequently, during the wet season the topi, kongoni, and whatever zebra and wildebeest have stayed in the woodlands remain on the short grass near the hilltops. Then, with the onset of the dry season, they disperse slowly toward the long grass in the valleys because they have eaten up their preferred forage on the slopes. Most wildebeest, zebra, Thomson's gazelle, and eland migrate, spending the rainy time of the year on the plains and retreating to the woodlands only when the grass dries and water disappears. Ceaselessly on the move even in the woodlands, the migratory herds orient their existence to the green grass that may sprout after a local shower. It may be that the animals see the towering thunderheads balanced on the black pillars of rain that advertise such a shower, and perhaps they also smell moisture in the wind. Whatever, thousands of animals may crowd into a few square miles where none were a day earlier.

The wildebeest pervade the Serengeti by their sheer numbers. Though predators may have the most visual impact on visitors, it is the huge, amorphous mass of the wildebeest population that permeates the thoughts of residents. Either the animals are present, inundating an area with black bodies, the air trembling with their grunts, or they are conspicuously absent, not a single individual as a reminder that the species exists. Bernhard Grzimek, Lee Talbot, and Murray Watson have outlined the general pattern of wildebeest movements. From the plains the animals sweep westward into the Corridor, where the herds break up and move in small groups north toward the Kenya border. There they tarry until once again rains signal them to return to the plains. Why do they surge back to the plains at the first opportunity, leaving behind ample grass? Perhaps the short species of grass are particularly nutritious. It is also possible that tradition plays an important role in their movements. Wildebeest prefer open habitats, and the eastern plains may have been their ancient ground when the rest of the Serengeti was more densely wooded and provided only a temporary retreat in seasons of exceptional dryness. Whatever the reason, their movement may be essential to the well-being of the grasslands. Hubert Braun, a Dutch botanist who with good-natured resignation always identified the wilted and battered remnants of plants I brought to him for identification, studied forage production in the park. He found that if he repeatedly clipped his experimental grass plots on the eastern plains at varying intervals, the total yields were the same for each plot. However, in the long-grass areas, which cover the western plains and woodlands, the yield decreased sharply with the frequency of cutting, indicating that if all the wildebeest and zebra were to remain in these areas throughout the year the range might well deteriorate under the constant heavy grazing.

The wildebeest is a strangely fashioned antelope, looking as if assembled from the leavings in some evolutionary factory. Its head is heavy and blunt, and it has a shaggy white beard and knobby, curving horns that give it a petulant mien. Its stringy black mane is so sparse that it seems to compensate for this thinness by having several vertical black slashes on its neck, an arrangement comparable to someone simulating a toupee by drawing black lines on his pate. The bulky shoulders give way to spindly hindquarters and a plumed tail that flails about as with a will of its own. Wildebeest alone seem rather woeful, but *en masse* they convey a strange beauty and power. Occasionally I walked among them. Retreating a few hundred feet to let me pass, the animals near me stood silently, their horns shining in the sun. Those farther back continued their incessant grunting, sounding like a chorus of monstrous frogs. Now and then several animals dashed off in apparent panic only to halt and stare back at me. The air was heavy with odor— earth and manure and the scent of trampled grass.

Wildebeest herds on the march are at their most impressive. Trudging along in single file or several abreast, they move in a hunched gait, only to break suddenly into a lope as they pour over hills and funnel down valleys, herd after herd, a living black flood tracing the age-old trails of their predecessors. This immutable urge to stay with the herd, to move in the direction of the others, causes them to press forward regardless of obstacles in their path. One day several lionesses settled by a brushy ravine that had been crossed by several herds during their erratic trek. In the course of a few hours the lionesses captured six wildebeest, yet, after hesitating briefly, each succeeding herd rushed recklessly ahead, deterred neither by the bodies of their compatriots nor the smell of blood and lions. If a river bars their way, they plunge in, disregarding all dangers, and many may drown. One day I watched about a thousand wildebeest gallop in a long line toward the Seronera River, a mindless mass in motion seemingly without reason or purpose. Those in the lead hurled themselves down the embankment, hit the water, and swam to the opposite side where its steepness halted them. The horde swept in behind and soon the water was crowded with thrashing animals, rearing up, climbing over each other, desperate in their attempts to scramble up the slippery sides. Some were pushed under so far that only their noses and bared white incisors were visible as they strained to stay above water. High-pitched bleats reached a frantic crescendo when those in front turned and met the rest still pressing ahead. Finally some gained the far bank and the others surged back past me with frantic, rolling eyes, still racing with implacable urgency except that now they headed in the direction from which they had just come. Seven dark bodies floating silently in the river attested to their violent passing.

Zebra have a steadier personality than wildebeest, less given to energetic mindlessness. Perhaps the family units in which they live promote stability. As discovered by Hans Klingel, zebra families consist of a stallion, several mares, and their foals. Adults retain their ties for life but young stallions leave on their own initiative to join other bachelors, and young mares in estrus are abducted either by stallions from other families or by bachelors with a longing to start a family on their own. Even when a family unites with others, forming herds with as many as five thousand or more animals, each retains its identity, recognition perhaps aided by the fact that the stripe pattern of every animal is as distinctive as a human fingerprint. The migratory pattern of zebra is more diffuse than that of wildebeest. Herds are generally small and widely scattered. Zebra are frequently the first to move off the plains at the onset of the dry season, eating those coarse grasses that other species may disdain. They stream by, their black-and-white columns in the flat light making one so dizzy from the motion that only the zebra appear stable in a moving world. I particularly liked hearing zebra bray at night, their wild and haunting calls filling the void between stars and earth. There are some feelings inaccessible to reason, and the zebra's braying always made the perfection of a Serengeti night complete.

Spending the dry season near the woodlands' edge, most Thomson's gazelle do not migrate as far as the other two species. They are the last to move off the plains, following the trampled swath left in the wake of the zebra and wildebeest. Gazelle dislike high grass, for aside from the fact that they prefer to eat tender shoots, they are unable to see well when grass reaches a height of three feet. But then neither can a lion. To observe a lioness stalk gazelle in such a situation is like watching a deadly game of chess. The gazelle takes a few steps, halts, tests the air, and strains to locate the predator by ear, then perhaps walks off to one side, stops again, and moves on. Meanwhile the lioness cranes her neck to peer above the level of the grass and maybe sees the black horn tips of the gazelle meandering among the yellow stalks. But by the time she has inched closer, her prey has moved and the whole process begins again. Most such hunts end in failure, but the suspense, the tension of the participants, each engaged in the one encounter for which thousands of generations of selective breeding have prepared it, impressed such scenes indelibly on my mind.

The August rains in 1966 were not widespread enough to permit the migratory herds to move out to the plains. The skies cleared and the dry season continued unabated through October. Some rain usually falls in November and December, and this enables the animals to venture from the woodlands. According to expectations, storms burst over much of the park in early November. But rushing to the woodlands' edge, the herds met only desiccated grass. They milled and waited, but not until mid-December were they able to leave the trees behind. A week later they were forced to retreat, the green grass gone, the sun blazing out of a clear sky once more. January came and went and still dust hovered over the parched earth. Animals were lethargic, plants dormant, people irritable, as everything waited for the rain to continue the usual rhythm of life.

Most wildebeest calves are born in late January and February. In 1967, for the first time in years, the wildebeest had to calve in the woodlands. Their calving season is one of the most inspiring and at the same time most tragic spectacles in the Serengeti. I watched one cow give birth, remaining far from her but with my eye steady on the scope until it ceased to exist and I became part of the scene. She stood quietly, breathing heavily. Soon two feet appeared, the hooves strikingly pale, and then the head and body encased in a luminous gray sheath. It dropped limply onto the grass, breaking the cord, and the cow lowered her broad muzzle to nibble at the fetal membranes and then lick the wet hide. Within seconds the calf raised its head, and, seeing its mother looming above, tried to rise. Shakily it raised its rump, toppled, tried again with the same result. But its racial wisdom urged it to struggle on, to gain its feet at all cost, until finally it stood unsteadily, legs spread and body weaving, a personal victory which I silently cheered. It fell again and again, yet each time regained its feet with greater ease. Within ten minutes after birth it stumbled along, its frail body pressed to the side of its mother. This calf aroused little interest in the other wildebeest, but those born early in the season often receive the fascinated attention of yearlings and adults. Crowding around, they butt the new arrival gently, sniff it, or perhaps buck and abruptly leap backward. The first commandment of a calf is to get on its feet, the second is to remain close to its mother. With herds large and constantly on the move, a calf that becomes separated from its mother by even fifty feet may never see her again. No cow will accept a stranger, and, as an outcast among the multitude, a lost calf slowly dies of starvation unless rescued from this fate by a predator.

Cows with small calves tend to aggregate into highly skittish herds. Tourists drive unheedingly through such herds and planes buzz them, spreading confusion and panic during which some calves invariably become lost. For these and other reasons, orphans are a common sight. A lost youngster at first dashes back and forth frantically bleating, but its voice is lost in the rumble of pounding hooves; it repeatedly runs up to strange wildebeest only to be rebuffed with a butt. Exhausted, the calf finally falters in its determination to join someone, and while the others recede into the distance, trailing a vane of dust, it halts, a small light-brown spot alone on the immensity of the plain. However, its urge to follow something, anything, is strong. I have seen calves attach themselves to zebra and eland, plodding behind the herd, quite ignored. The first time I took Kay to see the wildebeest herds massed near Naabi Hill, an orphan galloped up to our car as if this steel monster were its mother. Kay all but burst into tears at the sight of the forlorn animal, and when by the end of our day she had met several more such youngsters, she refused to ever visit the calving herds again.

Once a lost calf trailed two male lions for one and a half miles, trotting eagerly to within fifty feet of them. One or the other of the males made futile attempts to grab it, but, heeding its inborn warning to avoid anything that approaches rapidly, it lightly sidestepped the lunges. When the lions resumed their walk, it trailed them once more. The lions then reclined and the calf, losing interest in them, drifted onto a rise. And there, on the opposite side of a gentle valley, stood another orphan. Excitedly the calf looked toward this potential friend and with a burst of exuberance ran toward it, ran on in its escape from loneliness, oblivious to everything, even the lionesses that rose as if out of the ground and after a brief chase pulled it down. As the lioness held its throat until the new life faded from its eyes, hopefully the last thing it remembered was the other calf also hurrying to this ill-fated rendezvous.

At the height of the birth season the predators and scavengers can for once eat to satiation. Hyenas waddle along with their bellies almost touching the ground, lions stand panting, unable to recline comfortably on the monstrous bulge of their abdomen, and vultures flap awkwardly near carcasses, too full of offal to ride the currents into the air. Man sees himself reflected in nature, and, conscious of my ties to a hunting life, I could not but find satisfaction in the repletion of these animals.

Wildebeest calves are so vulnerable that many factors decimate them. Predation is one, disease another, accidents a third. One day, early in February 1968, a herd of wildebeest forded shallow Lake Lagaja, the adults plowing through the mud and turbid water without heeding the floundering calves. Several days later the writer Peter Matthiessen and I walked along the shores. Bloated carcasses floated in the shallows and the rotting remains of others were strewn along the banks, surrounded by myriads of vultures and maribou storks who had congregated there for this interminable fête. We counted 549 bodies and a tally by someone else a few days before had given 685. Several weeks later the wildebeest crossed there once more, with a loss of another three hundred calves. But in spite of this tremendous attrition of calves, the wildebeest have been increasing in number more or less steadily during the 1960's from an estimated 222,000 animals in 1961 and 382,000 in 1965 to over 500,000 in 1970. This overpowering throng is the more precious because it has endured in the face of a constant threat of death.

After eddying irresolutely back and forth, the migratory herds were able to move to the plains in March 1967 with the arrival of the main rains, which lasted to mid-May. In contrast, the next dry period ended on schedule and the wildebeest were able to use the plains from early December to the following May. But in 1969 the main rains almost failed, causing the herds to withdraw to the woodlands in April. A wildebeest's life is regulated by a movable feast in the form of a constantly changing pattern of available forage. About thirty inches of rain fall at Seronera during an average year, some forty to fifty percent of it from March to May and the least during June and July. The eastern plains receive about one third less rain than Seronera. These yearly differences in the amount of rainfall have an important effect on grass growth. Hubert Braun found that during the dry year of 1966–7 the grass had only 83 growing days in the woodlands near Banagi and 56 near Naabi Hill on the plains. The following year the figures were 198 and 183, respectively. Since grass seems to grow at roughly the same rate each day, over twice as much forage was produced in the latter year, a difference that may well have represented life rather than death to many herbivores.

The rainy season in March with its resurgent life is worth waiting for. On the plains a green carpet of grass stretches to the distant hills that stand out sharp and hard in the clear air. The earth exhales a new fragrance carried by fresh breezes. Once a herd of zebra pounded heavily past me, crushing some aromatic herbs with their hooves, and the air was then filled with a mintlike perfume. Scattered herds move over the expanse of the plains with the shadows of flat-bottomed clouds. *Rhampicarpa* flowers litter the green turf like discarded pieces of tissue paper, those on the rises being white and those in moist depressions pink even though all are of one species. Here and there a *Crinum* lily of the amaryllis family adds a splash of color. At times one glimpses a flash of red, and, kneeling down to bend aside the tall vegetation, one reveals the fiery scarlet flower of *Striga*, a plant that is parasitic on the roots of grass. Early in the morning, when the land is still hushed and no breath of wind stirs, a fog often lies low over the plains. Animals appear like phantoms only to dissolve again, and moving through this calm featureless world one seems to be afloat. But soon the sun melts the mists, and then the grass sparkles with silver dew.

Listening in the morning stillness one sometimes hears a mysterious boom, an ethereal drumming that seems to come from everywhere and nowhere. It is the call of the Kori bustard, a strange heavy-bodied bird that attains a height of almost five feet and a weight of twenty-five pounds. With the onset of the rains, usually in November or December, each male establishes a territory, preferably one with a hill-top that provides a wide view. On it the male struts back and forth, his tail raised to reveal the white undertail coverts. These function like a heliograph, the glistening white spot visible for miles as it flashes in the sun. Occasionally a male stands bolt upright and slowly inflates his white-feathered throat sac until just before it seems ready to burst he opens his beak, then snaps it shut, producing the unearthly boom. Thus having advertised himself to any wandering females and neighboring males, he stands motionless, waiting like some gray post, his black-crested head almost hidden in his semi-inflated neck. Once I saw a male encroach on another's territory, and the two males then fought by firmly grabbing each other's bills while pushing with their chests, each methodically gaining and losing some ground without violent motions, until finally one broke away and retreated, still walking with stately grace as if nothing could ever ruffle his composure. Males displayed until the end of the rains, but long before then the females had laid their two olive-brown eggs on bare ground and begun to incubate. I found eggs and small young only from February to April 1968, a very wet season. In the other two years the bustards either had little success in hatching eggs or they may have almost failed to breed because the rains were shorter than usual.

The rains signal the advent of the breeding season for many other birds too. Flappet larks rise into the sky and then slowly descend, beating their wings in such a way that they produce several curious clapping sounds. Male red bishop birds advertise their gaudy black and crimson plumage by clinging to the tops of swaying reeds, and the harsh calls of Coqui francolins and gray-breasted spurfowl ring insistently along the riverine thickets. The francolins and other gallinaceous birds are particularly dependent on the rains for successful breeding. For example, I often saw certain flocks of helmeted guinea fowl along the Seronera

River. When the short rains of November–December 1966 failed, the flocks delayed their breeding until the following April when the grass was high again. That autumn the short rains began on schedule and so did the breeding, with flocks raising at least two broods in succession.

The prolonged rains in 1967–8 also benefitted the *Arvicanthus* mice, which thrived in the security provided by the rank grass. The mice became abundant, particularly on the long-grass plains, where one could see them scurry back and forth across the roads in the daytime. News of this local food source must have spread beyond the confines of the Serengeti for that June saw the sudden influx of two kinds of birds of prey. One was the long-crested hawk-eagle, so named for the tuft of feathers that dips jauntily forward like that of a cockatoo; the other was the black-shouldered kite, a dainty gray and white bird. I enjoyed watching kites as they hovered over the plains, their eyes fixed on the grass below, silver stars against the blue sky, until suddenly they plummeted intent on a vulnerable rodent. But of twelve such attempts I witnessed only two resulted in a kill, the kite rising from the grass with a mouse in its tiny talons. When by September the grass had been burned and the mice reduced in number, these birds of prey vanished again except for rare stragglers.

When the first clouds swell on the horizon hopefully heralding the change from dry to wet season, winter has just begun in northern climes. Many birds have winged south from Europe and some come to the Serengeti, either as temporary residents or as casual visitors. European bee-eaters and spotted cuckoo tarry there, and Caspian plovers skim in tight flocks over the plains. The most conspicuous arrival is the European stork. Arriving with the first rains in November, they wheel as mere black specks in the sky until, turning around, their bodies gleam white in the sunshine. These storks originate in eastern Europe—two banded birds recovered in Tanzania had been ringed in East Prussia and

Poland—and fly over the Balkans before crossing the Bosporus and continuing south through Turkey. I always thought it rather incongruous to see storks stalking these plains surrounded by wildebeest and zebra rather than the bucolic meadows and villages of their summer home. Storks raised in the denatured environment of Europe have little to fear from predators and when they arrive in Africa they tend to be naïve about them. The Seronera leopards caught four storks and stored them in the branches of trees. Most of these visitors move north by May, but some, presumably subadult birds, remain behind in the dry season. About one hundred storks were at Seronera one day in August 1968, catching mice that were fleeing the flames of an advancing grass fire.

Because the woodlands became almost impassable to a vehicle during the rains, much of my work at that time of year was confined to the plains. Brown water filled even the smallest creeks, and seemingly solid earth would detain the car with wheels spinning futilely. To dig the wheels free, jack up the car, and cut brush for placing under the wheels was a tedious task, often requiring several hours of work, and, if the mire failed to release the car, the whole process would have to be repeated. Even the plains had their treacherous ground as this woeful tale from the monthly park report of March 1968 shows:

> On 12th March an air search was launched for the Planning Adviser, Mr. Thresher, overdue at Seronera from Lagarja [sic]. He was located 4 miles beyond the Eastern boundary in the Conservation Unit area hopelessly bogged. An International 4-wheel drive truck with Warden Nawaz was sent out to assist. This also got stuck. Warden Nawaz returned next day to Seronera after an epic night walk to Naabi Hill, and again returned to the attack, this time with a Land Rover and "Dungu," the Field Force 5-tonner. Both these vehicles got stuck but managed to get Mr. Thresher

and family to Naabi Hill from where they returned to Arusha by air. The final day was spent extricating one Land Rover and two lorries with the last remaining Seronera transport.

Most roads, too, became impassable or barely so. Unfortunately the park lacked regulations concerning travel after heavy rains, with the result that vehicles churned up the tracks or drove parallel to them. Some roads grew into morasses over a hundred feet wide. Cars that drove cross-country left deep ruts. Seen from the air, Seronera was a slum of roads and trails. Impassable roads were abandoned to erode into deep ditches, new ones were sited by cars merely following the tracks of a previous one. Tracks around Seronera increased tremendously in number while I was there—none planned, almost none maintained. Gravel for the few roads that were kept passable was dug from conspicuous pits, ugly scars that brutally violated the pleasing contours of the terrain. The Serengeti is beautiful because until now man has had limited opportunities to destroy it. The Seronera area has been spoiled through thoughtlessness and lethargy, through seeing and treating it as was done thirty years ago, not as it should be maintained, when over twenty thousand visitors come there each year. Fragile land must be handled gently.

The transition from the rainy to the dry season is gradual, without dramatic points of reference. By mid-May the long grasses have changed from intense green to a soft green and various shades of yellow, sienna, and brown. The hills have begun their retreat into haze. Though occasional veils of rain may still hang over the eastern plains, the animals there know that a forced march westward is imminent. There is a galvanic excitement in the air over the impending change. During this time the wildebeest reach the peak of their rut.

Many wildebeest bulls establish small territories when

they are at least three years old and from these they expel
other bulls but attempt to retain any cows that enter. Richard
Estes found that in Ngorongoro Crater, where wildebeest
are resident, some bulls may remain in their territory for
two or more years. But in the Serengeti, with its migratory
population, bulls cannot establish themselves permanently,
at least not if they hope to have cows visit them. Instead
they set up temporary territories. Choosing a piece of turf
perhaps 100 to 150 feet in diameter near a herd, a bull
stands in its center, very erect and with head raised, advertising his size, his power, his glossy hide. Occasionally he
paws the earth, then kneels and rubs his forehead on the
ground, depositing the sweet and slightly musty odor from
his facial glands. Repeated pawing and rubbing soon form
a bare spot and on it the bull urinates and defecates, further
enhancing the site with his odor. Sometimes he canters
around the border of his territory in a peculiar rocking gait,
and should he meet a neighbor during this patrol, both may
drop on their knees facing each other and vigorously belabor
the sod with their heads and horns. Having asserted their
rights, and while still on their knees, they may then nonchalantly nibble at grass, an incongruous gesture quite out
of context with the situation. Finally they leap up, bucking
and cavorting, freed from the tension of the territorial confrontation. But at times the preliminaries are followed with
a bashing of horns and a pushing match, tests of strength
that seldom result in an injury. When a herd of cows moves
through a territory, the bull places himself expectantly in
front of them, though as often as not they flow around him
as if he were an inanimate object. However, as the rut
progresses, as many as ten to thirty cows with their calves
may remain in the territory. The bull tries to prevent their
leaving by constantly prancing around and herding them
into a tight cluster. He is continuously in motion, fighting
neighboring bulls, chasing a straying cow. It is a scene of
organized pandemonium, with animals everywhere in cha-

otic motion and the air vibrating with grunts and bellows, yet it somehow suits this zany animal. After a few hours or days, the cows move on, and the bulls must pack up too, perhaps to establish a new territory closer to the herds.

Then, toward the end of May, the migratory zebra and usually a few gazelle arrive at Seronera, the air above the herds filled with dust. The sky is pale, seen as through a luminous gauze, and the yellow grasses whisper when the wind strokes them. Speckle-fronted weaver birds and red-cheeked cordon bleu come again to the bird bath in the garden, and at night we can hear hyenas lap water there. With these and other signs, we know that the rainy season is at an end.

LIFE IN THE PRIDE

A STUDY IS MOST SATISFYING AND INTERESTING WHEN ONE knows animals individually, and one of my first tasks around Seronera was to find a means of identifying the lions there. Since lions lack a distinctive coat pattern, such as the stripes of zebra or splotches of giraffe, I concentrated on such characteristics as torn ears, scars, and other blemishes. It did not take me long to recognize the thirty or so adult lions that roamed in the vicinity of our house. There was Flop-ear, for example, whose left ear was bent over at the tip. She was the every essence of a lioness, a lovely animal in the prime of life. The Old One had worn canines and the heavy tread of the aged, the local matriarch who was approaching the end of her life. One-ear and One-eye were rather runty lionesses, named for obvious characteristics, who usually traveled together as if the deformities were a basis for their bond. Sleek and russet-colored, The Young Female was perhaps three years old and she had not yet given birth, judging by her taut abdomen. Also using the area were three males with huge manes, an aristocratic trio that roamed through

44

their domain with an insolence based on eons of inviolability. I knew them as Black Mane, Brown Mane, and Limp. A few lions displayed individuality, whether playfulness, reticence, or irascibility, which made physical features almost superfluous as a means of recognizing them. The lions soon became acquaintances whose activity I followed from day to day and whose joys and sorrows I shared. I gave names to some lions and referred to others merely by letter or number. The naming of a wild animal should not be done casually, for a name colors one's thinking about it forever afterwards. To burden an animal with a cute or inappropriate label merely for effect, as is sometimes done, reveals a condescending attitude and lack of feeling I find annoying. Consequently most of my lions received either descriptive names or innocuous designations.

The social system of lions seems perplexing at first. One meets a group, recognizes several individuals, and the next day these are associating with entirely different animals. Not surprisingly, most observers have been confused by such casual contacts. For example, James Stevenson-Hamilton, a warden at Kruger Park for many years, wrote: "Exactly how a pride forms and breaks up is not perfectly clear, and the probability is that there is no definite habit or custom in the matter at all." However, once I knew all lions around Seronera, it became obvious that only certain ones associated whereas others never did so. Those that met and interacted peacefully were of the same pride. Members of a pride may be widely scattered—I have seen them as far as ten miles apart—yet they still retain their pride ties. The whole pride may rarely be together. One usually meets groups of three to six animals, whereas the average pride size in the Serengeti is about fifteen.

The lions around Seronera belonged to two prides, the Seronera and Masai prides as I called them. In mid-1966 the former was composed of two adult males, six adult lionesses, two subadult males, ten subadult lionesses, and four small cubs. The subadults were known to have been born in March or April 1963. The Masai pride consisted of three adult males, six adult lionesses and a subadult one, and six small cubs. By watching these individuals intensively in the ensuing three years, I learned how their society was organized and how natural forces shaped and maintained it. Several other prides also used the Seronera area intermittently. To the north ranged the Loliondo pride, a large one that at one period numbered thirty-seven individuals; and to the west was the Nyaraswiga pride, whose interactions with the Seronera and Masai prides provided me with some of the most interesting and exciting glimpses into lion mentality.

The composition of the two prides at Seronera was typical, with adult females outnumbering adult males by a ratio of between two and three to one. In addition, some lions are nomads, they do not belong to a pride. Taking such animals into account also, the number of lionesses in the population exceeds that of males by a ratio of about three to two. As is the case in many species, male lions seem to have a higher death rate than females because they fight more and wander more widely, roaming out of the park where they are shot and snared. About half of the lion population consists of adults, about a quarter of subadults, two to four years old, and a quarter of cubs less than two years old, a vigorous population with good reproduction.

During the first year that I watched the Seronera and Masai prides no dramatic events interrupted the level tenor of their life, even births and deaths being only part of the inevitability of things. That year, five of the subadult lionesses and the two young males in the Seronera pride became peripheral and finally left the area entirely by the end of 1966, not as a group but singly and in pairs, to roam on their own, free from the restraints of a pride existence. They were just over three years old at the time. One of these lionesses returned the following June for a day, but the others I never saw or at least did not recognize again. At that time, too, One-ear and One-eye of that pride became peripheral in that they avoided contact with their friends yet stayed in the area. The remaining three young lionesses remained with the pride as full members. It puzzled me why some young lionesses left but others did not, for I could not detect a difference in the behavior of adults toward them. Some adult lionesses with small cubs at heel may repulse any young lioness that approaches, but one is as likely to be cuffed as another. Young animals may also elicit attack by acting unsure of themselves when meeting a pride member, by, for example, nervously glancing around. Lions have few distinctive markings by which they can recognize one another at a distance, and behavior is used as an important cue to determine whether or not an approaching animal is a friend. A pride member must join others unhesitatingly, it must act as if it belongs there, and I found it quite amusing to observe a sedate lioness run to a group after an absence, not out of exuberance or impatience, but to leave no doubt as to her status. A lioness who does not behave as expected is attacked like any stranger. Some young lionesses that have been assaulted several times may well become increasingly unsure of themselves and this in turn elicits further aggression, a vicious circle that can only end by their severing the familial bonds. Other young lionesses possibly shrug off, so to speak, the occasional attack, being temperamentally less nervous, and these steady animals remain to contribute their character to society.

Whether or not to remain in the pride poses no question to young males: all are expected to leave. At some time between the ages of 2½ and 3½ years, a young male abandons his home, either alone or with one or more brothers or pride mates of similar age, and takes up a nomadic existence. A combination of wanderlust and rather forceful hints from the adults in the pride seems to determine their seeking a wider horizon.

The departure of seven subadult lions from the Seronera pride early in the study raised the fascinating problem of what factors regulate pride size. This pride helped to provide some tentative answers. There were probably about six adult lionesses in the Seronera pride in 1963 but success in rearing several litters raised the number of lionesses to sixteen. Of these, nine ceased to be regular members and two died of old age, leaving a total of seven lionesses at the end of the study in 1969. Having fluctuated markedly over a period of six years, the number of lionesses dropped back to about its original number of six to seven, which probably represents an optimum for that pride. Since all young males leave the pride, they have no influence on its growth or decline. Some biologists suggest that social factors are mainly involved in determining the optimum number of animals in an area; others contend that food is critical. In spite of the fact that the Seronera pride, and others as well, increased its size temporarily, it did not use a larger area during that period. Prides remain in a certain locality for years, possibly centuries, and their optimum size and the amount of terrain they occupy may be adapted to periods of prey shortage, which occur only at intervals of years. Yet something tends to reduce pride size to the optimum even in years of prey abundance. Some behavioral mechanism operates in the pride, resulting in the emigration of young lionesses, but I do not know what determines how many animals must leave. Thus both food and social factors have an influence on pride size.

In field work one is first of all a seeker of small facts that, hopefully, will later give rise to generalizations. A lion spends its day rather pleasantly—sleeping, resting, and reveling in the intimacy of the pride. But lions in the daytime give as one-sided an impression of their behavior as would a group of people observed only at night. To find out about the life of lions at night as well as by day, I frequently remained with certain animals on a twenty-four–hour basis. The use of car headlights or other artificial source of illumination was an intrusion the lions ignored but to which all prey animals in the vicinity responded by becoming startled or alert. Consequently I could not use lights. Instead, my existence began to revolve around the moon, as each month I watched it grow from the first radiant sliver to lustrous fullness, so bright that I could observe lions throughout the night. I also rediscovered old pleasures while watching for the moon. I became aware again of evening shadows creeping over the plains, and of the occasional fireflies blinking their Morse code in the calm darkness before the moon rises; I became aware of the planets and stars and of the cosmic rhythm of life, which one disregards more and more as civilization encroaches insistently on the senses. One day in August of 1969, Flop-ear and Notch of the Masai pride rested along the Seronera River with their five cubs, seven months old. With the moon almost full, I decided to observe them for several days, to see how they fared at the height of the dry season, when Thomson's gazelle were the main prey available around Seronera.

All afternoon the lions rested beneath an acacia, only changing their sleeping site to follow the movement of the dappled shade around the tree as the day advanced. Listlessly they rose, ambled a few feet, and collapsed with an audible sigh, as if quite exhausted by their effort. Then they rested some more, utterly relaxed, only the twitching of their ears evidence that they were not oblivious to their surroundings. I waited through the early afternoon when the only sound was the buzzing of flies and everything looked wan in the dazzling light; and I waited through the evening, during the hush at dusk when the daytime sounds are replaced by those of the night. But the lions slept on. A scops owl hooted far away. I often heard these small owls but never saw one and after a while I did not seek a meeting, for it would have ruined the mystery of their haunting calls. The Masai pride males roared downriver, then roared again. The lionesses did not answer. The moon rose, suffusing everything with its soft light. Yet the lions slept on. Finally, at 10:10 p.m., Flop-ear and Notch rose, stretched, and ambled a third of a mile, leaving the cubs behind. The lionesses sat down for ten minutes, listening, as if waiting for something to interrupt the silence, then returned to their cubs. A little later The Young Female arrived and greeted everybody in typical cat fashion by rubbing her cheeks and forehead against them. Soon thereafter she vanished. Thoroughly awake now, Flop-ear spotted several gazelle, their white bellies gleaming along the river. Tensing immediately, she waited a minute, as if planning her hunt, then cut toward a nearby thicket, walking with head lowered. The cubs gamboled after her, thereby scaring the gazelle before she had a chance to stalk.

Suddenly all lions ran into a thicket. A porcupine rattled its long quills there, a sign that the lions were harrying it. A few minutes later the lions emerged—without having eaten. Notch had a quill sticking in her lip and she pawed at it until it came out. Fritz Eloff told me that the lions commonly kill porcupines in the Kalahari Gemsbok Reserve of South Africa. The Serengeti lions seldom manage to penetrate the prickly defenses of this rodent. Possibly lions in some areas learn special techniques for dealing with certain prey. Simon Trevor, Kay, and I watched a lioness one night as she half-heartedly attempted to subdue a porcupine. She walked up to the porcupine and tentatively raised a paw as if to slap, but it merely rattled its quills furiously and sidled toward her. She prudently retreated from this battery of miniature spears. After repulsing the lioness repeatedly over a period of half an hour, the porcupine was able to waddle off unmolested.

While the lionesses sat around, the cubs played, batting at each other with their clumsy paws and chasing each other with abandon through the moonlight. Flop-ear walked to a pad of fresh buffalo dung and sinuously wiped her face in the soft, odorous mass, then ecstatically rolled in it. I have been unable to fathom the reason for such behavior among lions. Perhaps the odor of buffalo dung has the same effect on them as catnip has on house cats. A bit later they all filed down to the river, and crowding along its edge, they lapped water. For a few minutes they seemed undecided about where to go as they stood or sat around, occasionally sniffing at a tuft of grass or bare spot on the ground. How I wished that our own sense of smell were more acute—what a new world would be revealed to us! Pride members can no doubt recognize each other by smell and they can track an old spoor as well as can a dog. A whole history of recent happenings permeates each piece of ground, yet we sense little or nothing as we hurry by, almost entirely limited to a world of seeing and hearing.

Just after midnight, Flop-ear and Notch walked alertly ahead until their shadows disappeared in some tall grass. I waited beside the cubs, feeling that the lionesses were hunting something I could not see. Suddenly the cubs bounded ahead, and, hurrying after them, I soon came upon the three lionesses, including The Young Female, who had materialized from somewhere, each biting into a Thomson's gazelle and straining to appropriate as much of the carcass as possible. They growled and yanked until the gazelle tore apart, Flop-ear managing to get a small piece, Notch a leg, and The Young Female most of it. Each retreated with her portion while the cubs squabbled over stray bits of viscera. Twenty minutes later, as Notch walked aimlessly around the kill area, she flushed a gazelle fawn that had crouched there motionless. Chasing it about a hundred feet, she bowled it over with a swipe of her forepaw and grabbed it by the neck. Carrying it alive and still bleating to her cubs, she dropped it before them, an unusually generous gesture for a lion. She stood and watched them as they mauled it, snarling and slapping at each other. At such moments friendship becomes an intangible to a cub and the only reality is getting a bite of meat. After a minute Notch snatched the gazelle away, and, while the cubs clamored around her, she calmly consumed all of it herself. Content for the present with these snacks, the lionesses reclined and the cubs did too, at seven months of age still fully dependent on their mothers no matter how hungry they might be.

Over an hour later, at 2:30 a.m., about thirty Thomson's gazelle wandered over a rise one or two at a time, briefly silhouetted as they moved against the starry sky before dropping into the shadows of the slope. Flop-ear hurried toward them in a semi-crouch, the muscles beneath her sleek hide rippling in the cool light like water flowing over a submerged rock. Lions fully reveal their power and beauty only at night. At that time their indolence of the day is transformed into an implacable mien, into an aura of boldness and tension, even when they are at rest. And when they stalk into the night, all the mystery of their being is distilled to its essence. Notch trotted to the right in an obvious attempt to head the gazelle off should they flee that way after sensing Flop-ear. Suddenly Flop-ear sprinted and after a brief chase captured a gazelle fawn. This she ate. Afterwards the cubs crowded around her feeding site looking for scraps.

It was now 3:00 a.m. and the group moved upriver. There the two lionesses began to stalk a gazelle herd in the open without success, the animals perceiving danger when the lions were still 250 feet away. All then rested. Other pride members roared nearby and the two lionesses answered, whereas the cubs took no part in this vocal display. A few minutes later the lionesses roared once more and a male replied. Lions often advertise their presence by roaring toward dawn, and this enables scattered members of the pride to meet and rest together in case they wish to do so. At 5:15 a.m. the group continued its excursion, along the riverbank, down through the dry streambed and past a thicket until they came to a spit of land at the confluence of two creeks. Several gazelle grazed there unaware of the lions. Flop-ear walked toward them, gliding gently forward, using

In popular mythology a lioness has somehow become the epitome of the concerned mother who will care for her cubs even at the expense of her own life. Lionesses may, of course, defend their cubs, and they will suckle them and lead them to a kill, but the most striking aspect of their behavior is self-indulgence: they seldom permit the needs of cubs to conflict too much with their own desires, especially when these concern food. Being basically adapted to capturing and feeding on large prey, where the need to provide cubs with meat is not essential because these can compete for their own portion, lions have never developed a strong habit of sharing. Consequently when only small gazelle are available, as they are at Seronera for much of the dry season, the cubs get little or no food. A forty-pound gazelle is just a pleasant meal for one lioness and she hoards it jealously. Afterwards, replete with meat, she is little inclined to hunt. Even if she does so and catches something, another pride member may arrive and take the spoils. And again the cubs get nothing. Once lioness A of the Seronera pride killed two gazelle as they crossed a deep gulley. She consumed one, but gave the other to her daughter, driving away other lions that attempted to snatch a bite. Though such an incident was rare, I thought better of lions after seeing it.

Each summer as the dry season progressed the pelvic bones of cubs grew more prominent. Their leg muscles shrank, making the cubs' paws look even more disproportionately large and ungainly. All play ceased. They plodded behind their mother, eyes vacant and hollow, with the hope of snatching a stray morsel should there be a kill. Toward the end of the dry season, the weakest cubs may stagger, and, lacking the strength to continue, they may lie down and watch the family retreat around a bend of the river without a backward glance. The cubs' lives then hang in balance. If luck is with them a shower will bring forth green grass, which in turn attracts zebra. A few meals rapidly transform them into plump and vigorous youngsters,

the cover of tree trunks and bushes when possible until finally she launched herself from a distance of three hundred feet. Under normal cimcumstances she would have little chance of capturing fleet quarry from so far away, but years of hunting in the area had taught her that gazelle seldom try to flee across creeks whose brush-lined banks may harbor leopards and in whose depths lurk crocodiles. The area was a deadly cul-de-sac from which prey had to escape by running toward the lions. As Flop-ear approached in her low, fast gallop, the gazelle scattered and all escaped except one male who lost his head and erratically dashed back and forth, unable to decide in which direction to run. Entering a reedbed in a depression he lost so much running speed that Flop-ear easily overtook him, her momentum bowling him over and a bite in the neck killing him.

Flop-ear began to eat immediately, cutting through the skin along the inner thighs of her victim and tearing out chunks of meat, as usual bolting it hurriedly as if afraid that someone would take it from her. Notch lay seventy feet away and the cubs hovered around, all watching Flop-ear eat but afraid to approach to claim a share. A cub finally sidled closer until a cough and a vicious swat from its mother drove it back. Limp, the male, and one of Flop-ear's grown cubs arrived a few minutes later. Without hesitation Limp attacked Flop-ear. She fled with the carcass and he pursued, running awkwardly with his gimpy leg, until after five hundred feet she relinquished the carcass. Withdrawing into some high grass, he ate noisily, cracking the slender leg bones of the gazelle with the sound of someone munching celery. The cubs crowded around the male. They knew that he was more tolerant than Flop-ear, even though he once slapped a particularly impudent youngster. However, when the young lioness came near he immediately lunged at her, chasing her twenty feet. While he did that, the cubs piled on the remains for a quick bite. Limp returned. He gave a few token slaps with retracted claws and ate briefly with the cubs before abandoning the carcass to them, a magnanimous gesture in sharp contrast to the selfishness of the lionesses.

It was 8:30 a.m. by the time the gazelle had achieved its physical reincarnation in the bodies of various lions and the morning coolness was already giving way to the heat of the day. Stephen Cobb and Clive Craik, two British students who assisted at the Research Institute for several months, relieved me of my vigil so I could attend to other tasks. As they watched the lions, an occasional cub suckled, but the shriveled breasts of the lionesses held too little milk to serve even as a supplement to the meager ration of meat they had had the previous night. The first twenty-four hours of observation ended as they had begun, the lions at ease in the shade of a tree. They had walked 4.7 miles and caught four gazelle, a good record except that two were mere *hors d'oeuvres*, most of the third one was eaten by Limp, and most of the fourth by The Young Female—the mothers and cubs had received little.

At 1:45 p.m. the two mothers walked for .8 mile upriver without the cubs. Seeing no vulnerable prey there, they reclined and slept. Flop-ear raised her head at 4:00 p.m. and saw several gazelle. She approached them slowly. The animals sensed her and casually retreated, knowing that with their speed a lion was unlikely to catch them after it had been deprived of the element of surprise.

In the evening I returned to the two lionesses for another night of observation and Stephen joined me. Most nights pass easily in the open. There are the lions to watch and, when they sleep, there are the stars, the Southern Cross, the Big Dipper lying on its back, and the many others far beyond, their light touching me after millions of years of travel. The appalling vastness, the meaningless reach of the universe, produced a sense of loneliness, a feeling that all struggles mean nothing. Yet at the same time I came to terms with my dreams and I found a sense of peace. I

thought about the past and the future and about t I love and hate; I became a wanderer in search of and in the end my broodings usually ended in exh as I looked around at this, my kingdom, where I w and free in the night. One night spent awake is a to two in a row is tedium, and I was glad to have Steph me to pass the weary hours after midnight. It is surp hard work to stay awake for more than one nigh watching sleeping lions. When I submitted at times insistent temptation to close my eyes for just a few mi the lions would almost invariably vanish silently in darkness.

Flop-ear and Notch slept on into the night withou cern for the cubs that had been waiting for their mo return since 2:00 p.m. Finally at around 10:00 p.m lionesses rose, yawned cavernously, and ambled ba their offspring, who greeted them excitedly, no doubt l to be led to a meal. A few minutes later one of Flo grown cubs and Limp joined the group. These new drifted off again when at 11:45 the lionesses and cubs a mile upriver, as usual following the dirt road for ience. After this exertion, all settled down and the on and on until a pale line on the horizon announ next day, their night interrupted only by a visit fro Mane and two lionesses. At dawn the cubs listless to play, more out of habit than conviction, and t stopped. Having fasted for a whole day, they tried a drink of milk, but as often as not received a pu face from a hindpaw instead. Finally all slept. In ceding twenty-four hours the lionesses had walked They had failed to make a sustained attempt at hui though the ribs of their cubs were outlined clearl unkempt hides and their flanks had the hollow s malnutrition. Although we followed the group f two whole days, these examples suffice to show t routines during the dry season.

their period of deprivation forgotten. But if the drought continues there is no reprieve for some. Finally, unable to stand, their young lives retreat into the shadows. Flop-ear's three cubs starved to death in 1968 and Notch lost her single cub for the same reason in 1966. One out of five cubs born around Seronera died from lack of food.

The annual period of starvation presented me with a moral dilemma. Visitors complained vehemently to the park authorities and to the Nairobi press about the deplorable condition of the Seronera lions. Traditionally the park wardens shot prey to feed such cubs. I was against this practice for several reasons. The Serengeti is not a zoo, and, that being so, animals should be allowed to regulate themselves, to live or to die, without interference whenever possible; if left to herself, nature establishes her own *modus vivendi*. A park is a place where one can come into direct contact with unadorned nature, but, judging by the reaction to the emaciated cubs, man cannot stand much reality. The lion population was healthy. Taking into account the survival rate of cubs and the death rate of adults, the annual increase in prides was about 5.5 percent. Since prides tend to stabilize around an optimum number of animals, an artificial increase in surviving youngsters would simply mean that the excess animals would emigrate, possibly to be killed by man when they leave the park. It is in the areas surrounding the park that a disproportionately large number of lions die, and anyone truly concerned about saving lions and increasing their abundance in the Serengeti area should devote all efforts toward controlling illegal hunting there. To shoot perfectly healthy prey animals, disrupting their society, merely to feed lions whom fate has destined to die is wrong too. Is a lion better than a zebra? Of course, the whole problem could be solved by killing the starving cubs, but to annihilate all such animals, some of whom would surely have survived, merely to placate the sensibilities of a few visitors was not a solution that pleased me. My research had provided me with information that placed logic on my side. Yet when I saw a starving cub, whose development I had watched from woolly toddler to sleek youngster, whose vigorous play had brought me delight, whose unheeding explorations had caused me apprehension, I felt a deep anguish. My emotions were with the individual and not with the species. Yet choosing to argue from the basis of fact rather than emotion, I perpetuated the myth of the dispassionate scientist.

A cub's life is not just one of hardship. As a counterpoint to the grim dry season, I would like to describe a lion's day when, far out on the plains, the Masai pride had much food available. The five cubs of Flop-ear and Notch were four months old at the time. One day at 11:00 a.m. I met all members of the pride, except Limp, at rest by a waterhole. They were sprawled here and there, some on their backs, others on their sides, legs and bodies touching as if contact enhanced the pleasure of their repose. Only Scruffy, a young male, remained at the periphery because Flop-ear and sometimes Notch were antagonistic toward him while they had small cubs. He was almost two years old at the time, normally old enough to assert himself a little, but starvation had left him runty and the growth of his mane retarded. A few months later he was again tolerated by the lionesses although he continued to remain uneasy in their presence. Both at 12:30 and 2:00 p.m. several cubs became restless and tried to suckle on Notch. As usual they squabbled, trying to elbow each other aside, until Notch became annoyed at the sharp claws raking her breasts and drove the youngsters off with bared teeth and a snarl. Ignored by the adults, some cubs played gently. One bit a grass stalk and shook its head as if subduing an opponent, two slapped each other, a fourth caught the flicking black tassle at the end of a lioness's tail and bit into it, no doubt assuming that this delightful appendage was designed solely for its pleasure. A snarl from the owner quickly convinced it otherwise.

Toward dusk the pride stirred. Some animals wandered off to one side and defecated. They scratched themselves and stretched, and drew their unsheathed claws through the sod. Then they greeted each other, rubbing cheeks not leisurely but with a certain tension that foretold a communal endeavor. Such a greeting represents a subdued pep rally in that it reinforces the social bonds of the pride and gets the members into the unified mood needed to accomplish something together. Abruptly they departed from the rest site, leaving the cubs behind. These, on their own accord, sought a hiding place in the reeds bordering the waterhole. Cubs respond to their mother's subtle signals in deciding whether or not to follow her. By walking away silently and rapidly, a lioness conveys that she does not want the cubs with her and these then conceal themselves, or, as they grow older, merely lie in the open to await her return. But if the lioness walks slowly, uttering soft grunts—uh-uh-uh —it means "come" and the youngsters bound along behind her.

A broad valley stretched to the west. Gathering at its rim, the lions surveyed the scattered herds of wildebeest and zebra and then waited while the plains changed slowly to a shadowy purple and finally grew dark. As if on signal, the lionesses fanned out and dissolved in the grass, each moving toward prey on her own, yet each taking part in a cooperative effort whose strategy was predetermined by many hunts. I waited beside Black Mane and Brown Mane, who stood there staring into the night with inviolable dignity. Suddenly hooves drummed and the wild scream of a zebra shattered the darkness. The males and I hurried in the direction from which the sound came. Driving rapidly cross-country without lights, never knowing when the car would drop into a hyena warren or straddle a termite hill, was a minor adventure in itself. When I reached the kill site, the air was already heavy with the odor of blood and rumen contents. The tawny mass of lions filling the night with menacing growls, as each animal fought for a share of the meat, was a drama of such naked emotion that the hair on my nape and back raised itself in subconscious apprehension for my safety. I was witnessing a pitch of passion that was almost foreign to human experience. Thirty minutes later the zebra was dismembered and each animal was cleaning meat off some bone; Brown Mane with a lunge and growl had taken possession of the whole ribcage, neck, and head. I felt myself relax suddenly and realized for the first time the silent and ancient fear this primitive scene had evoked for me. It is not so much what we see but what it suggests that arouses us. Almost palpably my racial memories rose of a past when man crouched vulnerably in the dark, listening to the growls of his enemies, and of a time when the smell and sight of red meat meant survival. Here under a pale rising moon the past met the present.

It was now 8:20 p.m. Notch headed toward the cubs a mile and a half away, and Flop-ear soon followed. All returned at 9:30, the cubs trotting eagerly ahead of their mothers. No meat was left for the cubs except that which Brown Mane had appropriated for himself. Brown Mane was a beautiful animal in his prime, with a rather bemused expression and a huge mane that had no equal in this part of the Serengeti. But instead of giving him a regal appearance, that mane somehow made him look cuddly and kindly. The cubs joined him on the kill and were permitted to eat. After the last bones had been rasped clean, the cubs sought out their mothers and suckled in spite of being gorged.

I drove slowly to the remains of the carcass and quietly stepped from the car. Several quick strokes with the hatchet severed the zebra's head from the vertebral column and I had another specimen to age and sex. By checking the sequence of tooth eruption of young animals and the relative degree of tooth wear of adults it is possible to determine the approximate age of an individual; zebra stallions can be distinguished from mares by the fact that they have large canines. After collecting many zebra skulls, I would be able to note if lions captured proportionately more of one age or sex than of another, an important factor in evaluating the effects of predation. The lions usually permitted me to take the head of a kill without objection after they had finished eating. However, once I was impatient when a year-old cub tarried over the remains. I pulled on the skeleton while the cub was still eating. It merely clutched the bones and hung on grimly as I dragged them toward me. Finally it was at my feet, glaring up at me malevolently, and even when I placed the sole of my shoe against its nose and pushed gently it still did not want to relinquish its property. Never had I seen such combative force in so small a form.

At 1:20 a.m. the pride moved on. Again the cubs stayed behind, sleeping in a furry pile against the night chill. Topping a ridge, the lions saw a herd of wildebeest grazing in desultory fashion below them. The lionesses spread out over some eight hundred feet of terrain and waited, only their heads visible as dark lumps above the level of the grass. For once there was no wind and the herd moved imperceptibly closer without sensing danger. The lions waited for nearly two hours until finally a careless wildebeest stumbled on a hidden lioness. Within fifteen minutes the carcass was torn apart. Flop-ear departed this time to fetch the cubs. Ten minutes later they arrived, joining Black Mane on the remains he had taken for himself. Black Mane had an unusually dark mane for a lion in the Serengeti, where yellow and brown manes predominate. He liked to wander off by himself, at times for days disdaining the company of his friends. Coupled with his rather withdrawn personality, he had a severe and determined mien, and I would have expected him to rebuff the cubs. But he shared his meat. The first light of day found all at rest and happily glutted. They roused themselves just enough to greet the rising sun with a communal concert of roars before sinking into contented oblivion that lasted at least to midday. In twenty-four hours they had walked 2.4 miles, eaten twice, and each cub had suckled an average of fifty-three minutes.

Lion males have an unenviable reputation. They are considered to be shiftless and lazy, letting the lionesses do all the hunting. And they are said to bumble amiably through life doing little except procreate. There is some superficial truth to this impression. Males do permit the lionesses in a pride to hunt whenever possible. When a male fed on a gazelle the odds were seventy-six percent that he had taken the meat from a lioness, twelve percent that he had scavenged it, and only twelve percent that he had caught it himself. Limp, for example, dogged the steps of lionesses during the dry season, and when a gazelle was caught he did his utmost to obtain a portion—or, preferably, all of it—often at the expense of a starving cub to whose death he thereby contributed. Limp had an afflicted hip joint that at times hurt him so much he could barely hobble. He always seemed to have fresh cuts in his tattered hide, the result of some squabble. Since Limp lacked the stately appearance of Black Mane and Brown Mane, I somehow found it less easy to forgive him his transgressions. But his behavior cannot be interpreted through human values; it must be viewed objectively in the context of his society. As Henry Beston expressed it beautifully in his book *The Outermost House*:

> For the animals shall not be measured by man. In a world older and more complete than ours they move finished and complete, gifted with extensions of the senses we have lost or never attained, living by voices we shall never hear. They are not brethren, they are not underlings; they are other nations caught with ourselves in the net of life and time, fellow prisoners of the splendor and travail of the earth.

With time, as I began to better understand lions, the males provided me with some of the finest moments of revelation.

When a pride sets off on a hunt, the lionesses walking tensely in front, the cubs bounding playfully in the middle, and the males in the rear, their heavy heads nodding with each step as if they are bored with the whole matter, it is easy to castigate them for slothfulness. But males are bulky and adorned with such a voluminous mane that they look like wandering haystacks, in contrast to the sleek, lithe lionesses. In a business which for success places a premium on being cryptic, agile, and fast, it is of advantage to the pride that males remain mainly spectators. In addition, by bringing up the rear the males act as inadvertent guards for the cubs, which when small are vulnerable to marauding hyenas and other dangers. This is not to imply that males are incapable of hunting well: they can support themselves and indeed must do so when as nomads they may have no lionesses handy to provide them with a meal.

Frequently the cubs do not go with the pride during a hunt but stay patiently somewhere waiting for their mother to return and lead them to a kill. They may have a long wait. If the kill is small, the mother usually eats it up; if it is large she first gorges herself and then thinks of her cubs. By the time she has walked perhaps a mile or more to retrieve her offspring little or no meat may be left for them. Here the males come to the rescue. As I described earlier, males may drive the lionesses off and appropriate the remnants of a kill. Lionesses are not allowed back to the carcass, although one may try to inch closer on her belly in hopes of snatching a bite, behavior which the male discourages with heavy clouts. But small cubs are permitted to eat. The male's actions, no matter what their basis, are of subtle evolutionary benefit to the pride. At first, I had reproved males for their selfishness, and it was with total pleasure that I discarded that opinion and accepted a new truth.

With snapping jaws and flashing claws lions crowd around a kill, each fighting for its portion, each thinking only of itself, not even giving the cubs priority. I often had to remind myself that such seemingly excessive aggression must be adaptive or it would not have persisted. One wonders what would happen if lions had a rigid feeding hierarchy, the males eating first, then the lionesses, and finally the cubs, a system that popular supposition erroneously ascribes to them. Given their present size and temperament, such a system would probably lead to the disintegration or at least reorganization of the pride. Males have such a gargantuan capacity for meat that most kills are not large enough to feed more than two or three of them and perhaps a few lionesses too. Animals low in the hierarchy, young adults, subadults, and cubs, would seldom obtain a meal. With each lion fighting for a portion such inequity is partially removed. By virtue of their size and strength, males get more than their share of meat, and it is common, for example, to see one rip a gazelle from the grasp of a hapless lioness. However, his aggression is tempered by the knowledge that his opponent is also armed with formidable weapons and few inhibitions about using them. To attack a lioness may not only arouse her but also several other lionesses, and even a male avoids having the communal passions turned against him. A cub, too, may give a male a stinging blow on his nose while fighting for its rights over a piece of meat. Consequently lions hesitate to attack those that can retaliate most effectively. Two males prefer to share a carcass, though reluctantly, rather than dispute it, and their harsh growls will seldom erupt into a serious argument at such times. When a kill or part of it is small, one lion may keep possession of it without having its rights to the kill challenged. Once, for instance, Limp scavenged the remains of a gazelle from a cheetah. First Black Mane and then Brown Mane arrived at the site, but they merely reclined and watched Limp eat. Brown Mane approached Limp to within fifteen feet but a growl and lunge drove him back in spite of the fact that Limp was the weaker animal. Yet on subsequent days the other males may assume temporary dominance over some possession. It is a system of uneasy peace based on a balance of power, something not unknown in human affairs. The system obviously functions well, although the vigor of disputes seems excessive at times and I could think of more amicable solutions to the same problem. Only if the delicate equilibrium of adaptation is somehow upset, such as when available prey is below optimum size, does this lack of sharing harm the pride with the result that cubs may starve.

Because of such strife over food, a lion may at times try a simple deception on others that have taken part in the hunt. Having caught an animal in high grass and dispatched it, the lion will sit down casually and look around as if the chase had been a total failure, completely ignoring the kill hidden at its feet. Not until the other pride members have moved away will it surreptitiously begin to feed.

While starvation is an obvious cause of death among cubs, it is not the most important one. Of 79 cubs that were born to the Seronera and Masai prides during the study, 67 percent died of the following causes: killed by lion, 11 cubs; killed by leopard, 1; killed by hyena, 1; starvation, 15; unknown (not starvation), 25. Many cubs simply disappeared, sometimes whole litters of healthy youngsters. In some instances hyenas may have found them unattended and devoured them. But I think that most were abandoned by their mother. Until cubs are fully mobile at the age of around two months, the lioness must remain near them rather than return to the pride, which may be miles away. Unwilling to restrict the conviviality of her social life, or perhaps merely uninterested in her cubs, she leaves them to die in the obscurity of a thicket.

Cubs may also become separated from their family. Once a lioness with three small cubs from the Plains pride, which lived around the Simba kopjes, crossed a ravine. While she halted to drink, one adventurous cub drifted off on an exploration of its own. It continued to putter around, unaware that its family was departing. Suddenly it realized that it was alone. Frantically it ran up the ravine, then down it, then up again, miaowing first softly then harshly. From the embankment it could have seen its mother and two siblings depart across the plains, and its cries might have been heard if the wind had not been so strong. But fate was against the cub. After a while it just sat and cried where its mother had paused. Should I capture it and unite it with its family or should I gamble on the chance that its mother would return in search of it? Perhaps callously, I chose the latter course. I never saw the cub again. Its two siblings also vanished. In three years this lioness lost three litters and all except one cub of a fourth, an unenviable but not unusual record.

The fate of a litter in the Seronera pride was tragic too and illustrates the many dangers that beset cubs early in life. Lioness A was elderly, with a blunt and confident manner that would seem to presuppose competent motherhood. She had raised one cub since I met her, subsequently lost a whole litter, and a week previously had given birth again. Driving along one dawn I was startled to see a tiny cub lying in the road. It grunted harshly as I picked it up and deposited it into the safety of some tall grass a few feet away. Wondering whose cub it was and why it was carelessly left in such an exposed position, I waited for its mother to return. The cub in the grass miaowed shrilly at times, thereby revealing itself to any hyena that might pass. Finally at 1:00 p.m. several soft grunts heralded the arrival of a lioness. Lioness A stopped, called, listened intently, walked a few steps and grunted again, obviously not certain where she had left her cub. But when it miaowed once in answer, she hurried to it, and, picking it up by the scruff, carried it up the road. After walking .8 mile, she reached a solitary tree in the plains. Beneath it was a dead wildebeest, from which only a little had been eaten, and there, too, was a dead lion cub and a leopard, which fled up into the branches at the approach of the lioness. Here was a perfect situation for the mystery novel devotee: two bodies had been found, two suspects were present, neither of whom would talk, and several plausible motives existed. I was faced with one of nature's small but not uncommon mysteries and had to deduce the course of events from the available evidence. On the throat of the wildebeest were four indentations in the thick skin where canines had grasped the victim. The size of the bite and distance between the teeth indicated the size of the predator. The killer—lion; the cause of death—strangulation. The cub had been mauled to death, but only dissection could reveal the details. The wildebeest had died before the cub, judging by the stiffness and temperature of the bodies. Who had killed the cub? What was the leopard doing here? Norman Myers, at that time visiting the Serengeti to photograph wildlife, came forward as a witness to the crime, and his testimony, together with circumstantial evidence, told a story of theft and interspecific murder.

Sometime during the night, lioness A had captured a wildebeest. She ate a little and rested, and finally decided to fetch her cubs, most unusual behavior, for the cubs were much too young to eat meat. While the lioness was gone, a leopard found the kill and helped itself to a free meal. When lioness A returned with one cub, the leopard retreated into the tree and waited while the lions rested. Norman arrived on the scene at that time. At 11:00 a.m. the lioness wanted to fetch her second cub. But she was in an obvious quandary. Able to carry only one cub at a time, how could she bring the second cub and still guard the first one from the leopard? She took a few steps, returned to her cub, glanced up at the leopard, then turned as if to leave. After vacillating for half an hour she departed. When she was about three hundred feet distant, the leopard cautiously descended and pounced on the cub. It squawked loudly. Emitting coughing roars, the lioness returned at a run and the leopard dropped its victim and fled. The lioness licked and pawed the cub gently, but it was dead, bitten deeply into the chest. Finally she sought her other cub and that is when I met her. While she was gone the persistent leopard ate from the wildebeest, ignoring the dead cub.

All that day and into the night the lioness and her surviving cub rested by the kill, while in the tree above them the leopard lay draped along a branch, afraid to descend. At 8:00 p.m. a pride member roared nearby and lioness A answered; after that she fed for an hour before going to sleep, the live cub beside her. At 4:30 a.m. the leopard inched cautiously down the trunk and with a wild leap vanished into the grass, its departure speeded by a growl from the lioness. While on a dawn patrol of their domain, Black Mane and Brown Mane discovered the kill and partook of a snack. As they carelessly flopped down to rest or unheedingly rolled over, one of the males somehow squashed the remaining cub to death. Lioness A paid no attention to her dead cub and I removed it. As I stroked the tiny lifeless body, it seemed sad that only I should mourn its passing. But four and a half months later its mother had another litter.

In describing the life of any animal there is always the danger of dwelling on the unusual and striking at the expense of the mundane. This is especially true with respect to lions, whose existence of indolence is disrupted by such dramatic moments that the incidents sear the mind. Most violent eruptions are at kills. Yet lions feed on an average of only forty to fifty minutes per day. Being adapted to a feast or famine regime, a lion may have no meal for four or five days but then spend several hours in a bacchanalia of meat-eating that ends with the lion's abdomen grotesquely distended. I do not know precisely how much a lion can consume in one meal. Once I gave Black Mane a weighed carcass in the evening and by the next morning he had devoured everything edible—seventy-three pounds of meat and he had not been particularly hungry when he started. One night, at 2:20 a.m., Brown Mane appropriated a Thomson's gazelle that a cheetah had just killed. It took him 2½ hours to eat it. Walking along afterwards he surprised a gazelle crouched in the grass, either sleeping or hiding. In any event, he ate it too. Subtracting the 18½ pounds of stomach contents and bones which were discarded, Brown Mane had consumed about 62½ pounds of food in 5½ hours. Two days previously he had gorged on a zebra.

When not eating, a lion may walk in search of prey, a pride member, or perhaps in a patrol of its territory, but for whatever reason it exerts itself as little as possible. Lions plod along, as if weary, at about 2 to 2½ miles an hour, often breaking their journey with impromptu rest periods. In contrast to the light, dancing steps of a cheetah, or the smooth gliding motion of a leopard, the lion walks ponderously, a heavy-weight who has power rather than subtlety. In the silence of night the footsteps of a lion are surprisingly noisy interruptions. A lion may walk only a few minutes in the course of a day or for as long as six hours. In a sample of fourteen whole days, the Seronera pride lionesses averaged 2.8 miles of walking per day with a variation of .8 to 5.6 miles, and in a sample of five days the Masai pride males averaged 5 miles with a variation of 1.2 to 9 miles. Lions are obviously sparing in the expenditure of their energy.

The cats spend some twenty to twenty-one hours per day at rest. Much of the time they lie around with their eyes closed or gaze vacantly into the distance. Hours may pass without more than the most cursory stirring. A gorged lion, on the other hand, appears to be most uncomfortable: it turns and twists in an attempt to settle the bulge of its belly and finally it may stand up to permit the load to sway freely. Usually a lion is indifferent to the sun in the Serengeti highlands, where shade temperatures seldom climb above 90°F., but a bloated one suffers from the harsh rays. While shade is usually available, the extra effort that may be required to reach it seems to be too much for some lions and so they stand panting, saliva trailing from their slack lips until dusk brings relief. Cubs may also suffer from heat. At times they may escape the sun by sitting in the small patch of shade cast by an adult, and those at Seronera occasionally crawled beneath my car where I could hear them thump the floor with their heads as they changed position.

There was little for me to do as I sat near such resting lions, yet I had to wait. The most interesting incidents always happened unpredictably. Sometimes I read or wrote a report; at other times I merely sat there, my mind wandering from topic to topic, though always returning to lions. I wondered if lions dream. I wondered what they thought of me, or even if they considered me at all. Day after day they looked toward me with a vacuous gaze that went through me and around me and beyond me, a disconcerting glance that seemed to deny my existence. Their mien conveyed utter indifference and I never knew if they recognized my car and face. To stare rigidly at another individual is a mild form of threat in lions, as well as in man, and by looking at something in a detached manner the animals can see what is happening without seeming aggressive. I wondered also how much lions actually slept, but it is difficult to distinguish a dozing animal from one that merely has its eyes closed. Measurements of the brain waves of domestic cats in sound-proof cages showed that on an average day the animals were awake for about 8.4 hours, lightly asleep for 12 hours, and deeply asleep for 3–6 hours, figures that may also apply to lions. I wondered how lions perceived their environment. For example, the tree beneath which they rested was an important object to them, one that had many dimensions. On the rough bark they could sharpen their claws, and it was a site at which they could deposit scent and could check who else had marked the trunk recently; it was a vantage point from whose branches prey could be spotted; it was a retreat that provided shade; and it was also a landmark by which the animals could orient themselves. Pride members chose the tree again and again for various activities, thereby rein-

The Masai pride during its noonday rest.

A cub visits Brown Mane of the Masai pride.

A male and cub yawn in unison.

A lioness sits by her newborn cubs.

A playful cub bounds against its mother.

Crowded flank to flank, the Masai pride eats.

Several Masai pride lionesses accompanied by their cubs move out to hunt.

A lioness carries a six-week-old cub by the nape.

A lioness grabs a fleeing zebra with her forepaw.

A lioness pulls a zebra down by clutching its neck and biting its nape.

Several lions squabble over a warthog.

Two male lions harass a bull buffalo.

A nomadic male rests on a kopje.

forcing their attachment to the area. The tree helped give the lions an identity.

Merely to watch the constantly changing facial expressions of lions when they interact or respond to their surroundings is a fascinating way to spend the hours. The face of a lion is a marvelously subtle yet clear conveyor of emotions. Kipling's observation that "The beasts are very wise / Their mouths are clean of lies" applies particularly to cats, for they express themselves so unambiguously, their features and sounds mirror their minds so precisely, that only the most insensitive of persons could grossly misinterpret them. It is no coincidence that a lion has black lips and a black patch on the back of each ear. These markings enhance the vividness of those parts of the face that are among the most important in communication. When a lion notices something of more than passing interest, its bland eyes seem to harden, a delicate change due more to a tensing of the skin around the eyes than to a difference in the eyes themselves. The most conspicuous expressions are those of aggressive threat and defensive threat, as Paul Leyhausen calls them. An angry and purely aggressive lion lowers its neck obliquely and stares fixedly with eyes wide open at its opponent; its ears are erect and its lips are brought so far forward that they are almost in a straight line, hiding the teeth from view. Growls or coughs may accompany the expression. When a lion looks like that it is time to retreat and quickly, for attack is imminent and may not be limited to a bluff charge. The lion intends to convey emphatically, "Leave me alone; go away or I will see to it that you do." In a defensive threat, the animal retracts its ears, bares its teeth, snarling or miaowing while doing so. This expression, like most others, has many gradations. At a low intensity, a male may lift only one corner of his lip to expose a huge canine at a bothersome cub. But when highly upset, the animal opens its mouth wide, exposing all teeth in a massive display of weapons, and this gesture may be reinforced with snarls and a slap or two. The head is often turned to one side, and, if the lion becomes even more frightened, it may turn more and more, until it rolls onto its back, facing its tormentor with exposed teeth and claws. Lions that bare their teeth are somewhat fearful and in effect they mean, "I hesitate to attack you, but if you persist in annoying me I will do so in desperation." Emotions are seldom pure and static. A lion's conflicting impulses for flight or fight shift constantly in intensity and these changes are clearly expressed in the movements of the face, in the sounds, and finally in actions. Shifts in mood during an interaction occur so often and are so sudden and uninhibited, ranging in a second from violent passion to serenity, that it is difficult for a human observer not only to keep track of all the nuances but also to comprehend behavior that is so much a product of those emotions we tend to suppress in ourselves.

Sometimes, when the meaning of some behavior was obscure to me, I wished that lions could express themselves with more than growls and snarls and roars; I wished that they could impart to me the bases for their traditions. But on second thought I was not certain this would be helpful. In spite of his verbal virtuosity man is just barely beginning to understand himself. The thoughts of lions would no doubt be unimaginably different from ours, for each species sees the world in its own fashion. Furthermore, language is a mask that helps to obscure feelings and thoughts. The truth of an animal's existence is more likely to become clear from its gestures.

Cubs most often played at dusk and dawn, and I eagerly looked forward to their antics. Their capacity to have fun, happy in their youthful strength and lust for life, was so infectious that it always gave me unalloyed pleasure. One day three lionesses of the Seronera pride rested while their seven cubs played around them in the grass. I kept notes on the bewildering variety of play of one of these cubs—a male, six months old. I had not named this cub, nor any of the others, for the death rate of youngsters was so high that my notebooks would have consisted of obituary columns of deceased friends; I preferred to keep mere impersonal notations of demise. At any rate, the cub was now a vigorous one with a cocky expression and a slight unkempt ruff, the first intimation of his mane. These were his actions during ten minutes of play:

He pawed a twig, then chewed on it. When another cub passed by, he lunged and bit it in the lower back. The assaulted cub whirled around, slapped our hero in the face and walked off. He sat as if planning some new devilment. Suddenly he crouched and slowly, very slowly, stalked toward an unsuspecting cub. Finally he rushed. The two tumbled over and grappled before separating amicably, our cub now biting a tuft of grass instead. Tiring of this, he flopped first on his side, then rolled on his back and waved his paws in the air. Several cubs played near him and these he watched intently. When one cub ambled closer, our cub hugged the ground behind a tuft of grass and waited. Bounding out of hiding with exaggerated jumps, his mouth open and lips drawn back in a smile, he swatted at one cub and after that turned on another and nipped it in the flank, a form of greeting which led to his being clouted on the head. Two cubs wrestled gently nearby and he entered the fray enthusiastically, only to be slapped in the face, rebuffed again. A cub trotted by, intent on some errand. He lunged and tried to grab it with his forepaws, but missed. Both cubs then reared up on their hindlegs, and, leaning into each other, cuffed clumsily until the other one fell on his back, our cub on top trying to bite its throat with mock severity. Then they sat side by side, looking for new worlds to conquer, unaware that they were being stalked until our cub was hit on the head from behind. Failing to see the humor of the situation, he turned with a snarl and swiped the air in futile fury as the silent intruder vanished in the grass. He then reclined, his playful mood seemingly dampened, but suddenly he grasped a twig with both paws and bit it, shaking his head from side to side. The twig at least would not hit back.

The most common form of play among cubs consists of chasing wildly through the grass, of wrestling, pawing, and stalking. Small cubs, those less than six months old, are particularly fond of wrestling, but as cubs grow older they seem to prefer games with less body contact, such as stalking. Sometimes a cub picks up a branch and runs with it, and others then acquire an irresistible urge to possess it too, with the result that several may pursue, the chase ending with a tug-of-war during which each cub hangs on grimly as the branch is pulled this way and that. From a cub's point of view, males must be surly brutes, for most attempts to draw them into play are rebuffed with a slap or growl. Yet cubs are strangely drawn to these strong and withdrawn members of the pride. They like to sit by males and imitate them by, for example, yawning or sharpening claws when they do. The lionesses are more tolerant of playing cubs than are males, although their patience must be severely tested at times. A cub may leap onto a sleeping lioness with a thump that audibly knocks the air out of her, it may drape itself over her face, almost smothering her, it may pull her leg, bite her tail, and in general make a nuisance of itself without eliciting more than a mild reprimand. In fact, a lioness may reciprocate by slapping a cub hard but with restraint, first feinting with one paw and, when the cub's attention is diverted, clouting it with the other; she may cover it with her 250-pound body, lying as if dead, waiting for it to squirm free after much straining and wiggling; and she may pummel, maul, and chase it until it finally reclines on its back, exhausted, begging for peace. At night, when the moon stares in silence at the earth, a whole group of lions may gambol on the plains, sometimes dark shadows, sometimes shimmering silver spirits, the magic of such scenes never growing less with repetition.

Play is a fascinating form of behavior. It is obviously

important to the animal, or it would not be so widespread among mammals. Yet its functions remain obscure. Patterns used in play developed originally for other purposes. Lions, for instance, slap each other playfully as they would in serious combat and they drag sticks as they would a kill. They may have exaggerated certain gestures, and behavioral sequences may be arranged somewhat differently, but there are no new ones. However, the original source of some play gestures is not always easy to pinpoint. When a cub chases another cub, slaps it, pulls it down, and bites its throat, are the actions derived from hunting prey or from fighting between lions, circumstances that involve quite different emotions? These forms of behavior can be readily distinguished among adults by facial expressions alone: prey is captured unemotionally, silently, and with bland features, whereas bared teeth and ferocious snarls accompany fights. From this it might be deduced that stalking, chasing, and so forth in cubs were derived from the hunting pattern, as is generally thought. But a basic characteristic of play is that the animal behaves in a certain way without the corresponding emotional state; that is, play-fighting cubs do not snarl with exposed teeth. Thus, I found it impossible to trace this form of play to its origin, and, in fact, it may not be possible to do so by observation alone.

Play is commonly thought to be a form of practice that helps a young animal to prepare for life. For instance, a cub that has learned to stalk another cub efficiently may be successful later in capturing prey. However, it is by no means clear that play actually benefits a cub. I was puzzled by the fact that wrestling, which is of little use to adults, is a much more common form of play among small cubs than stalking. Subadult lions are inefficient hunters and killers, and any practice they may have had in play is not evident. And why do lionesses play? They certainly do not need the experience. Play expends excess energy. It is a friendly activity that perhaps strengthens social bonds. Possibly it also helps to

Adult lions playing with cubs. Top—a male invites an approaching cub to play by lowering his forequarters; middle— a male clouts a cub lightly on the head; bottom—a lioness and a large cub slap each other playfully, using positions typical of fighting lions.

coordinate complex patterns of movement in maturing cubs and keeps them from atrophying, since some, such as stalking, appear long before they are needed. Through play, cubs may also learn the rules of pride life. While play is not essential for such learning, it provides an innocuous alternative to the adult pattern, one not likely to be misunderstood: a playful approach with exaggerated bounds and a nip will elicit a less violent reaction than an unexplained attack.

There is only one form of behavior that keeps lions actively interested throughout the day and that is courting. Lionesses usually reach sexual maturity between the ages of three and four years. For example, of four young lionesses in the Seronera pride, two conceived for the first time at 3 years 6 months of age, one at 3 years 8 months, and one at 4 years 2 months. Lacking cubs, an adult comes into heat every three weeks on the average, but individual variation is great, with some doing so at intervals of only two weeks and others at eight weeks or more. And a few lionesses, especially old ones, may not come into estrus for years. For instance, Sore-ear of the Masai pride, an elderly female with swollen and bruised ears, seemed to have left the rigors of childbearing behind her, when suddenly in late 1968 she produced a litter. The males quickly detect a lioness who is coming into heat, probably by the smell of her urine, and one male then becomes her consort, lying beside her when she rests and following her closely when she walks, ready to mount at the first opportunity. But she may not be receptive to such positive overtures and she easily stymies his ardor by sitting down. Or she may tease him, as, for instance, lioness C did when Black Mane showed interest in her. She trotted to him and turned abruptly by his nose, her tail enticingly raised, rolled over and finally crouched, presenting herself. When he stepped closer, she first rolled on her back, then rose and ambled off nonchalantly. Bounding back suddenly, she circled him twice, lightly rubbing her body against his, and ran ahead again. However, he merely lay down, as if he had had enough of her coyness. She returned quickly, almost touched noses with him, only to race away once more. Losing his patience after several minutes more of this, Black Mane pursued and mounted her, but she twisted aside, her face in a snarl, and he desisted to wait for a more congenial reception.

A lioness fully in heat is restless, changing her position often and sinuously rubbing herself against the male, while he lounges around, a besotted look on his face. Either she presents herself to him at intervals or he rises and nudges her gently, a signal that he would like to mount. She emits a rolling, ominous growl almost continuously as she is mounted. At some time during the copulation, he may grasp her nape with his teeth. Young cats become immobile when their mother picks them up by the scruff. It seems likely, as R. F. Ewer pointed out, that the neck bite of the copulating male induces temporary passivity in the lioness. He needs those extra seconds of peace, for as soon as he advertises his climax with a prolonged harsh miaow she whirls around with teeth bared and may slap him if he does not quickly dismount. Though copulations are brief, lasting on the average about 21 seconds, they are repeated often. We observed one courting male continuously for 55 hours. In that period he mated 157 times, once every 21 minutes on the average, throughout the day and night, 145 times with one lioness and 12 times with another one that visited him briefly. Female cats need the stimulus of repeated copulation in order to ovulate. Such heroic passion must be rather wearying on a male, and he may become a reluctant suitor after a day or two unless vigorously importuned. In some instances he may abandon the lioness, making it necessary for her to find someone else. Lioness I of the Seronera pride once went through a nymphomaniacal period lasting over three weeks, during which she courted interchangeably with Black Mane and Brown Mane so often that her rump sported a smooth, shiny spot from constant wear. Although one lioness switched males no fewer than four times, most of them mate with only one or two males in the course of an estrous period that may last between one to eight days, with an average of about three to five days.

Because courting couples remain intent on their own business, other pride members usually drift away, leaving them alone. Pairs usually do not hunt except when a good opportunity presents itself. Once a male interrupted his courtship to capture a gazelle that had imprudently gone to a waterhole nearby. He carried his prize to the lioness and permitted her to eat it all, a touching and striking token considering the fact that he was hungry. For one adult lion to give meat to another is the ultimate gesture, a negation of one of its basic tenets. On another occasion, a lioness suddenly became aware of several gazelle in high grass near her. She crouched immediately. Her consort, misinterpreting her intention, eagerly mounted her, only to have her shoot out from under him in a futile rush at the prey. He stood there with such a bewildered expression at her sudden departure that I burst into laughter.

Often another male rests patiently near the courting pair, sometimes for several days, without trying to usurp the lioness. I wondered if he was a beaten rival for her affection or if he merely awaited his turn should his friend falter. To see what would happen if I separated the courting male briefly from the lioness, I tranquillized him on two occasions by shooting a syringe containing a muscle relaxant into his flank. Both times the extra male immediately claimed the female and she readily acquiesced to this change in partners. When the first male revived after about twenty minutes and saw his lioness in the paws of another he calmly accepted the situation and made no attempt to evict the intruder. Possession of a limited resource confers temporary dominance with mates just as it does with food, and this keeps strife to a minimum.

About eighty percent of the courtships did not result in

births. Occasionally a lioness was already pregnant or she had small cubs when she mated, and at other times she failed to come fully into estrus, but in about a third of the cases she passed through a typical heat without producing young. I do not know the causes for this. In a few instances courtship behavior may have had no direct relation to estrus. When a lioness meets a strange male or when for some reason she feels insecure in a male's presence, she may appease him by presenting herself sexually to him. Such a pair may for a few hours give the impression of being sexually involved when in fact they are mainly cementing their friendship. Among man, too, copulation has ceased to be simply used for procreation. It seems likely that early man used copulation to strengthen his social ties with particular women, especially after returning from a prolonged hunt, just as modern man copulates to reinforce a mutual attraction.

The sight and smell of one lioness in heat seem to stimulate other lionesses to come into estrus too, as long as they lack cubs. Consequently several litters may be born at the same time. It is not unusual to find three, four, even five litters all of about the same age in a pride. Such concurrent births are of advantage to cubs, in that all mothers guard, suckle, and hunt for them fairly indescriminately. Late in 1968 the Seronera pride had a population explosion, with seven lionesses giving birth to eighteen cubs. Lionesses B and H mysteriously lost their litters. Instead of their milk supply drying up, as would usually be the case if there were no cubs in the pride, they continued to lactate for four months, donating their milk to the other cubs.

Cubs may be born during any month around Seronera, but there were two definite peaks—one in January, the other in August–September. Two possible reasons for the peak became evident from my data. If, for instance, the survival of litters was poor the previous year, perhaps due to starvation, then a number of lionesses would be ready to have cubs.

Although a lioness may mate within a week after she loses her cubs, most delay estrus or conception for several months. As I described earlier, several lionesses may then come into heat simultaneously and cause a peak. Environmental conditions also have an effect on sexual activity. The periodic arrival of the migrating herds provided a superabundance of food to which lionesses responded by coming into estrus. Thus, the timing of birth peaks is somewhat accidental and may vary from area to area and year to year.

The reproductive potential of lions is great. The average litter size around Seronera is 2.3 cubs, with a variation of one to five. If a whole litter dies, a lioness may have a new one within four months, since the gestation period is only 3½ months. From figures such as these one would expect that most lionesses would be accompanied by cubs. But they are not, one reason being that they practice a physiological form of birth control about which little is known. After a whole litter died, an average of nine months rather than the expected four months elapsed before the next litter was born. If even one cub of a litter survived, its presence inhibited the mother from coming into estrus again until it was at least eighteen months old in most instances. In addition, seventeen percent of the lionesses in the Seronera area produced no litters, some no doubt because they were old. Each lioness could reasonably raise 1.2 cubs per year to independence. Actually only one fourth of the expected total grew up, both birth control and death regulating the number of cubs in the population.

Kay and I visited Nairobi National Park in 1960 and there met a pleasant-looking lioness. We watched her and admired her but we had no intimation that when she would die her life history as recorded by Charles Guggisberg, Rudolf Schenkel, and others would provide a unique record. Blondie, as she was called, was a member of a pride in the center of the park and spent most of her life within an area of fifteen square miles. Her published history starts in

July 1955, when she had two cubs, both of which died. Conceiving again immediately, she had four more cubs and these she raised successfully. Between late 1957 and mid-1958 she had two litters but abandoned them both. Yet another litter was born in March 1959, and it too was abandoned; her next cubs, born in July of that year, disappeared. After this dismal record, she raised two cubs between 1960 and 1962, her final effort, perhaps because of old age. She died in 1967 at an age of possibly twenty-two years, for she is said to have been fully grown in 1947. Over a period of twelve years Blondie had had seven litters of which she raised two, totaling six cubs. A species that lives a long time and has few enemies cannot afford to raise an indiscriminate number of young.

Statistics such as these take years to gather and are rather dull to read, yet they represent some of the most important information that emerges from a study. Without a knowledge of birth rates, for instance, a species cannot be managed adequately. But as one studiously adds columns of figures and applies various mathematical techniques to the results with the hope that something meaningful might emerge, it is important to remember that one is dealing with complex beings, each of which has its own strengths and weaknesses and each of which leads a life of playing, mating, hunting, and so forth that is its own, shaped by both a personal history and that of its species. As T. Blackburn noted in the journal *Science*:

> However, by relying lopsidedly on abstract quantification as a method of knowing, scientists have been looking at the world with one eye closed. There is other knowledge, and there are other ways of knowing besides reading the position of a pointer on a scale. The human mind and body process information with staggering sophistication and sensitivity by the direct sensuous experience of their surroundings.

I was interested in lions as individuals and the statistics were almost byproducts of watching certain animals for years, some from birth to adulthood.

Nevertheless, in working with animals one soon comes to expect certain reactions in particular situations. In fact, the accuracy of predictions is a measure of how well one knows the species. One lion, however, reminded me very well of his individuality. Driving across the plains, I saw a young male limping from a fresh wound in his hindleg, obviously in a sour mood. I stopped eighty feet from him to watch his progress. He would have none of me. He bared his teeth, hissed, and, when I did not promptly retreat, he charged. I thought it was bluff, but soon learned otherwise. He lunged for the car, placed a forepaw on the fender and punctured the metal with two of his canine teeth. Then he trotted off, still disgruntled, leaving me somewhat shaken. Yet on subsequent meetings he showed me no malice.

A lioness's breasts enlarge a few days before she is due to give birth, and I then watched her expectantly, hoping to find out where she had her cubs. The Seronera lions preferred to hide their offspring in the dense thickets of fever trees growing along the creeks or in the thick brush of kopjes. Weighing a mere three pounds and barely able to crawl, cubs are quite helpless at birth, but if disturbed or hungry they open their mouths, showing pink, toothless gums, and emit piercing miaows. At times I crawled into a thicket to count the cubs, and these calls made me distinctly uneasy, for I never knew when the mother of the cubs or one of her friends might return and find me crouched there, hemmed in by thorns. A cub's eyelids usually open three to fifteen days after birth to reveal eyes gray-blue in color, which slowly change to amber in the following two to three months. The first incisors erupt about three weeks after birth and at that age too the cub is able to walk unsteadily. Lionesses are not bound to a certain lair, and they move the cubs to a new one every week or two as the mood strikes them. While a mother feels protective toward her cubs, often warning some leonine intruder away with threatening growls, she may also permit some pride members to visit them. In this way both youngsters and adults have a chance to become acquainted. But a cub's world usually begins and ends with its mother until at the age of about five to seven weeks it is sturdy enough to follow her to the pride. What a traumatic experience it must be for a cub to be suddenly confronted with a shaggy male, to compete for the first time at a kill, and to be crowded away from the milk of its mother by a strange cub.

One morning I met lioness B of the Seronera pride with two new six-to-seven-week-old cubs tumbling at her heels, obviously delighted with their first long excursion from the dark recesses of the kopje where they had spent their early life. She led the cubs to a spreading acacia in whose shade rested six fairly large cubs while they awaited the return of their mothers. Cubs always seem to be filled with a vague and nameless apprehension when they are alone, but this mood is replaced by unbounded exuberance when an adult arrives. Excited by lioness B and the potential playmates they had not previously met, the six cubs ran up to greet the newcomers as soon as they hove into view. But the small cubs fled, unused to strangers, much less uninhibited ones. One hid in a thicket for the remainder of the day while the other sought refuge behind its mother's bulk when she reclined. The large cubs inched closer on their bellies, craning their necks in curiosity, yet slightly apprehensive of the lioness. The small cub snarled and swatted at them until finally an angry cough from the lioness sent them scurrying backwards. After an hour of proximity, the small cub grew courageous and cautiously, one step at a time, ventured to within a foot of another cub before losing its nerve and dashing back to its mother, where it gained reassurance by vigorously rubbing cheeks with her. Five hours after its first meeting with the strangers it triumphantly touched noses with one, a momentous occasion in its short life. And 1½ hours later, it suckled contentedly while lying flank to flank with one of the cubs, its integration well advanced.

> Three and a half months after a lioness has left the pride, with one of the males on her nuptial excursion she will be ready to leave it again to have her cubs. She will take with her one of the older lionesses, too old to bear any more cubs of her own . . . This lioness will help her to hunt and protect her cubs and act as nursemaid when they are older. These attendant lionesses are well known to all bushwhackers and are referred to as "Aunties."

The literature is full of such references to "aunties," yet I found little evidence of their existence. Some lionesses in a pride do form special friendships that may last for months, but these may persist whether or not cubs are present; sometimes a childless lioness is seen with cubs, perhaps waiting to meet others or too indolent to go hunting with the rest, but she has no special attachment to them and the next day may find her many miles away. Of course, her presence does provide cubs with inadvertent protection, but whenever a childless lioness has joined cubs it would be wise to suspect her motives: selfishness is more prevalent than altruism. Such a lioness does not lead cubs to kills, nor does she share food with them if she can avoid doing so; rather, she deprives cubs of their portion whenever she has the opportunity.

At times one lioness may help the cubs of another lioness, though this is seldom done graciously. Flop-ear and Notch, for example, became joint step-mothers to one of Sore-ear's cubs. When old Sore-ear had two cubs in August 1968, they were postscripts, appearing several years after any previous litter. Less than a year later she vanished with one cub and I suspect that she might have been killed in an inter-pridal fight. Her surviving cub attached itself to Flop-ear and Notch, the latter having two cubs of her own. It trudged behind the group, dependent on it for food and protection, a sad little creature whose overt attempts at friendliness were tolerated but usually ignored. Then one day it also vanished. One cub belonging to lioness A, whose loss of a newborn litter I described earlier, fared somewhat better. Lioness A became pregnant again when her cub was only fifteen months old, not quite old enough to take its place in the pride completely unassisted, yet she lost all interest in it and seemingly refused to associate with it. So the cub joined lioness B, who had a cub of the same age. The two cubs, both females, became inseparable companions, and later they left the pride together at the age of thirty-two months.

Cubs live wholly on milk for the first weeks of life. I never saw lionesses regurgitate meat for them, as they are often said to do. But at the age of five to seven weeks the cubs may follow their mother to a kill for their first meal of meat. At that age, too, several lionesses may combine their litters and raise them communally. Though loath to share meat, lionesses readily permit cubs of other litters to suckle on them. With as many as ten cubs tapping the same source in the course of an hour, the supply is soon exhausted. However, a lioness may give her own cubs priority, keeping others away with snaps—essential behavior, for a small cub is unable to compete with large pride mates for one of the four nipples. While cubs often suckle until they are seven to eight months old, at first to obtain milk and later for social contact too, meat soon becomes essential to their survival.

Rebuffed at kills, their portion snatched by adults, cubs quickly learn that their existence must revolve around the quest for meat. Until they are about four to five months old, cubs seem oblivious to adults during a hunt as they miaow and run in play around the stalking lionesses, behavior which may alert the prey. But cubs older than five months usually follow the hunt silently and then wait, staring alertly into the darkness, while the lionesses creep forward during the final stalk. Cubs sometimes watch the details of a hunt, but they do not participate in the pride effort until they are over a year old. By that age they have probably learned most of the correct techniques through observation and only some practice is then needed to perfect them. At the age of fifteen months, one of Flop-ear's cubs snagged a gazelle during a communal hunt, perhaps her first kill. She dispatched it with a quick bite, then sat by the carcass with a surprised look on her face.

As cubs reach the age of fifteen to eighteen months, their mother is less and less interested in them. She does not bother to lead them to kills nor does she carry meat to them. They may still follow her and rest by her but even this contact becomes more tenuous when she has another litter. At the age of about two years the cubs become subadults, full participants in pride affairs without special privileges. This does not imply that the youngsters know all the fine points of hunting, and they are in fact often inept, rushing at prey too early, failing to judge its speed correctly, or unable to subdue a large animal efficiently. However, such errors in performance are not critical because the adults are there to help or to provide meals in the event of failure. Young lions are dependent on adults for an exceptionally long time. Tiger cubs begin to lead their solitary existence by the age of 1½ to 2 years. Possibly lions need a prolonged childhood to learn the elaborate cooperative hunting techniques. Finally, at the age of 2½ to 3 years, when some cubs leave the pride to take up a life of wandering, they are reasonably adept hunters secure in the knowledge that they can subsist by their own efforts.

Facts such as these about lionesses and their cubs reveal little of the effort needed to collect them. First of all, one must of course find the lions. This may require hours of diligent searching, though with time, as one grows attuned to the surroundings, the task becomes easier. The perceptions heighten so gradually that one is not aware that the harmonious relationship between the land and the life it supports has somehow pervaded the subconscious. What to a visitor in my car is a meaningless spot on the distant plain is to me unquestionably a male lion resting beside his wildebeest kill. The tension that ripples through a gazelle herd on first sensing a lion is almost galvanic, yet the newcomer to the Serengeti may notice nothing.

Lions keep to their own erratic schedule of life, and I had to adapt to it. One of the joys of being a field biologist is the freedom to spend the day as one pleases, but this does not eliminate the need for a routine. I rose invariably at dawn, often awakened by the strident call of a striped king-fisher in the tree beside the house, and hastened without breakfast in search of lions. At this time of day one often becomes the witness to the final act of some nocturnal drama that is lost to those who sleep an extra hour. Having found lions or other predators, I watched them and took notes, and, after a while, perhaps searched for other animals. If, as often happened, the lions settled down by late morn-ing, I went home to eat, have the car serviced, or take care of the many daily tasks with which any project is burdened: writing up notes, doing correspondence and reports, pre-serving specimens, and so forth. By early afternoon I was in the field again, usually until darkness and occasionally far into the night. However, if something of interest happened in the morning, I remained out all day and night, observing the event continuously. A box in the back of the Land Rover contained a blanket, a spotlight, some food in the form of biscuits, raisins, and chocolate, a spare notebook, some water, and other items of use for a long vigil; I carried extra cans of petrol too, as well as various tools for the car, such as a powerful jack and a tire repair kit. Kay was never sure when or even if I would be home that day.

The notes one takes are the most important part of any project. At all times I carry a notebook into which I jot down the details of any event as it occurs or immediately after-ward. If the action is quick and prolonged there is time to write only the barest outline, a few key words, which must be elaborated later. With memory being imprecise, even an hour's delay may cause distortions and errors. The literature on Africa is full of reminiscences by hunters and game wardens. I mistrust the accuracy of these, not in broad outline but in detail, unless the author is known to have recorded his observations in the field. Every day, whenever I have time, the rough notes are transcribed into another book. This gives me an opportunity to elaborate and comment on the original material, and, above all, to record data neatly and legibly. Even I have trouble deciphering my own handwriting after taking notes in the dark while following a lion at night. A duplicate set of notes also provides some insurance that not all one's research results will somehow be lost or destroyed. To prevent this from happening, I always keep each set of notes in a separate building and ship them home by different means.

Perhaps the main difference between the observations of a naturalist in the past and one of today is the kind of event that is recorded. Once the dramatic anecdote, the subjective impression, the broad generalization based on an incident or two were the bases upon which animals were described. Today's researcher approaches the task differently. First, he or she records observations in elaborate detail. To note, for instance, that several lions are feeding on a zebra is not enough. Time of day, number and sex of lions, height of vegetation surrounding the kill, age and sex of victim, distance of kill from water, other prey in the vicinity, and so forth need to be written down. While some details seem irrelevant at first, they may raise important points later. Second, incidents are written down systematically, recording the same event again and again, until one can use a large sample from which to deduce patterns and derive conclusions. In one book published in 1933 is the unadorned statement: "After satisfying their hunger, lions invariably made straight-way for water." Is this generalization likely to be true? I watched the Seronera and Masai prides for thirty whole days, during which they ate twenty-five animals. Only once, or possibly twice, did lions drink within an hour after eating. Perhaps lions behave differently in other areas, but only a quantitative record can show whether they do so. A large sample may also reveal previously hidden facts about an animal's behavior. Not until I had laboriously recorded who licked whom during friendly contacts between lions did I discover that youngsters less than about six months old seldom initiated such contacts. They seemed content merely to absorb affection and it was not until later that they regularly licked other members, having finally become fully integrated into the pride emotionally as well as physically. Like most research results, these findings have little importance in themselves, but ultimately such fragments of trivia contribute to an understanding of an animal's society.

My existence revolved around lions, I was wholly saturated with them: I observed them, talked and wrote about them, and thought about them, sometimes in the abstract terms of predator–prey relations, at other times as individuals. Such immersion into another species helps one to enter its world; the animals become sentient presences rather than just creatures to peruse from the perspective of our intellect. If I interrupted my routine to take the family to Nairobi, climb Mt. Kilimanjaro, or make a similar journey, the spell was broken. It then took me days to find my way back to the world of the lion.

A few times, though, I saw too much of lions. Once Bill Holz, who assisted the project for several months, and I decided to track a lion continuously by radio for several weeks. We chose for our experiment male No. 159, a ragged old fellow who had set up a temporary territory around Naabi Hill. We tranquillized him and placed around his neck a collar to which we had attached the radio. Then we followed his steps, day after day, night after night. We worked in twenty-four-hour shifts, relieving each other at noon. Sometimes Bill remained with the male for forty-eight hours to give me a chance to continue my other work. It was easy to stay with the male in daytime, for we could doze beside him as he slept. But at night we had to remain alert, trying to gauge his position from the beeps of the receiving set in the car or perhaps to glimpse his shadowy form. The first few days were rather pleasant, at least for me. I had stayed awake for as long as three consecutive days with a lion before, and, besides, I found delight in delving deeply into the life of the animal, to learn whom he met, how far he traveled, how often he ate. As the days passed this delight vanished, and we went about our task with grim determination to add yet another twenty-four hours to our record. We were weary. Our eyelids and hands would almost refuse the commands of the mind. I would look at my watch, and soon look again only to discover that an hour had passed and I had been asleep though seemingly fully conscious. I would eat biscuits, tap my foot to some soundless tune, compose phrases and sentences that might suit some future writing task, anything to keep the body from winning its revolt in demand for sleep. And there was the torture of the receiving set, the incessant beep-beep that permeated the night until the modest sound became the throbbing of an infernal machine. I covered the set with a blanket, but the faint signal still grated until I was tempted to hurl everything into the darkness. The effort to stay awake left me so tense that sleep became difficult at home. I would walk around, doing my chores automatically, seemingly quite rational until a slight disturbance, such as a little bickering between Eric and Mark, would cause me to react with unfitting violence. I was grateful to Bill, Andrew Laurie, Stephen Makacha, and other assistants who at one time or another relieved me of such nightly vigils. But enough. We stayed with the male for twenty-one consecutive days and suffice it to say that for once I had a surfeit of lions.

NEIGHBORLY DISPUTES

THE SERONERA PRIDE, MASAI PRIDE, AND OTHERS EACH
confine their activity to a certain area, the lionesses remaining in one locality for life and the males sometimes for
several years. Such residency has several advantages. Scattered pride members can retain contact, something that
would be difficult if they roamed at random, and the chances
of meeting outsiders are reduced—an important consideration, for pride members tend to be intolerant of strangers.
Furthermore, by knowing an area well, lionesses discover
the best places for hiding their cubs and learn the most advantageous ambush sites and routes along which to stalk
prey. Such information is not only to their own advantage
but also to that of their offspring, which then learn these
pride traditions. But when adults are lean and cubs are
starving one wonders why prides cling to their areas rather
than migrate with the wildebeest and zebra. Some hyena
clans break up in times of food shortage and follow the
prey, according to Hans Kruuk, and a few hyenas also commute from their clan area some twenty or thirty miles to a

prey concentration, gorge, and return to their den a few days later. Lions are unable to use the latter system because they do not have the stamina of hyenas, who can quickly cover great distances at a steady lope. To remain sedentary would seem to be detrimental to lions, and to me one of the most interesting findings of the study was that lions must have a stable and secure social environment if they are to raise cubs successfully. They need an environment that is protected from intruders by pride males, and one in which cubs are fed and guarded by several lionesses, even though this is frequently done inadvertently. Nomadic lionesses lack the benefit of a stable group life and they are consequently less successful in rearing their cubs. And selection is for reproductive success.

To survive, a pride needs water and ample prey within its area throughout the year. In areas where these requisites are unavailable, which is the case over much of the plains during the dry season, lions are unable to establish themselves permanently. The woodlands are wholly settled by prides, and these have taken up all suitable space to such an extent that new prides cannot find room unless they squeeze themselves into occupied terrain. The Nyaraswiga pride, which consisted of just two males and two females, was able to hold sway over the western corner of the Loliondo pride area for well over a year before the males were pushed out, presumably by the owners. The size of the area claimed by each pride varies considerably and depends to a large extent on the amount of prey available during the leanest time of the year. Around Seronera and in most of the woodlands this lean time is during the rains, when the migratory herds are on the plains. Both the Masai and Loliondo prides used about 150 square miles of terrain; the Seronera pride roamed over at least 70 square miles, sometimes disappearing into the hills to the west, where I could not find it. For comparison, two prides in Manyara National Park, which lies on the eastern side of the Crater Highlands, each needed only eight square miles of woodlands because several large buffalo herds provided them with unlimited food.

That the number of lions in an area is fairly well correlated with the total weight of prey or biomass they have available is evident from the following figures:

AREA	APPROX. PREY BIOMASS IN LBS./SQ. MILE	NO. SQ. MILES PER LION
Ngorongoro Crater	58,000	1.4
Manyara Park	45,000	1.0
Serengeti Unit	24,000	4.1–4.8
Nairobi Park	17,000	1.7
Kruger Park	6,000	6.5

Ngorongoro Crater has an exceptionally large hyena population whose presence no doubt has an influence on the number of lions the area can support, because both compete for the same resources. The Serengeti also has fewer lions than expected because the migratory herds are unavailable to most lions for much of the year.

To lay claim to an area is one thing; to control it by keeping out intruders is another. Lions, with their leisurely view of life, are obviously not eager to patrol daily all the extensive borders of their pride area. Males may plod along for a while at night, listening, sniffing, obviously checking on who is around or has visited recently; occasionally they may flush an intruder and escort it toward the borders. However, lions prefer indirect methods for advertising their presence, methods which space animals out without the inconvenience of an actual encounter. Their most conspicuous signal is the full-throated roar, a thunderous sound that can be heard for at least two miles at night, especially when a whole group calls together. Most roaring begins spontaneously, but sometimes lions answer distant roars or they may even be stimulated to vocalize by the whooping of a hyena. Lions prefer to roar at night, and the frequency with which they do so varies considerably. Several lionesses of the Masai pride, which we followed for four consecutive days, roared twice the first night, eleven times the second, not at all on the third, and once on the fourth. Male No. 134, a nomad in the process of establishing a territory, averaged twenty-nine roars a night. The meaning of a roar depends on who hears it. To a pride member, secure in the knowledge that it belongs in the area, a distant roar merely conveys "Here I am," and it may be answered or ignored. But to a stranger a roar indicates "This land is mine, mine, mine"; it is a warning trespassers heed, though often they do so in no obvious manner. They may simply circumvent an encounter with the owners by remaining alert or they may veer from their route of travel to seek less dangerous terrain.

The mere tracks of pride members communicate their presence to outsiders, for lions have an excellent sense of smell. In addition, a lion may enhance the odor of a trail by marking its route with scent. Stopping at intervals, a lion rakes the ground with its hindpaws, leaving the soil scarred; at the same time it may urinate, sometimes mixing the fluid with scent from its anal glands, which are located near the base of the tail. Or a lion may first rub its face languorously against the branches of a shrub or small sapling, behaving as if the contact was infinitely pleasurable, and then swivel around, wriggle its rump close to the bush, and with raised tail repeatedly squirt a potion of urine and scent against the leaves, an odoriferous calling card. Such behavior is especially common among males, and a squirt by one will often stimulate his friends to mark the same site, creating a powerful scent post no passing stranger can fail to detect. Males mark not only their trails but also the vicinity of estrous lionesses and kill sites; they squirt after fights and during meetings with friends and, in fact, during any situation in which their claim to ownership or right to be there might be questioned. Scent marks are in effect physical extensions of

Strutting and scent-marking postures of lions. From top to bottom: a male struts before a lioness; a male scrapes the ground with his hind paws; a male squirts from his caudally directed penis; and a lioness urinates.

the animals themselves, in that they communicate to others that a lion lives there, how recently it has passed, perhaps who it was, and, in the case of a lioness, whether or not she was in heat.

Roaring and marking are such efficient means of advertising that pride members seldom meet intruders. This does not imply that nomadic lions or neighboring prides hesitate to trespass: it merely shows that they are adept at avoiding the owners. Each time I encountered a lion around Seronera, its location was plotted on a map. By the end of the study I was able to delineate the boundaries of several pride areas fairly precisely. The most striking fact about these pride areas was that they overlapped so extensively that there seemed to be no discrete boundaries between them. However, prides intruded on the land of a neighboring pride mainly while it was temporarily in a different part of its range. When during the rainy season prey grew sparse, the Masai pride shifted its position eastward, and the Seronera pride would promptly begin to use the vacated portion only to retreat as soon as the actual owners returned. Confrontations were also uncommon because each pride spent most of the year in its center of activity, an area within its range that contained ample food and water at most seasons, and this center did not overlap with the centers of its neighbors. It is an eminently sensible system of land tenure, spacing prides out yet allowing them to adjust their activity to changes in the available resources. Pride males generally roamed more widely than did the lionesses, and their explorations often took them into the occupied terrain of a neighbor. Venturing westward, the Masai males often penetrated a part of the Seronera pride area that the Masai females never used. But the males were nervous there; they frequently had a furtive look and at the first hint of trouble fled, looking anxiously back over their shoulders. Not until they were once again on home ground would they roar a challenge toward their distant foe. Such excursions help males become acquainted with the strengths and weaknesses of their neighbors, knowledge that some day might be needed to acquire another pride. A pair of huge males who lived with a small pride of lionesses near the Moru kopjes apparently ousted the males of another small pride that centered its activity on the Simba kopjes, with the result that they had two distinct prides of lionesses under their jurisdiction. These lionesses never associated even though they had the same overlords.

With a pride area often so large that its owners tend to use only a small portion of it at a time, nomads may sometimes exist as squatters for weeks without being detected. The Masai pride, for instance, spent about three fourths of its time in the western third of its pride area, leaving the eastern portion unoccupied. Once I made a census of nomads in that area and found a total of seven males and seven females, some with cubs, living there singly and in groups.

Tremendous strength, long canines, and hooked claws have made lions rather too well adapted to injure or kill each other, especially since inhibitions to use these weapons are weaker than they might be. Consequently pride members prefer to bluff an intruder out of their area rather than fight. They may roar or rush ferociously at such an interloper, or a male may stand broadside to it with head raised and chin tucked in to display his fine mane. Such tactics usually succeed, because the possession of land automatically increases the authority of a lion. Once four Masai lionesses were hunting gazelle in high grass. Having just made a futile chase after a fawn, one lioness looked around for another quarry only to see a male watching her, a handsome one with a golden mane and a jaunty look. She took a hesitant step in his direction, as if not quite believing that a stranger would so boldly trespass, but then she turned and fled. Alerted by her behavior, two other lionesses spotted the male, still standing motionless. They approached him hissing, with their heads held low threateningly, until his courage failed and he trotted off. Lions, like man, have two systems of morality, one for dealing with group members and the other for strangers.

Although at first lionesses tend to be unfriendly toward a strange male, they will soon tolerate his presence, especially if he observes lion etiquette by not forcing himself on them too quickly. He may rest near the lionesses, seemingly oblivious to them, though inching closer at intervals until rows of gleaming teeth hint that he has approached near enough. Antagonism is tempered by the inherent knowledge that males are essential to the well-being of the pride and that the replacement of pride males, which occurs every few years, would be difficult if strangers were rebuffed too vigorously. A lioness in heat readily accepts a casual visitor should the pride males fail to guard her closely. Pride males also tolerate trespassers of the opposite sex, especially if these are in estrus. One afternoon, Black Mane of the Masai pride met female No. 78, a nomadic lioness whose peculiar predilections will be related more fully later. She was at a zebra kill. Whether attracted by the food or her charms I do not know, but in any event they copulated, and not, I suspect, because she was in heat but as a friendly overture. They remained by the kill for much of the night. At 5:15 a.m. the lioness suddenly fled and a few seconds later several members of the Masai pride arrived.

The outcome between intruder and pride member may be amicable if they are of the opposite sex but not if they are of the same sex. A pride male is unlikely to tolerate a nomadic male and trespassers are often evicted with much commotion. Roaring hoarsely, a pride male may pursue a stranger until after a long chase he stands exhausted, with chest heaving and flecks of saliva on his lips, having seemingly done his utmost to annihilate his opponent but failed. However, males usually take care not to run fast enough to catch anyone, and it amused me to watch a pursuer slow down as soon as his intended victim did so. Combat makes little sense when the same purpose can be served in other ways.

Lionesses also help to keep the integrity of the pride area intact by harrying intruding lionesses, but their antagonism is also tempered by respect for the others' weapons. Late one afternoon, lioness A of the Seronera pride found a zebra that had died of disease in an area belonging to the Masai pride. She ate a little and then left the carcass to fetch her four small cubs. Several vultures promptly descended to the unattended body and these were spotted by Flop-ear, Notch, and Sore-ear of the Masai pride. Lioness A returned with her cubs shortly after dark. Seeing the shadows of lions around the zebra, she hesitated, then roared softly, announcing her arrival. But her answer was an ominous silence. Two Masai lionesses walked toward her stiffly, as if barely able to contain their urge to attack, and lioness A departed rapidly with her cubs. She returned to her pride and induced six lionesses to follow her, a feat of communication that I unfortunately did not witness. Somehow these lionesses had sensed trouble, for they advanced through the grass toward the zebra on a broad front and finally rushed at the Masai lions, chasing them away without a fight. Although the Seronera lions had priority to the carcass, they were still trespassers. Recognizing this, they hurried home after their meal.

In describing encounters such as these, one tends to think of them as isolated events rather than as having historical depth. However, the behavior of lions is shaped not only by immediate circumstances but also by the past, by friendly or hostile meetings certain individuals may have once had. This may make it difficult to interpret some incidents. The repeated meetings of male No. 61 with the Masai pride is a case in point. In October 1966, I first met a nomadic lioness who had three offspring about 2½ years old, two females and a male. I placed tags in the ears of this male and he forthwith became No. 61, an innocuous designation for a nondescript youngster. Using the same area was female No. 78, who for unknown reasons was particularly attractive to subadult males. She had a cub of her own, a male just over a year old, and another male about three years of age also accompanied her. This trio fed on a kill at 10:00 p.m. on November 1 when male No. 61 suddenly appeared alone, having apparently abandoned his family, and later that night he was accepted by the group. Female No. 78 and her three male companions wandered over the plains and along the woodlands' edge during the next six months, meeting other nomads on occasion. In May 1967, the female parted from her masculine company to lead a solitary existence, although she sometimes met her old friends casually. Male No. 61 had formed close ties with one of the males, No. 55, and these two traveled around together. They were near Seronera in October 1967. One day, Sore-ear had caught a gazelle, and its dying bleats attracted the male Limp, two lionesses, and several cubs—as well as male No. 61. Limp, as usual, attacked the lioness, relieving her of the kill, quite oblivious to the fact that male No. 61 stood nearby. But the startled lionesses stared at him. Into this tense confrontation bumbled a small cub, belonging to The Young Female, intent only on reaching the kill site as quickly as possible. Male No. 61 pounced on the cub without warning, bit it, shook it, then dropped it and retreated when a lioness charged him with a furious cough. I think that the attack by the male had no vicious intent, merely affording him an outlet for his tensions. He ambled off. Pursued by another lioness, he whirled in midair, slapped at her, and continued on. Limp ate without interruption as if nothing had happened. And the cub miaowed and miaowed, blood seeping through its fur, quite ignored by the others. It later died.

The following day, attracted by some vultures, male No. 61 found the remains of a Grant's gazelle. Three Masai lionesses hurried up too, from another direction, only to face their old nemesis. They lay down and watched him, and he in turn tried to show his friendliness by ambling closer, quite casually as if they did not exist. But when they hissed at him, he reclined and waited awhile before approaching a little closer. Some 3½ hours after meeting the lionesses he was still fifty feet from them. In subsequent months I occasionally met male No. 61 with his friend on the plains. Then, in April 1969, he visited the Masai pride again. Only his ear tag enabled me to recognize this tawny-maned adult as the scruffy adolescent I had first seen in 1966. He tried to join the lionesses—eight of them this time—by moving closer to them a few feet at a time while they had their daytime rest. He spent at least ten hours at the task, finally approaching to within ten feet of a lioness, but they were not friendly toward him. I wondered if they recognized in him a figure from the past, a figure tragically linked to their pride history.

While lions have covenants that help them to avoid fights, no system functions without errors, and the Seronera and Masai prides provided me with a dramatic example of the consequences when the balance between aggression and restraint is upset. During the first year of my study I never saw these two prides meet, and in the ensuing months they had only two brief spats. The males of the two prides were about a mile apart on September 1, 1967, the Seronera males in a corner of their range that the Masai ones also included in their peregrinations. The Seronera pride had a zebra kill and one lioness was in heat, a potentially explosive combination. When I checked the kill site the following morning at 6:35, there, lying on the ground, was Yellow Mane of the Seronera pride, his body covered with blood and his hide riddled with punctures and cuts, mute evidence of a titanic struggle. A deep gash angled across his brow and a fist-sized hole penetrated his chest. He reclined quietly, the wan rays of sun touching the scattered tufts of his mane, turning them into flecks of gold. Lioness A came from a nearby thicket and sniffed his mane, emitting a plaintive moan as she did so, a sound such as I had never heard from a lion before. Suddenly she growled and fled. Standing at the edge of the thicket was Black Mane, his head held high, imperiously surveying the battle scene. His sleek hide was unmarred. Slowly he walked to his vanquished enemy and gazed down at him. Yellow Mane gave him a baleful glare and a faint growl. I had not been particularly fond of Yellow Mane, for he was neither attractive in appearance nor in his rather morose disposition. But now I marveled at the enigma of his courage. Without hope to sustain him and too late for fear, he had become a realist, fighting for survival even in his last moments, not frantically but calmly and with dignity. And Black Mane retreated.

Yellow Mane raised his head three times in the next half hour, but the last time he lowered it with a groan. Soon after that his breathing became feeble as life ebbed from his mauled body almost imperceptibly. Finally his pupils grew very large, and the amber fires faded from his eyes.

The three Masai males availed themselves of the zebra remains and the lioness in heat. Only one showed any evidence of the fight—a cut in his paw. Lioness A also made friends with her powerful neighbors, but the other lionesses remained aloof from them, preferring to remain with Yellow Mane's companion, whose only memorable act the previous year had been to stumble into a nest of bees. With his face puffed and lumpy, he had wandered about for several days able to see out of his swollen eyes only by raising his muzzle high into the air. Now, with his friend dead, a dramatic change came over him. Apparently feeling himself threatened by the males of the surrounding prides and knowing that alone he could not defend his territory, he lost all assurance. His eyes became shifty as he glanced around at the slightest noise. When he heard roars he slunk away rather than answer the challenge. He had good reasons for this apprehension. Not only did the Masai males tarry in his territory, but now the Kamareshe and Nyaraswiga males also penetrated it, something they had not done before. Somehow a message had reached them that their neighbor was vulnerable and they had immediately taken advantage of the situation. Yet they remained uneasy about the intrusion. One day, lioness C of the Seronera pride killed a zebra by a waterhole. With their extraordinary ability to ferret out a free meal, Black Mane and Brown Mane soon showed up. But at 8:00 p.m. they suddenly jerked to attention, then fled roaring. Arriving from downstream were the two males of the Nyaraswiga pride. But when they heard the roars they too promptly fled, with the result that both sets of trespassers bolted in opposite directions. The Masai males regained their courage first, and, sensing that the others were in retreat, they turned and gave chase. As if to compensate for their momentary cowardice, they now blustered, roaring extra loudly. However, the Nyaraswiga males sneaked across the river while the pursuers, intent on making noise, failed to note this and ran on downstream another mile.

These intrusions affected the Seronera pride in other ways as well. An unknown assailant, a lioness judging by the tracks, ran down three cubs and one at a time bit them to death, the bodies and scuff marks in the dust revealing the grim tale. At dawn, on December 8, I saw the two Kamareshe males in pursuit of the remaining Seronera male in the middle of his own territory, an ignominious situation. He trotted along heavily, panting from the exertion, heading up a rise, past several lionesses whom he either did not see or ignored, and on toward the broad valleys beyond. I never saw him again. The Kamareshe males halted, and I traced their route in the dew-soaked grass to a fallen tree where lioness D had hidden her three small cubs. They were dead, killed by the two males. These now returned to the scene of their carnage. One of them, an old fellow with blunt canines, ripped open a cub and ate its viscera; the other, also a male past his prime, picked up a corpse and carried it off like a trophy. He kept it all day, sometimes nestling it gently between his paws, and I never discovered its ultimate fate. This sequence of events, more than any other, helped me to reach an understanding of the importance of pride males in lion society: they are responsible for maintaining the integrity of the territorial boundaries and, by extension, the safety of cubs.

One cub was left at the kill site. I waited by it all day to see how lioness D would respond when she found her dead offspring. I did not know what to expect—indifference or sentiment. She came just as the last light faded. After sniffing the carcass and licking it briefly, she ate it. Fifteen minutes later only the head and forepaws remained, and as I sat there in the dark listening to her crunch the bones, I realized that I still had not penetrated the mystery of a lion's mind. Once I thought that lions refrained from eating members of their own pride, that cannibalism was reserved for strangers, but lioness D refuted this generalization. Cannibalism is rare, and I still do not know why a body is sometimes consumed and sometimes not. Research is a Gordian knot whose loose ends trail off in so many directions that no one project can hope to untie it.

The Masai males moved east with their pride during the rainy season, and the Kamareshe males also left the Seronera area. Yet no new males established themselves with the Seronera pride. The following June both the Masai and Kamareshe males continued to indulge their dilettantism with their neighbors. These accepted their part-time masters, even to the extent of mating with a male of one pride one day and with another the next. Only poor Limp was often rebuffed, several lionesses attacking him in unison, perhaps because of his poor physical condition and because he was so persistent in stealing their gazelle kills. His depredations came to an end in mid-1969. I think he had had a fight with Black Mane and Brown Mane, for I found him one morning sick and broken in body beneath the sparse shade of a tree. He dragged himself off that night and probably died in the depth of some thicket.

It was not always easy for the males to avoid contact. Once Black Mane followed a female in heat, as usual oblivious to everything but her. She led him straight to the old Kamareshe male, who lay asleep in the high grass. Suddenly he reared up and the two then stood broadside a few seconds, showing off their physiques and manes. Lunging forward, the old male gave a deep growl, and Black Mane, though younger and stronger, lost his nerve and fled for over a mile, abandoning his claim to the area and to his lioness. His bold demeanor with that edge of menace fronted a rather timid personality; his lush mane was more bluff than substance, useful for intimidating a stranger but not an animal who had previously taken his measure. His ultimate strength as the owner of a pride was derived from his association with Brown Mane. After that incident I could never again take his dignity quite seriously.

During an encounter such as this the males display their manes prominently—status symbols that hopefully will intimidate their opponent without the need for more direct methods. Lionesses also seem to be impressed by large manes, for I never saw one present herself sexually to a subadult male. The mane also enables lions to distinguish the sex of individuals at a distance, an important consideration in a society where strangers of the same sex are not tolerated by pride animals and a case of mistaken identity could lead to a severe fight. Males also find manes of advantage during spats, the thick, matted hair absorbing blows harmlessly. However, I have been told that in some areas, such as Tsavo Park, adult males may lack manes. The position of such animals in lion society has not been studied, but an interesting incident of relevance to this question was reported from Nairobi Park. Two pride males there were exceedingly aggressive, killing two lionesses and a subadult male of another pride in 1961 and 1962. Rudolf Schenkel, who was studying the lions at the time, reported the subsequent events:

> The park authorities and their advisers were convinced that the stronger of the two males was "abnormal" and that castration was the appropriate remedy for his abnormality, a remedy which had the added advantage of saving the imposing animal as an attraction for park visitors. The castration was performed, but the expectations proved futile: the male, after having lost his mane within 4 months as a result of the successful castration, together with the other adult male killed two more lionesses in 1963.

Even though the male lacked a mane he remained in the pride until the park authorities shot him for his extreme irascibility.

The intermittent association of the Masai and Kamareshe males with the Seronera lionesses continued into 1969. By the middle of that year, the Masai males spent more and more time with their neighbors, seldom visiting their own lionesses. And in August, almost two years after the death of Yellow Mane, the Masai males switched their allegiance completely. It had been a difficult two years for the Seronera lionesses. They had lost not only their males but also most of their cubs. Out of forty-six cubs born since my study had begun only fourteen were still alive and some of these too would die in the ensuing months, a survival record much poorer than that of the Masai pride. Both The Old One and Hump had died, apparently of old age. The health of these old lionesses had deteriorated slowly, even though they still hunted and fed on the kills of others, until finally their muscles grew slack and thin and they vanished. But now the future of the pride looked bright once more.

The deserted Masai pride lionesses were now without males, and to understand how their immediate future was settled it is necessary to trace the history of two nomadic males. Male No. 58 was a nomad in his prime or just past it, whom I had met for the first time in November 1966 with a huge, shaggy friend near Seronera. Their bond did not persist, and by the following February male No. 58 had another companion, this time an elderly male with a luxuriant dark-brown mane and with hindquarters so spindly that they seemed in imminent danger of collapse. A month later these two males joined three nomadic lionesses in a shallow valley just east of the Gol kopjes and formed what I called the Cub Valley group. These lionesses had various backgrounds. Lioness No. 69, a sleek, dark animal, was first seen near Seronera with two cubs in November 1966. Somehow she lost her offspring and the following February I met her on the plains, courting. A second lioness, No. 102, was alone near Seronera in December 1966. By February she had moved thirty-five miles to the east, where she joined for a while two lionesses with whom I was not acquainted. Chance took the two males and two lionesses, as well as a third one, to Cub Valley in late February and they met, perhaps when quenching their thirst at the permanent pool there, and they decided to remain together. By May, another male, No. 54, whom I had previously met around the Simba and Gol kopjes, had replaced male No. 58, who then roamed alone for several months. But suddenly the males changed positions once more, because one day No. 58 was back with the Cub Valley group and No. 54 had resumed his wanderings. I do not know what had precipitated the temporary switch. After it, the group stayed together. Forced off the plains during the dry season by lack of food, it tarried near the woodlands' edge until the animals could return to Cub Valley with the renewed rains. There the three lionesses had cubs, eight of them, which they kept hidden in the reeds bordering the pool.

Preying on straggling zebra and on occasional gazelle, the group clung to their valley far into the 1968 dry season, but finally they made their annual trek westward. With the rains early in 1969 having almost failed, the lions were unable to return to Cub Valley, and they merely shifted their position back and forth along the edge of the plains wherever food was to be had. From April onward they subsisted within the territory of the Masai pride, no doubt fortunate that Black Mane and Brown Mane were at that time infatuated with the Seronera lionesses to the west. When in August the Masai males abandoned their pride, the Cub Valley males grasped the opportunity as if they had been waiting for the moment. Deserting the three lionesses with whom they had spent over two years, they joined the Masai lionesses in a quick and smooth transition. Without qualms they had given up the freedom of their nomadic existence for the security of a pride. Considering their advanced age, it seemed likely that their tenure with this pride would be fairly brief, but even so they may have left a lasting imprint. Just before I left the Serengeti, two of Flop-ear's cubs came into their first heat. They were 3½ years old, and I had watched them grow from toddlers to sleek adults. Male No. 58 and the old one each mated with a young lioness, and perhaps after some three months a new generation would join the pride.

THE WANDERERS

"MAN IS BORN FREE, AND EVERYWHERE HE IS IN CHAINS," LA-
mented Jean Jacques Rousseau. There are those who yearn
for this vanished legacy, for the freedom to roam, and to
them a nomadic lion would seem to lead an ideal existence.
It may wander at will, without family cares, choosing
its company as it pleases among nomadic friends. However, just as man sought security first and only afterwards found delight in the freedom of the wilderness, so the
nomadic lion wants the bonds of a settled life, being
always in search of a piece of land. I spent much time
with nomads, for many followed the migratory herds to
the plains. Meeting the same animals time after time over
the years, I found my view of their way of life changing
from appreciation, perhaps a bit tinged with envy, to sympathy. Their existence was in many ways less carefree than
that of pride members. Harried when they trespass, never
certain whether a stranger will be friendly, with no one to
provide food when they are sick, shot when they leave the

park, their problems are many. Freedom is not just a matter of discarding all chains.

The nomads traveled so widely and I saw most of them so seldom that I needed an identification system that was more permanent and distinctive than one based on such physical blemishes as scars and cuts. Young males were particularly difficult to distinguish after a period of absence because the growth of the mane can alter an animal's appearance completely within a few months. To enable me to plot the movements of such lions, I placed ear tags on 156 of them, many of these being nomads. To tag a lion is a fairly simple process, once one knows the technique. First, of course, a lion has to be subdued and for this I chose the muscle relaxant succinylcholine chloride, which not only acts rapidly but also has no long-lasting effects. The method of capturing animals by shooting into them a muscle-relaxing or sleep-inducing drug was developed in the United States during the 1950's. In brief, a syringe is filled with a drug and then shot from a gun, using either a carbon dioxide or powder charge. On impact a small powder charge is set off in the syringe and it propels forward a rubber plunger that forcefully injects the drug through the needle into the muscles of the animal. With trapping, netting, and other cumbersome techniques of capture eliminated, wildlife biologists can now mark many animals in a relatively short time to study movements, longevity, social structure, and other aspects of behavior. Drug dosages depend on the weight of animals, and this is not easy to estimate accurately. An overdose may kill, for many drugs have no antidote. I knew of projects in which over half of the drugged animals died. I dreaded the thought of even one lion succumbing, and it was with great reluctance that I began to inject the animals.

Driving close to a lion, I fired the syringe into its thigh. The first few lions failed to relax completely and I dared not leave the car. By slowly increasing dosages,

I finally was able to determine the proper amount. While the animal reclined on its side, I clamped a colored and numbered metal tag in one or both ears and I also cut a small notch out of one ear, spreading a drop or two of the escaping blood on a glass slide. The blood would be checked later for disease organisms. After that I returned to the car and watched the lion carefully, ready to give it artificial respiration should its breathing falter. The tagging disturbed most lions very little. With the impact of the syringe, a lion occasionally swatted its neighbor, thinking that it had been responsible for the sudden pain. Seeing the syringe dangling from the thigh, a pride member sometimes tried to pull it out, but such solicitude was usually not welcome. As the drug took effect, the lion calmly rolled on its side, usually within five minutes of being hit, a typical position in lions that caused no alarm among the others. At times lions watched me from as close as thirty feet, their heads cocked quizzically, as I tagged one of their friends. Lions apparently fail to recognize a car and a person as separate entities as long as the two are close together and the latter does not display his silhouette. Hence the cats treated me as fearlessly as they would the car.

Although lions retreat hurriedly from a person on foot, they would no doubt become inured to such encounters if meetings occurred often. The behavior of lions in the Gir Sanctuary of India is of interest in this respect. The terrain in the sanctuary is rolling and covered with a scrubby acacia and teak forest. Some 120 villages are located within the five hundred square miles of the reserve and the 150 lions in it see people almost daily, especially since they prey almost exclusively on the thousands of domestic cattle and buffalo that use the area for grazing. Several groups of lions are fed by the forest department as a tourist attraction. Paul Joslin was studying the Gir lions when David Jenkins, Paul Leyhausen, and I visited his project in 1968 for a couple of weeks. Late one afternoon the local guides showed us three lionesses lying on the slope of a hill near a road, their pelage strikingly golden among the green teak leaves. The lions merely watched as a guide led us to within forty feet of them. I was uneasy: in Africa one does not wander that close to a wild lion on purpose. But when Paul approached to within twenty feet of a lioness, she rose and gave a sharp growl. It now being dusk, we expressed the hope that we might see these lions again the next day, and the guide assured us that this would be no problem. One guide fetched a goat, and, walking slowly with it, he lured the interested lions to a quiet place half a mile away. There the guides built a fire, substituted a young buffalo for the goat, and sat down to wait through the hours of darkness. And the lions also reclined nearby and waited, showing a remarkable patience, considering the fact that their meal was in effect dangled before them all night. When we returned at 6:30 a.m., one lioness was lying only fifteen feet from a guide who had placed himself between her and the buffalo to prevent a premature attack on the animal. It was decided to move the buffalo 250 feet into a small clearing. The guide walked ahead, a tall, gaunt fellow with a black beard, leading the docile buffalo, and, off to one side, padded the lionesses, all interacting with almost eerie casualness. When a lioness began to stalk and from a distance of fifteen feet seemed ready to rush, the guide shooed her back with a wave of his hand while he finished tying the buffalo to a tree. Finally, the lions were permitted to eat.

Although I tranquillized lions routinely for a few months, the operation could never be treated casually. An animal with too small a dose might suddenly rake the air with its claws, or, far more worrisome, one with too large a dose might have difficulties with breathing. To avoid potential crises, I preferred to work alone, remaining tensely alert and concentrating on every nuance of the lion's actions without distractions. Even Kay was somewhat irrationally banished after she emitted a small involuntary "oh" when an angry lioness reached through the open door of the car. Slight mishaps did occur. Once, as I gave a young lioness artificial respiration, not mouth-to-mouth but by alternately lifting and depressing her forearm, her mother charged me. I had just time enough to jump into the car. On another occasion a drugged lioness retreated into a swamp before lying down. I drove in after her and promptly became mired. Unable to extract the car, I set off across the plains on foot, my retreating form watched by three lionesses whom I had disturbed on their wildebeest kill. I had planned to walk to the main road and there hitch a ride back to Seronera. This I did. But in the meantime my absence had worried Kay, especially since it was now late afternoon and I had also spent the previous night with lions. She mentioned her concern to Hugh Lamprey. Hugh, with Myles Turner, left immediately by plane to search for my car. They found it. There was no sign of me, but beside the car rested three very gorged lionesses, a rather suggestive situation. Banking low, Hugh and Myles circled the site, searching the ground for tatters of clothing or any other sign of me. Meanwhile, I had returned home, news that was later received by my searchers with relief tinged with annoyance for the needless worry I had caused.

One day, accompanied by several visitors, I drugged a lioness and she died suddenly, possibly from an allergic reaction to the drug, for it was the only such mishap during the study. I loaded her into the car and transported her to Kiwawira, in the western part of the Corridor, where Rüdiger Sachs had a veterinary field station. He autopsied her, pleased to obtain the parasitological material. But her death greatly affected my attitude toward tagging. I must admit that in the beginning it did give me pleasure to kneel by a lion and stroke its slightly oily hide or caress the mane of a male. These gestures touched a deep atavistic cord within me, one in which I seemed to re-enact a primal victory over an ancient enemy. But soon I developed such a feeling of tenderness for lions that I found it abhorrent to disturb them; I came to detest tagging, and, after I had marked enough animals to give me the needed information, I tranquillized animals only in exceptional circumstances.

Animals in East Africa are commonly marked for identification without eliciting comment from the public: elephants walk around with white numbers painted on their sides and wildebeest have garish collars around their necks. But, as Evelyn Ames noted in her charming book *A Glimpse of Eden*: "Lions are not animals alone; they are symbols and totems and legends; they have impressed themselves so deeply on the human mind, if not its blood, it is as though the psyche were emblazoned with their crest." And to mark a lion is a desecration. Tour guides objected to the tags, a conservation organization questioned the propriety of marking lions, and, for a while, Myles Turner's lips tightened into a thin, hard line whenever he met me around Seronera. As I was tagging a lioness one morning, a car drew up beside me and a red-bearded face glared at me. Expletives aside, the spluttering voice conveyed that I was involved in a nasty business, the most disgusting thing he had ever seen, that he would rather shoot the lion than have it touched by my foul hands. I said nothing. On his car was the legend "Professional Hunter." Later, George Dove generously came to our house to apologize and to explain that to see me handle a lion, removing its aura of danger and freedom so casually, was more than his emotions could bear. I had empathy with his feelings, but I also needed the information that the tagged lions would provide.

For example, there was male No. 57, whom I tagged in November 1966, at Musabi, a small plain in the Corridor. He was about 2½ to 3 years old at the time, a rather untidy-looking fellow with tufts of mane on his cheeks and a rakish ruff down his nape; he also had a slight umbilical hernia. Twice more I saw him in the area, once alone and once with another young male. In March 1967 he appeared on the plains, some fifty-five miles east of where I had tagged him. His social life, like that of many nomads, was desultory, casual and indifferent associations with various animals for a few hours to a few days. He spent several days with a lioness in May, and on June 9 he rested with male No. 134, whom I will describe more fully later, as well as with two other males and two lionesses. With me that day were Howard Baldwin and William Holz. Since I had found it extremely difficult to locate the same lions day after day, a necessary requisite for studying their feeding rates and movements, I hoped to track some animals for months by attaching radio transmitters to them. This technique had been used successfully in the United States on many animals including bears, and the gently rolling Serengeti was ideal for sending radio signals and receiving them. Howard, at the invitation of John Owen, had initiated a radio telemetry project in the park in January 1967, by sending his two assistants, William and Suzie Holz. Unfortunately they failed to bring functional radios and their project had lain dormant for many months until Howard arrived with some new equipment. Male No. 57 was now chosen to wear a radio.

We attached the radio to a collar that was then placed around the lion's neck. He ignored this adornment and continued his daytime rest with his friends. These moved away early in the night, but he remained where he was, a fact evident from the steady beeping of the receiving set that Howard and Bill had with them in the car nearby. Around 5:00 a.m. the radio signal grew faint, an indication that the lion was finally traveling. By slowly rotating the directional antenna on the car until the beeps became loud again, it was possible to locate his approximate position in the darkness. Driving toward the signal, male No. 57 was soon found striding with determination up a slope and over the crest to a waterhole. Daylight found him ambling along rather aimlessly, and at 6:50 a.m. he lay down on a hilltop, having traveled three miles that night. As usual he spent the day

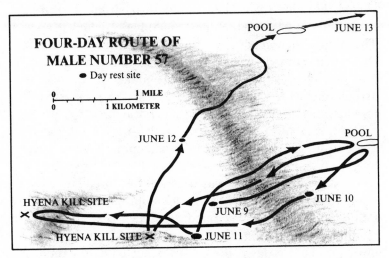

**FOUR-DAY ROUTE OF
MALE NUMBER 57**

● Day rest site

0 ———————— 1 MILE
0 ———————— 1 KILOMETER

POOL   JUNE 13

JUNE 12 ●

POOL

HYENA KILL SITE
✕

JUNE 10

JUNE 9

HYENA KILL SITE ✕   JUNE 11

Four-day route of Male No. 57

alternately napping or staring into the distance until after dark he headed for a while in the direction from which he had come the previous day. That night was mostly uneventful, except that shortly after 4:00 a.m. he met three of his former friends gnawing on the remains of a wildebeest they had scavenged from several hyenas. But male No. 57 remained aloof and soon left to spend the day alone near his rest site of June 9. The night of June 11 to 12 was an active one for the male, and he kept Howard and Dorothy Baldwin and myself awake and busy trying to follow the weak radio signal that transmitted for only about half a mile. Shortly after 7:00 p.m. a roar came from the darkness far away, faint and mournful, more like the hoot of an owl than a proclamation from a lion. Male No. 57 listened attentively but did not respond. Later, however, he roared several times and received an answer. And then at midnight male No. 134 suddenly arrived and the two reclined side by side. I was always impressed by how amicably nomads joined and parted, because their behavior was so strikingly different from the manner in which pride members treated strangers. The nature of nomads seemed to widen with their horizon. Of course, nomads were often acquainted, having casually met during previous years, just as male No. 57 was now associating with No. 134. Nevertheless the possession of a territory has a drastic effect on lion character.

After a short rest the two males moved off together, heading in the direction of some whooping hyenas. Several hyenas had killed a wildebeest, but by the time the lions reached the site not only was the meat devoured but also two other young male lions had already appropriated the scraps. Reluctant to dispute the remains, males Nos. 57 and 134 reclined 150 feet from the kill and waited over three hours, until just before dawn the others departed. After removing the last shreds of flesh from the bones No. 134 walked away, leaving No. 57 alone once more. At 7:30 a.m. he too abandoned the remains to the still-lurking hyenas and hiked two miles before beginning his rest. He had walked six miles that night. Much to my annoyance the radio had ceased to transmit properly and we had to abandon our efforts to track this male continuously. But we followed him long enough that evening to take part in a momentous event in his life. He returned to the pool he had visited the first night and at about 9:25 he met there another male of his own age. In the past he had always abandoned or been abandoned by his newly found friends. Yet this new young male was obviously special, though in looks and character he seemed rather unprepossessing, no different from many adolescents I had met. They shared a drink, they shared a rest site—nothing extraordinary, but by some intangible process they cemented a friendship in the course of a few hours that lasted until death.

The pair spent July to about December around the Musabi area where I had first met No. 57, and in January 1968 they trekked to the plains again with the migratory herds. There I met them occasionally, inseparable companions, now in the first flush of full lionhood, with fine yellow-brown manes that glistened as if curried. They swaggered along, powerful yet retaining their youthful grace. Their hides were still unscarred from internecine battles. Soon they might attempt to take over a pride, and I hoped that I might be present to witness their triumph. But it was not to be. I do not know where they spent the dry season. But I do know that on November 9, 1968, they were northeast of the park, outside its boundaries, and that they met a hunter in search of a trophy. A bullet slammed into male No. 57. The outfitter of the hunt sent the ear tag to the Research Institute and the scientist in me was grateful. But holding the blood-encrusted tag, I was filled with a terrible sadness, for I would rather have retained my image of the two friends roaming through their domain. Now he is one more lifeless hide imprisoned in someone's private mortuary.

The Ikoma area, where male No. 57 died, is a favorite hunting ground for those who like to shoot their lions with little effort. Myles Turner told me that at least eighty-five males were killed there by sport hunters in the year 1959–60, many of them illegally, and over fifty more were taken there in late 1966 and early 1967. Late in 1969, Marshal Tito of Yugoslavia is said to have shot two tame males near Lake Lagaja, just outside of the park in an area that is ostensibly protected. Nomadic males are attracted to terrain not occupied by other males, and heavy shooting siphons lions out of the park. Most of these lions are tame, for their years in the park have taught them that cars are harmless. Every hunter who feels that he must prove himself by obliterating a lion should first contemplate the animal for a while. As he gazes at his intended victim, a perfect and unique product of evolution, a being with its own aspirations and fears and joys, there may come a time when he suppresses his urge to kill and instead recaptures his sense of wonder and feeling of fellowship.

Actually, the days when hunters achieved status and acclaim for killing are over. With more than a quarter of a million tourists a year in East Africa enjoying the sight of lions at ease in their domain, no one is likely to be impressed with a hunter who has selfishly shot a lion for his own pleasure. Parties of hunters sometimes passed through Seronera. Sitting in their vehicles, self-conscious in their new khaki uniforms and with their arsenal strapped grimly within reach, they were a rather anachronistic sight among the tourists dressed in cameras and gaudy clothing; they seemed so lacking in imagination. Of course the hunting tradition is a part of us—without it man would never have become man. However, the mindless hurt inflicted by a child and the unquestioned satisfaction that hunting brings to youth are in many replaced by a feeling that to cause unspeakable pain to another creature, to kill it without purpose, not for food, not for hides, not for protection, for nothing except enjoyment, is a form of sadism. More and more people are renouncing carnage for contemplation, and therein lies a hope for man's fate.

My condemnation of killing for sport is based on a moral attitude, one each hunter must resolve within himself. Wildlife populations are not necessarily harmed by hunting unless the species involved are threatened with extinction. Licensed hunters in East Africa are so few in number that their impact on wildlife is negligible when compared to the amount of poaching that occurs. Indeed, the animals often benefit to some extent from hunting. In areas where predators are absent or for some reason are unable to keep the prey population from increasing beyond the limits of its food supply, shooting is a useful management tool. Many African countries are maintaining game reserves to cater mainly to foreign hunters, again a direct benefit to wildlife, for if such areas were opened to other land-use practices the animals would surely vanish. The mere presence of hunting parties in a locality deters poachers from operating there. The fact that male No. 57 died had little impact on the lion population in the Serengeti Park. There is a sharp distinction between considering the consequences of hunting on the well-being of a wildlife population and the moral implications of killing for pleasure.

Male No. 57 died before he could fulfill his territorial imperative, but No. 134, whom we met earlier, made an attempt to claim an area on the plains. Almost devoid of prides, the plains provide one of the few areas where lions can set up territories without intruding on occupied terrain. Of course they are temporary territories only, for there is not enough food for lions to dwell on most of the plains during the dry season. I had tagged male No. 134 in the woodlands west of Lake Magadi in January 1967, when he was about 3½ years old. He was alone then, a beautiful animal, unscarred and with a perfectly proportioned face. The next month he was on the plains, where he remained for the season, wandering aimlessly until he retreated to the woodlands in July. I saw him twice near Banagi, but after that he vanished for several months. The following December he returned to the plains, centering his activity on the Gol kopjes. He was almost 4½ years old now and adult in appearance. When he reclined on some granite boulder, his long silky mane streaming in the wind as his eyes searched the great vistas, he distilled the simple grandeur of the Serengeti to its most elemental. He was no longer alone but had formed an unusual friendship with lioness No. 60. Lions usually form close and lasting companionships only with members of their own sex. However, lioness No. 60 had a predilection for young males. She was a middle-aged animal with a rather coarse face and a bold and somewhat derisive way of looking at the car. I had known her since November 1966, when, as a lone nomad, she had been tagged south of the Moru kopjes. Soon after that she had

Facial expressions of lions. Top left—relaxed face of a dozing lioness; top right—relaxed face of a lioness sitting by her kill; upper middle—relaxed open-mouth face of a cub as it pounces playfully on another cub; lower middle (left)—alert face of a lioness watching prey; lower middle (right)—roaring face of a male; bottom left—yawning face of a lioness; bottom middle—grimace face of a male after sniffing scent; bottom right—tense open-mouth face of a lioness while guarding her kill.

R. KEANE

The bared-teeth face. Top left—a lioness bares her teeth in response to being greeted by a cub; top right—a male bares his teeth slightly while being attacked by a lioness after copulation; upper middle (left)—a male opens his mouth in response to a cub's greeting; upper middle (right)—a bared-teeth face with strong components of the tense open-mouth face by a male guarding a kill; lower middle—a copulating pair, the male with a bared-teeth face, the female with a tense open-mouth face; bottom left—a lioness deters a cub from suckling with her open mouth; bottom right—a lioness hisses at a male.

formed a friendship lasting several months with one young male. And now she and male No. 134 were closely attached to each other.

We placed a radio on male No. 134, doing so at night because I had found that lions are more approachable and less disturbed when handled in the dark. While Howard and Bill hurriedly attached the collar, I kept my eyes on the shadowy form of the lioness prowling just beyond the narrow arc of illumination cast by my flashlight. With darkness the assurance of man is replaced by apprehension, at no time more so than when faced by an agitated lioness who has not yet decided on a course of action. With relief we all returned to the security of the Land Rover. We followed the pair for nine consecutive days until the radio quit. But male No. 134 had many adventures even in this short period and these gave us fascinating glimpses into the life of a lion.

To establish a proper territory one must eliminate competition and proclaim one's presence—and this the pair did with a vengeance. On December 9, the day we placed the radio on him, male No. 134 had met a male of his own age. Although they maintained an uneasy truce during the heat of the day while resting on the same kopje, they slapped each other at dusk before parting. The following night, the pair crisscrossed the Gol kopjes, roaring again and again. At 10:10 p.m. the two heard many hyenas whoop and gibber over a mile away, a sure sign that a kill had been made. Male No. 134 and his lioness hurried toward the sounds and obtained a free snack. At 6:10 a.m., I saw several hyenas harass a wildebeest in the distance until one hyena bit it in the belly and with a powerful jerk pulled it down. The lions had also witnessed the spectacle, showing the interest of two gourmands over the preparation of their meal by several chefs. They appropriated the carcass. Coming from the opposite direction was a nomadic lioness with her seven-month-old cub, also intent on a share of the spoils. But lioness No. 60 attacked the newcomers and chased the other lioness vigorously. Whirling around suddenly, she clouted No. 60 on the head and followed up her advantage by biting her in the neck, drawing blood. When No. 60 tried to rise, a flurry of blows knocked her down again. The cub meanwhile had escaped the turmoil by running to a kopje and hiding itself in the dense tangle of a bush that grew on top of a steep-sided boulder. Its mother called softly, sniffed the ground as if searching for its spoor, and then gave up her efforts to find the cub. Instead she joined male No. 134, who reclined with epicurean ease by the kill. Lioness No. 60 had stood there silently after having been chastised, but now she seemed to seek vengeance for that inglorious rebuff. She searched around until she found the trail of the cub and then she followed it to the end. Unable to penetrate the bush into which the cub had retreated even farther, she lay down at the base of the boulder. She had patience, staying there all day; she was still waiting at 10:00 p.m., when I went home, having made arrangements to pick up a visiting scientist at dawn. Returning nine hours later, I found her with the cub, which was dead and partially eaten.

Howard and Dorothy stayed for the night with male No. 134 and his new friend. She made no further search for her cub, which at the time still huddled silently on its boulder nearby, and instead lounged near the kill. The male roared often toward morning, proclaiming his ownership of the territory and all it contained—but from the darkness came a challenge. It was the same male with whom No. 134 had had a spat a few days earlier. They met on a grassy slope at dawn. A blow knocked No. 134 down. He leaped up quickly, saved from injury by his mane, and lunged at the interloper, who first retreated and then charged in turn. Each having called the other's bluff, they then lay down side by side for half an hour. After that they renewed their contest for dominance. A tussle followed, and then another. Rearing up on their hindlegs, they exchanged a flurry of massive blows that ended only when the new male crouched down in supplication while No. 134 stood over him, his ear torn and a cut in his scrotum, but still master of his domain. He left the scene of the battle and found his friend No. 60, whom he had not seen all night. Spotting something furry and bloody between her paws, he pounced and snatched the carcass, always interested in a snack, no matter how full he might be. But he did not expect a lion cub. He stood stock still for a second, holding the tattered body in his mouth, then dropped it. Less fastidious in her tastes, lioness No. 60 resumed her meal.

A little after 6:00 p.m. many roars emanated from about half a mile beyond the kopje in which the male and female had rested all day. They answered many of the calls as they moved closer to inspect the new challengers. At 7:05 p.m. they met males Nos. 103 and 104, a pair of nomads whom I had seen before in various parts of the plains. They probably were brothers, both blond-maned and about four years old. Male No. 134 and his friend charged the powerful intruders without hesitation and these fled, much to my surprise. At first bounding, then slowing to a trot, the two lions chased the trespassers for two miles, roaring hoarsely, until finally they halted, panting from the unwonted exercise. They had relative peace for several nights after that encounter and they used this interlude to solidify their claim to the area. Patrolling the kopjes and roaring often, they let it be known that intrusions would not be welcome. One afternoon a young lioness came to within five-hundred feet of the pair and there she reclined, looking at them expectantly. I knew this lioness and wondered where her usual female companion was. A little later, the pair walked slowly toward this reticent visitor. She headed at a fast walk straight across the plains toward a kopje 3.3 miles away. The pair followed. The other lioness was at the kopje on a freshly killed zebra, which naturally male No. 134 and lioness No. 60 ate. I was puzzled by this incident. Why had one young lioness left a kill to walk over three miles in the hot sun to wait for two hours near the other lions before leading them without hesitation to the kill? Lions just do not invite neighbors over for a meal!

It was now December 17 and we had followed the male and female for eight continuous days. The radio had stopped. We were all weary from lack of sleep. I wanted to spend one final night with the pair by myself. Not only was it necessary to remove the collar from the male but I had also grown fond of the animals. They were not a particularly pleasant couple by human standards, brutal in their assertion of rights, preemptory in taking what they wanted. However, such judgments are irrelevant and I simply watched them to learn how they existed in their world. I also liked to be on the plains at night, where no cars, no airplanes, nothing violated the peace; I know of no solitude so secure. Everything was quiet except for the wind that blew in from the east bringing with it a fragrance compounded of grass and animals. Only the occasional yip of a jackal interrupted the silence. I huddled down in my seat, a blanket drawn tightly over my shoulders against the chill. When I closed my eyes in this boundless space I could almost sense the movement of the earth. Suddenly male No. 134 roared, startling me out of my reverie. The pair hurried off, breaking into a trot, obviously intent on something, since they sniffed and looked around alertly. After a mile they came upon male No. 88, a solitary nomad. They chased him for two miles until he finally crouched down and rested his chin on the ground, conveying his submission. The pair rested near him instead of attacking. With the first glimmer of dawn, male No. 134 and lioness No. 60 departed to spend the day in the shade of a nearby kopje. In nine days the male had traveled a total of 67½ miles. His daily maximum was 13 miles and his average was 7 miles. He had eaten on seven of the nights, three times on carcasses scavenged from hyenas, three times by joining other lionesses. Like most nomadic males on the plains he had shown little interest in hunting for himself.

During the following weeks I checked on the pair at intervals, curious to know how they fared in their territory, for the various males with whom male No. 134 had had altercations were still in the area. On December 19, male No. 134 had apparently fought with the same intruder as he did on December 17. The encounter had ended to his satisfaction. While the other male was on one kopje, a bleeding cut over his eye, he courted near another kopje with the lioness whose cub had been killed. But his time was running out. During the night of January 11 to 12 he must have met males Nos. 103 and 104, whom he had evicted a month earlier. During this meeting the outcome was reversed. That morning I came across him pacing back and forth in agitated fashion near the Gol kopjes until after 10:00 a.m. as if afraid to approach his usual haunts. That night he roared and roared, and when his challenge was answered by males Nos. 103 and 104 from the kopjes, he meekly turned and walked away. He and lioness No. 60 remained together for at least another year, but in that time they never tried to claim another territory. Males Nos. 103 and 104 remained in possession of the Gol kopjes at least until April, and during the next rains they came back, successfully taking over the same site for another season.

I encountered these males often because the Gol kopjes were one of my favorite areas in the park. Sometimes I drove there in the afternoon and climbed up on a kopje. The Land Rover is surely one of the most uncomfortable vehicles ever designed, and its jarring ride had given me a common East African ailment called "Land Rover back." My muscles were simply unable to adapt to the constant shaking and pounding on the hard seats, with the result that pain in my lower back was sometimes quite strong.

Only walking and other exercise brought relief. Aside from that, I was content to escape the insulation of the car. Feeling the rocks under my feet, seeing the vultures soaring stiff-winged in the blue space, I was projected into the environment, alive, my humanity regained after confinement. It is all too easy to become alienated from nature, smothered by the effluvium of culture, the noises of motors, the secure walls of our homes, even the thoughts that dwell more on irrelevant abstractions than on the basics of living. To perceive this land, the plains and sky fused into a calm whole, forces man to relinquish his dominance. Occasionally a car intruded, and I viewed it with selfish antagonism for breaking into my communion with the infinite.

The plains were at their most beautiful on moonlit nights. The kopjes were black masses of eternity and a single silence hung over everything. At times I left the car and climbed what was no longer a hill but a shining silver mountain. As I stood on top, exulting in the wind, there came over me the serenity and rapture that are said to be the symbols of religion. Not the self-interested Christian precept that commands man to "be fruitful and multiply, and fill the earth and subdue it and have dominion . . . over every living thing" but more in a Taoist ideal which exalts a life spent in harmony with nature. Religion is basically a search for understanding, a striving for meaning. Man's single most important task is to become sensitive to his role in his environment and to foster an attitude of gentleness with nature. Conservation then becomes the ethical criterion on which man's future depends; it is a religion based on moral, aesthetic, and practical values, which has no one object of reverence but which nevertheless quests for something holy, a spiritual unity with all life. Minutes passed. But then a primordial fear reasserted itself and shook my complacency. My imagination conjured predators prowling the shadows, and I hurried back to the car, back into my cultural bondage.

There, wrapped in my blanket, I stretched out in the back of the car and slept away the lonely hours until dawn again brought reassurance.

Male No. 134 won and then lost a temporary territory because he was unable to successfully assert himself against two opponents. Perhaps he would team up with a congenial male companion some day and take over a pride. The young Moru males showed me how such a transition is accomplished. I first met these animals at the Moru kopjes in March 1967. There were five males, about 3¾ years old, no doubt all members of the same pride who had left their ancestral home together. They were inseparable companions, an implacable team whose concerted demands no other lion could resist. That season they roamed widely over the plains in a typical exhibition of youthful wanderlust. The dry season found them back around the Moru kopjes. In December, at the age of about 4½ years, they followed the migratory herds back onto the plains, but this time they homesteaded the area around Naabi Hill. I often saw them there until the following May.

On September 10, David Jenkins of the Nature Conservancy and I were watching fifteen members of the Magadi pride including Silver Mane and Scar Nose, two of the three males that had been with the pride for at least two years. All lounged along the edge of a small marsh, keeping their eyes on a solitary bull buffalo who stood there belly-deep in mud and water. The bloody wounds on his shoulders showed that he had been attacked and mauled but had shaken off his assailants and retreated into the marsh. We waited for the inevitable action. It arrived from unexpected quarters. Suddenly, at 9:25 a.m., the five Moru males came at a trot, radiating power as they roared. Seeing this invincible phalanx, the pride scattered and fled. Only one lioness asserted herself by chasing a surprised male one hundred feet before retreating like the others through a thicket of whistling thorn toward the rocky slopes bordering the Mbalageti River.

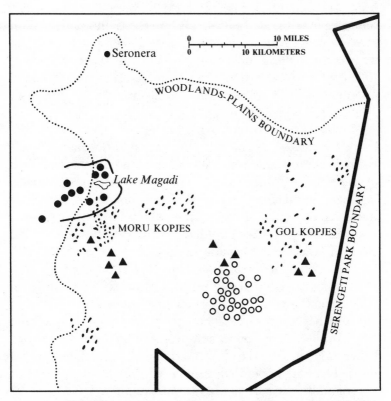

Movement pattern of a group of five males showing
their transition from complete nomadism (triangles—
March to October 1967) through temporary residency
on the plains (open circles—December 1967 to May
1968) to complete residency after they took over
the Magadi pride (closed circles—September 1968
onward). Each symbol represents a sighting.

Forty-five minutes later the victorious Moru males returned.
They sat by the marsh, hesitating to get their paws wet,
while the buffalo faced his tormentors with lowered head.
Then, inexplicably, he plodded toward them, committing
suicide with such serenity it was as if his end had long ago

been preordained. One lion grabbed his rump; another placed his paws over the bull's back, bit him there and pulled. With intolerable weariness the bull sank to his knees. There were no violent actions, no frantic tussles, as the buffalo was rolled on his back with impersonal force. Another lion joined and held the bull's throat, a fourth his muzzle. He died after a few minutes of suffocation.

At 7:00 p.m. a lion roared in the distance. Though victorious in battle, the Moru males still had the mentality of nomads and the solitary challenge made them nervous. Two of them fled for three hundred feet, but then their thundering communal reply restored their confidence and they lumbered off in the direction from which the roar had come. Later that night, after they had returned to the buffalo, an old and emaciated nomadic male joined them on the kill. Not yet accustomed to possessing their new territory, the Moru males permitted the newcomer to eat, something no self-respecting pride owner would do. Nevertheless, from that day on the Magadi pride had new overlords. Two of the former pride males I never saw again, but a few months after being evicted, Scar Nose was on the plains, alone, now a harried-looking nomad who along with his territory had lost his friends, his security, and his quiet dignity.

Scar Nose and other lions would seem to have few problems in life after they have passed their precarious childhood. Since food is plentiful and lions have no persistent enemies in the park, one would expect most of them to reach a contented old age and then, shrouded in their regal past, sink into oblivion. But the dead lions which I found or which were shown to me did not support this assumption. Some forty-one percent of the dead animals, aged two years and older, were in their prime and only ten percent were old; the others consisted of subadults, young adults, and animals slightly past their prime. Twenty-two subadults and adults died of the following causes: snared or shot, forty-one percent; fight with other lion, twenty-three percent; disease, eighteen percent; injured by prey, nine percent; and old age, nine percent. Nearly three quarters of these lions had died violently. Lions that venture to the periphery of the park or outside it may stumble into a snare set by poachers for zebra and wildebeest, or they may meet a trophy hunter. Hyena packs may attack a lion if it is sick. Myles Turner gave me this extract from his field notes:

> On the night of February 25th, 1961, at about 9 P.M. very loud hyaena howling and grunting broke out on the camp site ridge and continued on and off throughout the night. On investigating next morning we found the few remains of one of our fine resident male lions. This old lion had been very sick from a wound in his flank and we had been keeping an eye on him.

Lions that attack prey carelessly may be crippled or killed by hooves or horns. One male had a broken jaw, possibly the result of a zebra's kick, and I found the skeletons of a male lion and a bull buffalo side by side along the Mbalageti River.

Lions sometimes inflict serious injuries on each other, as the demise of Yellow Mane illustrated. Only their amazing recuperative powers prevent the death toll from lacerations and infections from being higher than it is. Of ninety-two lions resident around Seronera at one point, six were blind in one eye, four had the end of the tail missing, and one had lost an ear. I discovered one freshly dead lioness who had died of septicemia after she had been severely mauled in the neck. George Dove told me that on March 16, 1969, he watched a lioness walk then crawl toward a male on a kill. Suddenly the male attacked her, and, after a brief flurry, she quivered and lay still, bitten through the back of the neck. The male continued his meal unconcernedly and finally reclined by her body as if unaware that she was dead.

In 1962, unusual weather conditions caused a plague

of blood-sucking flies of the genus *Stomoxys* in Ngorongoro Crater. After witnessing swarms of these flies attack the lions, H. Fosbrooke wrote:

> Neither illustration nor description can adequately portray the condition of the lions in the crater during the *Stomoxys* scourge. The Assistant Conservator said that he observed a pride of six which climbed up the *Acacia* trees around the Seneto waterhole to a height of perhaps 40 feet and others tried to hide themselves in Hyaena holes in attempts to evade the flies.

The lion population dropped from an estimated seventy animals to about fifteen due to death and emigration. But the reproductive potential of this lion population was such that by 1969 it numbered about seventy animals again.

Biting flies did not unduly bother the Serengeti lions but another kind did so. Rüdiger Sachs checked the blood slides of lions I had collected and found that sixty-nine percent of the samples were infected with the trypanosomes of two kinds of sleeping sickness. Normally trypanosomes become infective in the mouth parts of tsetse flies and are transmitted when the fly bites an animal, but the protozoan may also penetrate lesions in the mouth of a carnivore that eats infected prey. The fact that most infected lions were in good condition indicates that the parasite usually does not affect a healthy animal. However, should the lion's resistance be lowered, perhaps by a serious wound, the disease might then prove fatal. Four out of seven blood samples checked for *Babesia* by parasitologist Alan Young were positive. This potentially deadly parasite is transmitted by ticks. It acts like malaria in that it breaks down blood cells, resulting in severe anaemia. Again, an animal is probably not susceptible unless already in poor condition from some other cause. Some forty-eight percent of the lions were infected with a protozoan called *Hepatozoon*, which encysts in the liver and may cause cell damage there. Lions may succumb to anthrax when they scavenge an animal that has died of the disease. The larval stages of various tapeworms encyst in the muscles of prey animals, the eggs of these worms having been ingested with the grass by their hosts. When a lion eats the meat, the worms develop into their adult form and infest the intestines. The eggs of the worms are eliminated with the lion's feces onto the grass, and their complicated cycle begins anew. Rüdiger Sachs found some strange tapeworm larvae inside the bony space of the sacrum in wildebeest, topi, and some other antelope. Somehow this imprisoned parasite had to complete its life cycle. Only one predator, the hyena, is strong enough to crush and eat the tough sacral bone, reasoned Rüdiger. He, therefore, examined several hyena and found in their intestines a new species of tapeworm that indeed was the adult stage of his mysterious larvae. Although knowing that nature abhors a vacuum, I still remain continually amazed at the ingenuity with which empty niches have been filled.

It is particularly difficult for a nomadic lion to exist when sick or injured, lacking as it does the inadvertent help provided by pride members. The Young Female of the Masai pride was bitten in the thigh during a scuffle. A canine must have injured a nerve, for her leg withered until she could barely hobble. Completely unable to hunt, she subsisted entirely on the kills made by others of the pride for nearly nine months before recovering the use of her leg. A nomad might not have survived such an ordeal. I remember one male, a nomad in his prime, whom I had never seen before. He was found lying in the grass beneath a tree near the Masai kopjes. Some disease must have prevented him from hunting, for he was now only a skeleton held together by a slack hide. But his large brown mane attested to his former glory. He reclined on his side, too weak to raise his head, only his eyes showing the final tenacity with which he clung to life. At dusk he heard distant roars and, with a last effort, he grunted weakly several times, trying to retain a vestige of contact with the community of which he had been a part. That night death came to him as he lay calmly alone beneath his tree.

THE HUNTERS AND THE HUNTED

MUCH OF THIS CHAPTER IS ABOUT DEATH, BUT A DEATH SO that others may live, death because of need, not pleasure. There is neither cruelty nor compassion in a lion's quest for food and this impersonal endeavor strikes a responsive cord in man the hunter. I enjoyed watching most hunts as struggles of life and death at their most elemental. It is a time when each animal uses to the utmost those attributes with which evolution has endowed it. It is also a moment when man, weak of body and slow of foot, can watch his limits transgressed, a moment which engenders not only humility for his own lack of prowess but also pride and exultation that he has managed to survive at all.

The life of a prey animal always hangs in the balance, for it never knows if it has made a serious error until a lion has flung itself into the final rush. Yet prey is not constantly alert; it does not anticipate momentary death. I wonder if these animals have fear as we know it. Fear is a subjective sensation, an anticipation of future feelings based on past events, but few animals have ever suffered the agony of a mauling and lived. No, the prey flees primarily because tradition passed down from its kind dictates that it do so when a lion is close and its heritage commands it to retreat when it sees and perhaps smells certain things. Prey leads a mundane existence of feeding, resting, traveling, courting, fighting. Evasive action is taken when needed. If a member of the herd dies, the others watch the event, then calmly continue with their routine as if conversant with the inevitability of death.

The prey animals have endured because they have evolved a truly remarkable array of behavior patterns that help them avoid predators or at least nullify their effectiveness. Some are designed for that purpose, others are used only secondarily so. The vital tension of most prey is the result of a constant predator pressure which has weeded out those that are stolid and slow. Without predators, antelopes would have no need to flee at forty or fifty miles an hour; they would have no need for bulging eyes that provide extreme wide-angle vision or a sense of smell so powerful that it can detect a lion several hundred feet away. The zigzag flight of gazelle, the twisting leap of impala, the bunching of wildebeest herds when pursued—all are traits that make it difficult for a predator to select and capture an individual. Herds tend to travel in single file, thereby reducing their chance of stumbling on a hidden predator.

Almost all species of hoofed animals, including the normally silent giraffe, may whistle, snort, or bark when they see a predator. Such sounds serve as alarm signals to others in the herd, and even to members of a different species, alerting them to danger. Alarm signals present an interesting evolutionary problem. Why does an animal make its presence known so noisily to a predator? An obvious answer is, of course, to warn others. But surely selection did not favor a form of altruism in which the most alert animal in a herd endangers its life by drawing attention to itself at the expense of its slow-witted associates, whether of its own or other species. Furthermore, even animals that normally live alone, such as the bushbuck, give a loud alarm call. One must find out not what good the signal can do for others, but what good it can do for the animal itself. If an animal calls after sensing or even suspecting danger, a lurking predator may simply give up a hunt, for it has learned that once prey has discovered its presence further efforts are almost futile. Several times I have seen a stalking cat stop a hunt prematurely on hearing an alarm call given only at the suspicion of danger. Had the prey remained silent, the cat would have stayed in concealment and perhaps been able to launch an attack later.

A female giving birth is highly vulnerable, but the young appears within a matter of minutes. Newborn animals are defenseless and fall prey easily, yet they too have their means of eluding capture. A wildebeest calf struggles to its feet within five minutes after birth; and a gazelle fawn spends the first week or so of its life crouched motionless and alone while its mother grazes in the vicinity. Solitary and fairly small animals, such as reedbuck and bushbuck, may also escape predators by hiding in the manner of gazelle fawns. One reedbuck crouched within twenty feet of three lionesses for over three hours without being detected. But when a reedbuck feels itself discovered by a lion, it explodes so suddenly from its retreat that the predator may just stand there, a bewildered look on its face. Reedbuck are highly alert too, picking their way carefully through thickets, their russet coats blending into the dappled shade. Another alternative for a hoofed animal is to form herds. Many animals are better at detecting danger than is one, especially since each individual must lower its head to eat, a period during which its vision is circumscribed. Lions are well aware of the fact that a grazing animal is less alert than one with its head raised, and they advance or halt accordingly during their stalks. The chances are good that in a herd at least one animal is alert, looking, sniffing. However, herd size alone is no guarantee of safety. Animals in small herds tend to be less vulnerable than those in very large ones. When many zebra are packed in a tight mass around a waterhole, they get in one another's way when attacked, giving a lion that extra fraction of a second advantage that may mean the difference between success and failure in a hunt. Each wildebeest in a huge herd appears to assume that its neighbor will warn of danger and consequently it is easier to sneak close to large numbers of these animals than to a few.

Prey may also inadvertently reduce its chances of a fatal encounter. Grant's gazelle do not need to drink and they can therefore avoid waterholes, where danger often lurks. Topi males advertise themselves and their territory by standing on termite hills, but they can simultaneously survey their surroundings. Zebra often rest their heads on each other's back, a friendly gesture that also gives them a 360° view. Wildebeest, warthog, and some other species have a birth peak that limits the time when vulnerable young are available to predators to a few months of the year. Horns evolved for intraspecific strife, but they are also useful for fending off predators, as many a lion has learned when trying to subdue a buffalo. When it comes to avoiding lions it also pays to be large and short-tempered. Rhinoceros and elephants have grown so large and have such formidable weapons that no predator can deal effectively with an adult.

However, even small animals may repulse a lion. One morning two lionesses came upon a monitor lizard basking in the sun along a riverbank. The lizard was at most three feet long. I expected it to scuttle into the water at the cats' approach. But it only puffed itself up, not even deigning to face its potential captors, and, after a lioness had approached stealthily to within about two feet, it suddenly lashed its tail back and forth once, flipping it past the nose of the surprised lioness. She leaped backward with a startled woof. When another approach was greeted similarly, she circled the lizard cautiously with a puzzled expression on her face and then joined her companion, who had watched the incident without participating. The lizard deflated and contentedly continued its sunbath.

Each individual prey animal must also learn the habits of the various kinds of predators. By watching its elders, a youngster finds out how closely it may approach a lion with impunity, and it learns to venture toward waterholes cautiously at the proper time of day. In fact, a young animal must first learn to view a predator as an enemy, and, after that, it must adapt its response to the actual danger involved. A Thomson's gazelle almost ignores a jackal, views a hyena warily, and prefers a safety margin of at least a hundred feet with lion and leopard and three hundred feet with cheetah. But at the mere sight of a distant pack of running hunting dogs, the gazelle flee far and fast.

As these few examples show, prey animals have evolved a truly remarkable array of defensive mechanisms against predators, some morphological, some physiological, others behavioral in nature. I was continually impressed with the many subtle ways in which nature has helped the animals to outwit death. Yet the behavior of an animal must be balanced between avoiding predators and fulfilling various daily requirements. Impala must drink, even if a herd member is captured; a topi male must establish a territory even if to maintain it alone makes him vulnerable to predation. Life consists of a series of calculated risks.

Selection is for conformity, and the animal that attempts something different is severely penalized. A gazelle that shows its individuality by veering from a bunched herd to seek its own escape route will be chosen by a pursuing cheetah or hunting dog. As I watched such rigorous repression of initiative from the norm, it occurred to me that at some stage in human evolution there must have been a dramatic and important change during which conformity was replaced by selection for the individual who had original thoughts and did novel things. This does not imply that animals merely abrogate themselves to the collective mentality of the herd but that their freedom to express themselves is severely circumscribed by biological pressures too great to safely ignore.

I found it fascinating to observe how lions used both brain and brawn to overcome such deficiencies as a lack of running speed in obtaining a meal. Being pragmatists, they are determined only that they shall eat, and they disdain neither animals dead of disease nor the scraps of a kill left by hyenas. The white-backed and griffon vultures often reveal the presence of meat to lions. Soaring on thermal upcurrents, they spiral slowly, monitoring the earth until their sharp eyes focus on a potential meal, perhaps a dying gazelle or a still-born zebra foal. The vultures then hurtle down to throw themselves upon the carcass, a hissing, struggling mass of birds whose unappeasable hunger can strip all meat off the bones of a wildebeest within half an hour. Lions have learned to heed the behavior of flying vultures and they sometimes arrive at a run to appropriate whatever is left. While vultures help lions to a few free meals, they deprive them of many others that ultimately they might have discovered without help. For example, I located a total of seventy-five zebra that had just died of disease or malnutrition and of these the lions found only fifteen before vultures cleaned them up or hyenas carried away the remains.

The spotted hyena also provide lions with meals, particularly on the plains. Hyenas are rather unprepossessing creatures. When disturbed they slouch off, tails tucked between their legs, looking back with moist, reproachful eyes. But at night they shed their subservient air and metamorphose into bold hunters. One dawn I watched a solitary hyena lope after a yearling wildebeest, a quixotic gesture it seemed, for the animal galloped along spryly. But suddenly the hyena raced ahead with unbelievable speed, grabbed the veering wildebeest in its side, and violently tore it down; another bite partially disembowled the animal. Although hyenas in the Serengeti kill primarily young animals, those less than three months old, and sick ones, this yearling showed no obvious disability. Such an incident engenders lasting respect. Hyenas are emotional creatures, given to whoops and moans as they crowd around a kill; sometimes one erupts into gibbering laughter, an indication of uneasiness, during a minor squabble. Any lion within two miles is certain to be attracted by the bedlam. Often, however, little is left by the time the lions arrive at the kill site. Bolting their meat, hyenas can clean up a carcass with remarkable speed, and, having powerful shoulders and necks, they can carry large pieces away to be consumed in peace somewhere else. Their blunt conical teeth can crush even the leg bones of large prey, something lions cannot do, and their potent stomach juices can dissolve bone, which enables their bodies to assimilate the organic matter from it. All that may remain of a skeleton are white fecal droppings of calcuim compounds that look like quartz pebbles strewn in the grass. Sometimes, too, the horns and tough parts of the skull, including the teeth, are left uneaten.

That hyenas are not primarily scavengers and that they sometimes actually provide lions with meat, rather than the reverse, was first documented in detail by Hans Kruuk in Ngorongoro Crater. The hyenas there live in eight distinct clans, each with ten to a hundred members. A clan occupies a territory in which the animals hunt and have their communal den site. Battles between neighboring clans in disputing a kill may result in an occasional death. The propensity of these hyenas to kill for themselves was first described by Hans in a 1966 article published in *Nature*:

> Of 1,052 hyaenas which were observed feeding, 82 per cent were eating from an animal killed by hyaenas, whereas only 11 per cent fed on animals killed by other predators (jackal, lion, wild

dog, leopard, cheetah); . . . However, during the day, 34 per cent of the feeding hyaenas were seen on other animals' kills and undoubtedly popular knowledge is derived mainly from such day-time observations. Often other "predators" scavenge on hyaena-kills; I have good evidence that the lion-population in the Ngorongoro Crater obtains its food largely in this way.

The Serengeti hyenas kill some two thirds of the food for themselves, according to Hans, a ready source of meat for lions. When I found a lion on a kill in the plains the chances were about even that the cat had scavenged the remains, as often as not from hyenas. However, lions in the woodlands were able to scavenge only about one fifth of their kills, not only because hyenas were scarce there, except during the dry season, when some follow the migratory herds, but also because the restricted visibility among the trees hinders lions in discovering kill sites.

Much to my surprise one or two lions were often able to drive fifteen or more hyenas from their kill. Armed with the most powerful jaws of any predator and weighing at least 125 pounds, an adult hyena could be a formidable opponent. But daylight inhibits their aggressive tendencies. Early in the study I noted that if one or more gorged lions out on the plains were resting beside a large kill in the evening, they seldom were still there the following morning. Puzzled about the fate of the carcass, I spent twenty-three nights watching lions in such situations. Seventeen percent of the kills were abandoned by the lions, and thirty-nine percent were eaten up, usually by visiting friends. The remaining forty-four percent were appropriated by hyenas, who simply drove the lions off. One afternoon I found two lionesses with a freshly dead wildebeest. Returning at dusk, Kay and I watched the peaceful scene, the lions sleeping, one hyena waiting patiently nearby. Then, as the darkness deepened, other hyenas silently arrived, one by one, as if summoned by some superior power to this rendezvous. A sweep of my flashlight revealed seventeen hyenas ringing the carcass with burning eyes, implacably quiet. Suddenly at 11:00 p.m. the lionesses intercepted some subtle signal from the hyenas, for they began to eat frantically as if anticipating the loss of their kill. And then, as if on command, the hyenas began to whoop and circle the carcass, drawing ever closer as they shattered the night with their unearthly din. Finally their bushy tails whipped up and they rushed the lionesses, who wisely fled.

Lions and hyenas share a mutual antipathy that may erupt in a fight even when no meat is involved. One lioness pursued a hyena and bowled it over with a sweep of her paw before biting it in the rump and abdomen. Two more lions ran up and mauled it in the face. Finally released, the hyena hobbled away bleeding from several wounds but still alive. Though lions win some rounds, hyenas even the score in others. Once I came across male No. 159 on the plains. He was an elderly fellow who had fallen on hard times. The previous year he had held a temporary territory with a friend around Naabi Hill, but he had lost both and now suffered a further indignity. Circling and whooping, a pack of hyenas taunted and threatened him while he crouched, his head resting supplicatingly on his paws. An attack by the hyenas seemed imminent when their enthusiasm was dampened by the arrival of five lions who were checking on the cause of the commotion.

Lions must catch most of their food for themselves. My records of kills for the Serengeti comprise eighteen kinds of mammals and four kinds of birds, including such exotic dishes as pangolin, hare, and saddle-bill stork. Charles Guggisberg reported python, catfish, locust, and a shirt as being on the lions' menu. Food habits vary from area to area within the park, depending on what is available. The following species contributed most importantly to the diet of lions around Seronera and on the plains in terms of animals killed and scavenged:

	SERONERA (SAMPLE OF 552)	PLAINS (SAMPLE OF 280)
Wildebeest	22.0%	56.7%
Zebra	15.8	28.9
Thomson's gazelle	50.0	7.5
Buffalo	2.4	0
Topi	3.2	1.4
Warthog	2.2	0
Grant's gazelle	1.3	1.1
Reedbuck	1.1	0
Eland	0	3.2
Others	2.2	1.2

Small kills are never fully represented in samples such as these because a lion may devour a gazelle fawn in five minutes, whereas a buffalo may last for several days, thereby increasing my chances of finding it. Wildebeest, zebra, buffalo, and topi are the lion's most important prey in the park as a whole. All are large animals that provide several lions with a substantial meal. It simply does not pay a lion to waste time and energy in pursuit of small prey such as Thomson's gazelle except as incidental snacks or in the event that there is little else. When several lionesses have a choice of hunting gazelle or wildebeest they will inevitably choose the latter. Availability naturally influences food habits, as is well shown at Seronera, where for much of the dry season lions have primarily Thomson's gazelle and a few buffalo bulls on which to prey. The total amount of lion prey in the ecological unit is on the order of 237 million pounds. Some two thirds of this biomass consists of migratory species. This has a profound effect on the lions, since most wildebeest and zebra are on the plains for part of the year while most lions remain in the woodlands. Some prides may not see a wildebeest for eight months out of twelve.

Ever alert for an easy meal, lions often capture the young, the sick, the old, or the careless. Nearly a quarter of the wildebeest killings that I observed were of animals physically below par. One afternoon, at 4:35, six nomads rested near Naabi Hill. Wildebeest passed by in long lines, the sun glinting on their hoary backs, but the lions seemingly ignored them until one stumbled, and stumbled again. A lioness immediately bounded after it. Running up alongside the animal, she placed a paw over its shoulder while clinging to its side, using her deadly weight to pull it down. It fell with legs flailing. First jumping nimbly back to avoid the tumbling body, the lioness then lunged in and placed her mouth over the wildebeest's muzzle, clamping its nose closed. Four minutes later it was dead of suffocation, a rather curious but effective killing method that lions use less often than the usual throat grip when dealing with large prey. Even as the wildebeest expired, a male lion had begun to feed on viscera. The others waited until this male was almost satiated before joining him in the feast. The banquet lasted until 8:00 p.m., when happily gorged they all went to sleep. At 3:00 a.m. a male snacked a little, and at 5:50 a.m. two lionesses checked over the remains. Shortly thereafter they departed, each with about thirty-five pounds of meat in its belly. Several hyenas scavenged the bones. Fourteen hours after the killing all that remained was a blood stain and a mound of stomach contents.

When toward the end of the study I lined up all the zebra skulls I had collected at lion kills and checked the teeth for age, it was apparent that old zebra fell prey proportionately more often than any other age group. This surprised me, for I had not expected lions to be so selective. They seldom chase an animal far and in the confusion of an attack one animal would seem to be as vulnerable as another.

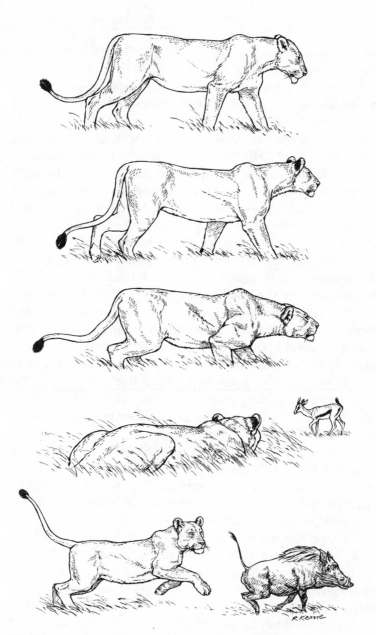

Walking and stalking postures of lions used during a hunt.

But apparently not. Old zebra have possibly lost some of their speed and agility.

One day male No. 134 ambled across the plains, seemingly not interested in food. Suddenly he saw a zebra foal so deeply asleep on the grass that it even failed to hear the alarm snorts of its family. The lion wakened it, briefly. Lack of vigilance is a fatal fault, especially among warthog. Once one of these pigs sauntered with careless abandon past several nervous gazelle to a waterhole and there its impetuous life was abruptly terminated by a lioness. However, at night a warthog withdraws into its burrow, where it is well protected unless a determined lion discovers the hole. One night the Masai pride had hunting difficulties. The moon was so bright that the lions cast shadows as they moved, and the short, brittle grass crackled under their paws. They had no hope of stalking gazelle, and nothing else was to be seen. The pride ambled along irresolutely just after midnight when Notch suddenly peered into a burrow and then began to dig, ripping at the sod first with one paw and then the other. Warthog burrows often consist of a single shallow tunnel, and, working with uncharacteristic vigor, Notch rapidly exposed it. The other pride members sat idly by, except for lioness P, who helped occasionally. At the end of half an hour, seven feet of tunnel had been opened up. Ducking into the hole, Notch grabbed at something and pulled. She strained and jerked, but the warthog clung to its violated retreat. Finally, after eight minutes of tugging, she hauled out a screaming pig.

To my puzzlement, man is not an important food item of lions even though no other large mammal is as defenseless and easy to kill. Perhaps man's upright stance baffles the uninitiated lion, who is accustomed to attacking animals that are built on a horizontal plane; perhaps lions are conservative, preferring the prey they learned to hunt as youngsters in a pride; or perhaps man's ancient ability and predilection to defend himself has imbued lions with caution. Lions readily capture and eat baboons and other monkeys, showing that they are not averse to primates. When lions face man they growl and snarl, behaving as they do toward a hyena or other predator, not as they do toward prey. Lions act as if they recognized in man his predatory past, and this after all is not surprising, because the two have competed for the same resources for several million years. However, a few lions do overcome their reluctance to kill and eat man. The reasons for this are obscure. Sometimes, no doubt, it is from hunger, caused either by a lack of other prey or the lion's inability to catch it. While a man eater may be old or in some way incapacitated, many are vigorous animals. I knew a male lion in Manyara Park who became a man eater, and his history is a fascinating one.

Manyara Park is small, consisting of thirty-five square miles of woodlands hemmed in between Lake Manyara and the wall of the rift escarpment. About thirty-five lions inhabit the park, and these are known chiefly for their habit of lounging around in trees during the day. When I heard that one of the tourist guides was keeping notes on the lions I went to visit him. Stephen Makacha is a remarkable person. Born and raised in an area northwest of the Serengeti, he later joined the park service and was posted to Manyara Park. On his own initiative he had learned to recognize most lions there and had kept a carefully written record about them. I encouraged him to continue his observations and this he enthusiastically did for over two years until he joined the Serengeti Research Institute.

The small Chemchen and Mahali pa Nyati prides used the northern half of the park in mid-1967. Both were under the jurisdiction of the same two males, Chongo and Dume Kubwa, who divided their attention about equally between the two sets of lionesses. At that time one of the lionesses in the Mahali pa Nyati pride had three cubs about 1½ years old, two females and a male. Satima, the young male, was a husky youngster, large for his age no doubt because Manyara Park contained so much prey, principally buffalo and impala. Cubs did not starve there. The death rate of cubs was nevertheless almost fifty percent, nearly as high as in the Serengeti. Some cubs were probably abandoned by their mothers and others were known to have been trampled to death by elephants and buffalo. At any rate, Satima survived, and by the following year Chongo and Dume Kubwa began to view him as a potential usurper of their territory. They chased him several times but without being able to drive him from the area. Then fate intervened. Dume Kubwa ventured out of the park in November 1968, passing the edge of a village as he swung around the northern end of the lake into an area where hunting was permitted. There a bullet apparently ended his life, for we heard that a fine and tame male had been shot there just when Dume Kubwa vanished. Chongo remained. In March 1969, a strange male intruded into the territory, the first time this had happened in at least two years, and soon after that a trio of males investigated the territory like prospective owners. Chongo was clearly on his way out. He then made a decision, an admirable one, for it showed his adaptability to changing circumstances: he teamed up with Satima, who was now about 3½ years old. Satima mated that June with one of his sisters while Chongo courted the other. I was delighted that Stephen had been able to record these unique changes in the pride, and now expected the animals to settle back into their humdrum existence.

The park unfortunately borders both a main road and a village at its northern end, and the Mahali pa Nyati pride occasionally strayed into that area. One villager was injured by a lioness early in 1969. At 11:00 p.m. on June 16 of that year, a struggle and growls were heard from a field. Investigating the following morning, villagers found the head, feet and hands of a Mr. Athuman Omari, who, a report on the incident stated, was going home intoxicated "from drinking the native beer." Since occasional stray lions visit the area, the Mahali pa Nyati pride was not directly implicated in the deed. A second killing took place in September, again of a person who was thought to have been drunk. Since the main road is used by many people at night, usually with impunity, it may be that an unsteady gait releases attack in lions more readily than a firm one, since in the normal course of events a staggering individual is sick, unable to flee and defend itself well. Soon after that a third person fell prey. And then in May 1970, Stephen sent me the following sad note: "Satima the young male among the Mahali pa Nyati pride has been shot when he was found eating another killed person near the Park Headquarters."

Lions kill primarily healthy and alert animals, and to do so they must use all their skills, creeping from bush to bush, halting whenever their quarry moves, then advancing again with such smoothness that one is barely conscious of movement. "There are certain things in Nature in which beauty and utility, artistic and technical perfection, combine in some incomprehensible way," noted Konrad Lorenz, and a stalking lion is one of these. While even the sight of a resting lion contributes to the authenticity of an African scene, a hunting lion adds that edge of vital tension which changes a mere experience to a revelation.

Unfortunately the majority of tourists never see a hunt in the Serengeti because they do not have the patience, or the interest, or the knowledge to wait with some predator for a few hours. They rush, rush, rush along in convoys of cars, shrouded in dust, halting a minute by some resting lions and the cameras go click, click. Then the cars race on.

"How many lions did you see today?"

"Twenty-two."

"*I* saw twenty-nine!"

Many tourists cruise from park to park, spending half a day in each one, just as they would go from cathedral to museum to castle in Europe, quite bored with it all, concerned with the quantity rather than the quality of their ex-

periences. Their recreation is mileage. The following incident reveals this attitude:

Tourist: "We saw an ostrich being attacked by a
leopard."

Lodge Manager: "What happened?"

Tourist: "I don't know. It was lunch time and we had
to leave."

The Serengeti seems desolate to many visitors, for they
see only scenery, not details; to them emptiness signifies
nothingness. One elderly lady to another after a morning's
drive around Seronera: "What did you see?" "Nothing." I
think that perhaps the contrast between city life and stark
wilderness, between the twentieth century and the Pleistocene, is a shock to many visitors. They feel lost and vaguely
apprehensive in this immense silent space. Silence is becoming the privilege of only a few in industrialized societies,
and, unable to adapt to the quiet of the wilds, some visitors
shout and laugh extra loudly and they play their radios, anything to banish their uneasiness. Then, too, in a society in
which the transcience of experiences has become a way of
life, many people are unaware of the joy that contemplation
can provide. Unfortunately the parks make little effort to
teach visitors to feel and understand their experience.

To the pride lionesses falls the task of catching most
prey, at least eighty percent of it. They support not only
themselves and their cubs but to some extent the males too.
It is therefore not surprising that they are consummate
huntresses who have learned well how to take advantage of
their environment as they approach prey for that final, fatal
rush. A lioness knows that darkness provides concealment
and she may merely watch a distant herd at dusk, waiting
until she can disappear into the night's shadows before
attempting a stalk. She has learned to conceal herself behind
bushes, and to wait until prey is inattentive before advancing.
These are basic rules for success, but there are many others
too. When running at prey from an angle, a lioness must

adjust her line of approach to the speed of the animal's flight; two lions working together are more successful than one working alone; and an upwind stalk is more productive than one from downwind. The value of adhering to certain rules is reflected in hunting success. Once lions have selected their quarry and have begun their final stalk, their chances of capturing it are as follows:

	% successful
Day hunt	21
Night hunt (mostly moonlight)	33
Little or no cover	12
Thickets along river	41
One lion hunting downwind	7
One lion hunting upwind	18.5
One lion hunting	15
Two lions hunting together	29
Hunting wildebeest in herd of two to ten	13
Hunting solitary wildebeest	47

Ideally, a group of lions should stalk a lone animal upwind in dense vegetation at night. Although highly adept in choosing advantages, lions have not discovered the value of wind direction. Contrary to popular belief, they stalk downwind as readily as upwind even though they are over twice as successful when inadvertently using the latter. The success rate also varies with the species of prey. For the bumbling and slow warthog it is 47 percent; for the migratory wildebeest, zebra, and Thomson's gazelle it is 32 percent, 27 percent, and 26 percent respectively; but for topi it is only 14 percent —speaking well for the vigilance of this animal.

Emotions cannot be re-created, but there are some hunts I remember with special clarity and feeling. One day Flop-ear plodded along the banks of the Seronera River in the midday heat. It was the dry season, and her paws raised

puffs of dust. With little cover and her golden hide quite conspicuous against the gray earth, the portents for a meal were
not good. The plains were empty of prey except for a few distant topi and an occasional zebra family. She met three of
her friends resting beneath a tree, all contentedly full on a
zebra foal they had caught just upriver. At first Flop-ear
was tempted to tarry, but then she trudged on. When she
saw four zebra—three adults and a foal—approach the
river in single file, heading toward a crossing, she began to
slink along the dry streambed, moving closer. Once, almost
imperceptibly, she raised her head to look over a tuft of
grass, then continued toward a clump of reeds near the
crossing. Holding her body low to the ground, she became a
part of the shadows of the fever trees and she fused with
the grassy stubble, flowing toward her goal. Undetected she
entered the reeds and waited. Still oblivious to danger, the
zebra approached the riverbank and after a moment's hesitation walked down the gentle incline. The tension of watching
their leisurely advance was almost unbearable for me, and I
felt my muscles grow rigid as if for a rush. Suddenly the
zebra last in line halted. I feared that Flop-ear had been
detected and the zebra would now wheel about and race
away. But the first three animals continued on through the
streambed and up the other side. One adult passed by her
at a distance of thirty feet and then the other. Last in line
was the foal. A tawny flash, a violent leap, and the lioness
hurtled through the air. She hit the side of the foal with a
loud slap and both crashed to the ground, the air rent with
its screaming. This, incidentally, was the only time I saw
a lioness actually leap at her prey.

Before going to Africa I had read a number of books
and articles about lions. Some authors described the wonderful way in which members of a pride cooperate while hunting
their prey, yet others considered such behavior accidental
or an outright myth. I too was somewhat skeptical about the
existence of cooperative hunting, but to my delight some of

the accounts were at least partially true. It has been said that the lionesses may hide while the male roars from the other side, thus driving the prey into the ambush. I have never seen this happen. Animals are not really afraid of a roar, unless it is exceedingly close, for, after all, once a lion reveals itself the prey is generally safe. Furthermore, a male rarely participates in a collaborative effort; he is likely to wreck a carefully laid ambush by indifferently startling the prey. Lionesses, however, may use quite sophisticated techniques when hunting together, each one watching the others and then patterning her actions to suit the situation. One morning lionesses Nos. 69 and 102 of the Cub Valley group were resting on a promontory when they saw two wildebeest bulls wending their way along a reedbed in their direction. Immediately descending from her vantage point, and, moving swiftly in a semicrouch, No. 69 crossed the reeds, halting to look back at the friend following in her tracks. She then crept over a strip of hard-packed clay into a patch of tall grass, where she flattened to the ground. No. 102 hid herself at the edge of the reeds, facing the other lioness. If the wildebeest held to their course they would be neatly trapped between the two cats. The lead animal stopped abruptly sixty feet from the ambush and glanced back at his companion as if checking to see if he sensed danger too. At that, lioness No. 69 rushed, streaking forward fast and low. Wheeling, dodging, and accelerating in one frantic series of movements, the wildebeest fled. One of them, for some reason, ran into the reeds, where in the thick vegetation it lost speed. Even so, its escape seemed assured until suddenly its forelegs dropped into a hole. Before he could fully regain his feet, one lioness grasped him by the neck and bit at his throat while the other straddled his back. Slowly all sank out of sight among the reeds and I could hear only the disembodied growls of lions on a kill.

Cooperation may also involve several lionesses. These

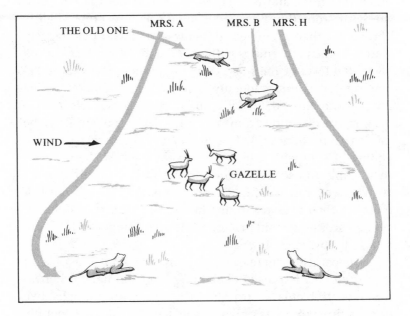

may fan out and advance silently in a broad front toward their quarry. Animals startled by one lioness may then rush into the arms of another. A herd may even be encircled, a strategy implying that lions are aware of the consequences of their actions in relation to both the other pride members and the prey. Once, for example, a small herd of Thomson's gazelle had congregated on an island of short grass surrounded by tall dry stalks. It was shortly after 8:00 a.m. and the gazelle either fed desultorily or stood around with only their constantly flicking tails an outlet for their nervous vitality. Four lionesses—The Old One, and lionesses A, B, and H—spotted the herd. Lioness A immediately advanced with her body held low, not directly toward the gazelle but to one side of them, until she was just beyond them in the high grass. She waited. Long association had taught the others to anticipate her maneuver, and lioness H encircled the herd from the other side; lioness B also crept slightly ahead, but then crouched motionless. The Old One lagged, watching the proceedings with only the top of her head raised above the level of the grass. Sensing danger, the gazelle became agitated and suddenly bolted toward lioness B. She lunged and missed, which caused several animals to flee back in the direction from which they had come, only to be met there by lioness A. She grabbed and clutched a male, ending his life with a bite through the back of the neck. In their panic to escape several gazelle veered toward lioness H, who was still waiting patiently. Spotting her at the last moment, they swerved around her but she leaped straight up, twisted around in midair, and after a few huge bounds bore a gazelle to the ground.

Cooperation increases not only the lions' success in capturing prey but also in subduing large animals. A lioness has few problems in overpowering prey that weighs two or even three times as much as she does, but she is generally unable to handle a fully grown buffalo or giraffe, which may scale a ton. On one occasion I came upon a lioness as she was biting at the rump and tail of a young buffalo bull who lay on his side as if dead. I had passed this spot half an hour earlier and cursed my fate for having missed the killing. But the buffalo was not dead; he had apparently gone into shock when suddenly attacked by the lioness. The noise of my car must have jarred him out of his trance, for he suddenly struggled to his feet, little hampered by the lioness, who desperately tried to pull him back down. He charged her and held her at bay for 1½ hours, whirling around to face her with lowered horns whenever she tried to approach, until finally she permitted him to retreat. The ease with which the five Moru males handled a bull buffalo was in marked contrast to this abortive attempt. With buffalo being one of the main prey species available to lions in the park, their cooperative efforts amply repay them in spite of occasional awkward times when several lions must share a puny gazelle. Indeed, the whole social system of the lion is no doubt an adaptation for hunting large prey in open terrain.

I have purposely described a number of hunts and killings because few detailed accounts have been published on this matter and the generalizations that have been made are often erroneous. One author, for instance, wrote: "Lions generally kill by seizing the animal by the nose with one paw, dragging the head down and biting through the back of the neck." Another claimed that the lion "pulls the head sideways and downward with such force as almost invariably to break the neck at once . . ." I never saw lions employ such methods, although their occasional use either by accident or design cannot be ruled out. Small prey, such as gazelle, are first grabbed or slapped down and then bitten in the throat or nape, or any other convenient spot. These two stages of subduing and killing may require considerable effort when a large animal is involved. To pull down a zebra or wildebeest, a lion usually hooks its forepaws into the rump or side of its quarry and then uses its strength and weight to throw the animal off its feet. After that, it lunges for and holds the throat, or more rarely the muzzle, preventing the animal from breathing. Death is from suffocation, a slow process, which may require ten minutes. Lions are tidy killers, not quick ones. Since a lion's teeth are neither long enough nor strong enough to bite through the thick muscles and massive vertebrae on the back of the neck of a large animal, the throat hold is an eminently sensible solution. In addition, the downed animal is unable to use its horns and hooves for defense.

A carcass is often eaten at the kill site, especially if several lions are present to prevent one from hauling it away, but on occasion it may be moved several hundred feet to the shade of a tree. Grasping a body by the neck and straddling it with his forelegs, a male lion can drag a six hundred-pound zebra in this fashion. In some parts of Africa, lions are said to disembowel their prey and bury the digestive tract by pawing earth or sand over it. Such behavior was rare in the Serengeti. Usually lions eat the viscera, and they may do so even before touching the rest of the carcass. The reasons for this puzzle me. Why should a lion gorge himself on intestines rather than on red meat, when the latter is more nourishing in terms of calories? Perhaps lions are after the deposits of fat in the mesenteries around the viscera. The meat of antelope and other wild animals in Africa is very lean when compared with that of domestic animals—about three percent of the body weight of a wildebeest consists of fat whereas the figure for a steer may be fifteen percent. Maybe lions require more fat than they get from red meat. It is also possible that lions obtain some needed vitamins from the partially digested vegetal matter, even though they manage to eliminate most of it from the intestines by using a special technique. Placing one end of a piece of intestine on their rough tongue, they make slight lapping movements. This draws the intestine inexorably into the mouth like a gigantic strand of spaghetti. By keeping its lips and teeth almost closed, the lion automatically squeezes out most of the contents.

While a lion will eat a truly large meal when it has the opportunity to do so, it may obtain only scraps on some days and nothing on others. Such an irregular schedule made it difficult for me to estimate how often and how much lions ate. My long vigils with certain lions combined with other information showed that those on the plains ate something every two to two and a half days on the average and that those in the woodlands did so every three to three and a half days. But I had no direct way of measuring the amount of meat that was actually consumed. On the basis of what is known about energy metabolism of animals in captivity, a lioness weighing 250 pounds would need some 7,300 calories per day and a male weighing 350 pounds about 10,300 calories. This would be about 11 to 15½ pounds of food in terms of the low-fat meat, skin, and viscera that lions eat. During his nine-day travels around the Gol kopjes male No. 134 had perhaps an average of twenty pounds a day, more than he needed. The two males and three lionesses of the Cub Valley group once killed four bull wildebeest in thirteen days. This gave the lions about fifteen pounds of food each, but some of it went to the eight cubs they had at the time. Perhaps more typical was the food intake of three Masai pride lionesses: they gorged themselves on a wildebeest one night, ate nothing the following four nights, then killed a zebra foal on the sixth, an average food intake of about eleven pounds per day. Sometimes lions get more than they need, at other times no doubt less, so everything probably averages itself out to about the expected daily requirements of 11 to 15½ pounds a day. However, a lion must kill more than that, for parts of the carcass are wasted, primarily the horns, hooves, large bones, and contents of the digestive tract, and these constitute some twenty to forty percent of the weight of a carcass. Taking this into account, a lioness needs 6,000 pounds of prey per year and a male 8,400 pounds. Converting poundage into actual animals, a lioness could be satisfied with ten adult zebra a year. Naturally she acquires a variety of prey from several sources, killing some, scavenging others. Cubs need less food than adults, but even so the 2,000 to 2,400 lions in the ecological unit require about 10,850,000 to 13,000,000 pounds of prey per year.

A priori reasoning would indicate that such a huge drain would have a strong impact on the prey population. But the intricacies of nature are not always revealed by simple human logic. A basic question that must be answered is to what extent lions remove individuals whose loss depresses a population to a level below the one it would maintain if there were no predation. When viewed in that perspective, much of the lion's food consists of surplus. Perhaps as much as ten percent of the food is scavenged, often animals that have died of disease. Lions commonly deprive hyenas of their kill, obligating the latter to kill more than they would normally. However, many of the adult animals that are captured by hyenas in the Serengeti are ill, probably soon doomed to die anyway, and such losses benefit the prey rather than causing it harm. The removal of those that are physically below par helps to prevent the spread of disease, and in times of food shortage it reduces competition by leaving the available resources to those who are most likely to contribute to the well-being of the population by producing vigorous youngsters. Lions kill sick individuals too, perhaps up to twenty percent of the adult zebra and wildebeest they capture being in that condition. Lions also take proportionately more old wildebeest, zebra, and buffalo. Such animals have passed their peak of reproductive life and they often face a slow death from malnutrition, for after years of grinding coarse grasses their teeth may be worn to the gums.

In a polygynous society, where one male mates with many females, there is an excess of males whose loss has little effect on the population. Lions tend to capture more males than females of several species, not because the former are preferred but because they make themselves vulnerable: they select against themselves. Wildebeest bulls are often alone or they are preoccupied with tending their cows during the rut, and lions take advantage of both traits. Consequently bulls fall prey twice as often as cows. Tony Sinclair found that many buffalo bulls leave cow herds permanently at the age of ten years and all do so by the age of twelve years, to lead a misanthropic existence either alone or with a similarly inclined companion or two. Lions find it difficult to select and attack an individual in a large and pugnacious herd, but solitary bulls are more easily subdued. Three times as many old bulls as cows were killed by the Serengeti lions. Having voluntarily chosen abstinence in matters pertaining to the propagation of their race, old bulls have forfeited their need to exist and their main importance lies in relieving herds of predator pressure.

Fires swept away the grass early in the dry season of 1966 and everything was exceptionally parched. Thomson's gazelle began to trek to the Seronera River at dawn. All day weary lines of animals filed to water, ignoring the scent of lions that permeated the air. I soon noted that the lions caught adult bucks more often than females even though the latter were more abundant in the population. When danger threatened, females and young dashed heedlessly away from the river and into the open, whereas bucks often tarried a fraction of a second, looking right and left as if to make certain that the effort to flee needed to be made—a fatal hestitation. Fritz Walther also pointed out to me that bachelor bucks are often displaced from the favored gazelle areas by bucks who maintain territories. Such bucks often wander along river courses and other localities with dense vegetation, thereby making themselves vulnerable to lion predation. In 1967 the dry season was not as severe as in the previous year, the grass was not burned over large tracts, and the gazelle did not congregate near the river. Under such conditions the bucks were not particularly vulnerable and lions caught them no more often than one would expect. Ecological conditions may thus have an important effect on prey selection, and I was reminded that one does not jump to conclusions on the basis of one season's work.

Lions kill a certain number of young animals but proportionately not as many as do hunting dogs, hyenas, and cheetah, who specialize in this age class. Nature is profligate in the production of young, and even should half of a year's crop succumb from one cause or another enough would most likely remain to keep the species at its customary level of abundance. For instance, Hans Kruuk calculated that hyenas may kill as many as nineteen thousand wildebeest calves annually in the Serengeti. Other predators also account for some. Yet in 1966 an estimated sixty thousand calves died, far more than could be accounted for by predation. Many calves become separated from their mothers and die of starvation, some have accidents, and many probably succumb from a combination of disease and malnutrition. All these losses did not prevent the population from increasing that year.

Though many animals that are killed by lions are in some way surplus individuals, healthy adults fall prey too. The total impact of such predation varies with the species. Lions probably account for about 9,100 to 13,700 wildebeest, including calves, a year, or only 2.2 to 3.3 percent of the population. Tony Sinclair, whose interest encompassed wildebeest as well as buffalo, calculated that in 1968 about 52,000 yearling and adult wildebeest died. Of these, lions accounted for fewer than a quarter. The hyena is the only other predator that preys on adult wildebeest to any extent, and Hans estimated that about 5,600 to 9,300 are taken by

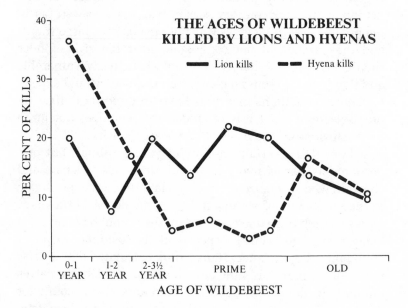

THE AGES OF WILDEBEEST
KILLED BY LIONS AND HYENAS

━━ Lion kills   ■■ Hyena kills

PER CENT OF KILLS

AGE OF WILDEBEEST

0-1 YEAR   1-2 YEAR   2-3½ YEAR   PRIME   OLD

them, many already doomed to an early death because of illness. As the graph shows, lions and hyenas select quite differently from the wildebeest population, with the latter concentrating on young and old animals and lions on prime ones. Although these two predators share the same resource, they hold competition to a minimum by concentrating their harvest on different segments of it. Predators account for only a third to a half of the adult wildebeest killed each year. Poaching also contributes to the total loss and the rest die of accidents, disease, and starvation. It is almost axiomatic that as the incidence of predation decreases the amount of disease increases. The Serengeti is full of sick wildebeest, a good indication that there are not enough predators; in Ngorongoro Crater, which has a high predator population, a sick animal is seldom seen because it is weeded out quickly.

The whole topic of predator–prey relations is made even more complex by the fact that animals may compensate for their losses by increasing the birth rate. In the early 1960's, when the wildebeest population was fairly small, about a third of the cows had a calf in their second year. By the late 1960's, after the population had dramatically increased, only about five percent of the cows had a calf in their second year. More predation would at this stage have resulted in more calves. But the wildebeest are a somewhat special case, for they escape the full impact of predation by migrating.

The sedentary buffalo have only the lion as a major predator. Almost 6,300 yearling and adult buffalo die each year and lions take fewer than 2,000 of these, the rest dying mainly of malnutrition and disease. I am indebted again to Tony for these figures on mortality rates in buffalo. One of the advantages of studying in the Serengeti was the presence of other investigators with whom one could share information. Tony's data on wildebeest and buffalo helped me greatly when trying to understand the effects of predation; conversely, my lion observations contributed to his analysis of the population dynamics of these prey species. Peter Jarman gave me useful information on impala and Ronald Skoog on zebra, and I reciprocated whenever I could.

Buffalo being so large that solitary lions hesitate to attack them, the brunt of lion predation falls on topi, kongoni, impala, and other species when the migratory herds are on the plains. I lack detailed information on these animals, but it is striking to note that a sick topi is seldom seen and that the resident prey populations have apparently not increased as much as have wildebeest and buffalo. I would guess that predation affects these species considerably. Locally, at least, lions and other predators may at times remove much if not all the annual surplus, keeping the prey population stable. Warthog around Seronera are heavily preyed upon, particularly by lions during the dry season, and every tooth and claw is turned against reedbuck in their restricted habitat along the river courses. In special circumstances, predation may even cause a temporary decrease in prey numbers, as reported by Bristol Foster with respect to wildebeest in Nairobi Park. A drought in 1961 killed many of these animals. The survivors were favored by lions either by preference or because they were for unknown reasons highly vulnerable. In any event, the wildebeest population declined until 1967. With wildebeest numbers low, lions had to turn increasingly to other prey such as eland, giving the wildebeest a chance to recover. The effects of predation vary from park to park, and may even differ in various parts of the same park, making anything I have to say applicable mainly to the Serengeti. My findings may, of course, also have relevance to other areas but more research is needed before it can be decided whether or not they do.

While predators may exert an influence on the number of prey animals, the ultimate controlling factor is the food supply. In East Africa the amount and distribution of rainfall has a profound influence on the available forage. The mid- and late-1960's were good years, with showers stimulating a growth of green grass whenever times became critical. As a result some species markedly increased their numbers as they are wont to do when somehow they escape the full impact of predation. Unless they are controlled in some way, hoofed animals tend to increase up to and even beyond the capacity of the habitat to support them on a long-term basis. Disease then becomes rife, and, with the food supply exhausted, many may die of starvation. One of the most important functions of predation is to keep prey species within the carrying capacity of the land, below a level at which disease and starvation can take effect. By taking a percentage of healthy, reproducing animals, predators help to prevent population explosions and the resulting crashes by dampening the rate of increase in the prey; they contribute to the maintenance of an equilibrium within the limits imposed by the environment. The lion and other predators are an integral part of the ecological community and must be present if the prey animals are to survive in all their vigor and abundance. The relationship between predator and prey is usually viewed as an interminable battle with the former killing the latter, striving for evolutionary success. But there can be no such winners in nature. All species are bound to each other in a universe of relationships and maintain a tenuous harmony, each dependent on the other for survival.

FAMILY NOTES

OUR LIFE AT SERONERA WAS BEAUTIFULLY BALANCED BE-
tween civilization and wilderness. We had the best of both
worlds, and it is always with nostalgia that we look back at
our pleasant and uncomplicated years there. Our home was
comfortable and we had good food, two important considerations when there are few diversions. A truck brought supplies
from Arusha to Seronera about once a week including whatever items we had ordered the previous week. Avocados,
bananas, lettuce, pineapples, mangos, and other fresh fruits
and vegetables could be had in marvelous variety, and
excellent beef fillet was available for the equivalent of about
eighty cents a pound. At times, too, I scavenged a zebra steak
or some other meat when a predator killed more than it
could consume. We ate better and more varied meals in the
Serengeti than we usually do in the United States. And there
was also Jackson Kyondo, our servant. He cleaned the house,
served meals, did the dishes and laundry, some of the cooking, and the many other tasks most housewives are happy
to forgo. A servant helps to set the tone in a home, and

Jackson's constant cheerfulness, efficiency, and readiness to help contributed greatly toward a pleasant atmosphere. We were so content that we left the Serengti as seldom as possible, taking a family trip to Nairobi or Arusha to buy clothes, shoes, and other essentials only once or twice a year.

I always departed at dawn to spend the morning with lions, and Kay often rose then too, to sit quietly on the veranda with a cup of coffee. Silence is an important value to Kay, but a peaceful hour is a rare commodity in a home with two active boys. The quiet minutes before Eric and Mark awakened gave Kay time to plan her day or to just sit, fondling whatever pet we had at the time, while watching the sunrise and the animals around the house. Swallows of three different kinds nested on our veranda at various times, and once a crombec, a stubby-tailed warbler, did so. The most elegant residents were a pair of amethyst sunbirds who searched for nectar and insects in the red-blossomed aloes we had planted beside the house. The raiment of the male was lovely, a shimmering black garment with a metallic green cap and an iridescent purple throat; the female was a drab olive-brown and heavily streaked. She constructed a nest in the vine that grew at one end of the veranda. Using only tiny feathers and spider webs to build the covered nest, she took four days to complete it. She then laid two eggs and incubated them, but after ten days they mysteriously vanished.

Kay also liked to inspect her small garden in the morning to see if perhaps a giraffe had trampled the flowers again or if some gazelle had found the herbs to their liking. Zinnias, geraniums, and other flowers grew alongside the house, and there was a small bed of herbs and another of vegetables. To plant something and watch it grow always makes Kay feel settled and contributes to her contentment even if the plot is tiny. Gardens do not thrive readily at Seronera, especially during the long dry season, and we had to nurture the plants carefully. We had dug in elephant droppings to loosen the earth, and used zebra dung as fertilizer. One day I was far out on the plains, walking along with a small shovel and a box, devotedly collecting zebra droppings, when a convoy of tourist cars spotted me and rushed over to investigate. One tends to feel a bit silly when stared at while standing alone in that vast space clutching a box of dung.

One of the charms of the Serengeti for Kay was that she could take the car when I was home and within minutes find some silent sanctuary where she could watch lions, zebra, or other animals. While she did that, I worked on my field notes and other tasks and kept an eye on Eric and Mark. Eric was almost 5 years old when we arrived in the Serengeti, and Mark 3½ years. They had no regular playmates of their own age until Ronald Skoog arrived two years later with his family, which included a son, Chris, who was Eric's age. Though surrounded by kopjes and other interesting sites, we could not permit the boys to explore them on their own. Two bull buffalo had settled down near our house and an occasional leopard spent the day on one of the kopjes; lions often passed by at night, and when the grass was high they might be sleeping unnoticed under a nearby tree. Although the superb starlings, speckle-fronted weavers, and other birds told us by their screeching and wild fluttering when a snake was on the move, boys have a propensity to poke around holes, the retreat of spitting cobras and puff adders. We saw few poisonous snakes, but some did visit us, including a mamba that measured nine feet five inches. So the boys had to amuse themselves by drawing pictures and playing in the yard around our house. After we had been there a year, Eric started school with Kay teaching him from a correspondence course. Mark was banished from the room during the lessons, which lasted a mere hour to an hour and a half a day. Soon Kay would hear a rustling by the window and then she would see Mark clinging to the sill, listening. In this way, and with occasional help from Eric, Mark soon taught himself to read. Sometimes I would take the boys with me to watch animals, but, having known little else in life, they were blasé about such outings. Instead of watching, they sat in the back of the car reading or doing their school work, happily oblivious to lions fighting on a kill outside the window.

Sometimes, when the predators were inactive, I came home at midmorning and invited the family to go on an impromptu picnic. More often than not, Kay was in the middle of baking bread, a task she could not drop at a moment's notice. But soon we set off, usually onto the plains, where on some barren kopje the boys could climb among the rocks. One of our favorite places was at the Moru kopjes. There, in a jumble of boulders, was a natural cave in which Masai had stayed while tending their herds of livestock. On one wall they had painted a hunting scene, using, among other substances, charcoal and red ochre for color. One episode depicts several men carrying huge shields while advancing with raised spears toward a lion. And there are other figures too—an elephant, some humped cattle, and little white stickmen with legs spread and hands on their hips, which, according to Myles Turner, represent Europeans in their typical stance of giving orders. These paintings are recent—bicycles and cars adorn walls at other sites—yet their history added a touch of intimacy as we had our lunch in these impersonal wilds.

Occasionally we took a short drive in the evening along the edge of the plains. With darkness one enters into a new world, a world of gleaming eyes imprisoned by the narrow beams of the headlights. Twin rubies may burn brightly in a fever tree along the river, the enormous eyes of a galago, and a pair of silvery lights may bounce across the open grasslands, tracing the path of a springhare. And then, far ahead, a whole galaxy of stars may flash across the horizon, as if the heavens have retreated into chaos, until finally the beams reveal a fleeing herd of gazelle.

To break the routine we would sometimes camp for a day or two with Eric and Mark. One afternoon, for instance, we pitched our tent on the plains at the base of a large kopje, and in the evening we built a fire with wood that we had brought with us. Huddled in the narrow circle of brightness, we felt content, drawn to the flames by an ancient force that probably had its beginnings when man first discovered how to turn night into day. Fire provides warmth, but, more importantly, it banishes loneliness and fear. Except for man eaters, nocturnal predators lose their boldness when they step into the light cast by the flames. We slipped into our beds when only glowing coals were left, and, with the breeze gently ruffling the tent flap, we soon fell asleep. Suddenly a roar and then another shattered the night, jerking us awake. Two lions had noted our intrusion and come to investigate. As they padded around the tent, continuing to proclaim their ownership of the area, the walls of canvas seemed thin indeed. Kay was apprehensive but the boys were delighted by this visit. The lions came and went several times until they finally departed, and all I remembered after that were their distant rumblings and the thunder of a fleeing zebra herd before it was time for me to make the morning rounds.

Kay enjoys having more frequent social contacts with others than I do. On previous trips we had sometimes been alone for months, and she had fervently wished for just one other woman with whom to talk. Things were very different in the Serengeti. Ros Lamprey, Jane Kruuk, Anneke Braun, and other wives of scientists were there, as was Kay Turner, the wife of Park Warden Myles Turner. Nani Croze might stroll over accompanied by her pet zebra and mongoose while Harvey was away observing elephants. At times Philip and Carolyn Thresher would fly in from Arusha and invite us on an outing, such as an evening bonfire at the Moru kopjes with steaks grilled over coals. Though isolated geographically, the Serengeti has become a crossroad of the world. The number of visitors to the Institute in the form of scientists, journalists, and just interested observers seemed endless. It was not unusual for us to have anywhere from four to eight guests for dinner, some of them unannounced. Certainly we did not anticipate such a hectic social life when we settled down in this remote wilderness. When the rains came and the influx of outsiders slowed down, almost everyone felt relieved. While many of these visitors were charming and interesting, it was pleasant to spend the evening once again in the intimacy of the family or only with friends.

When we arrived in the Serengeti there were few biologists, mainly Fritz Walther and Hans Kruuk around Seronera and a couple more that lived in the western end of the Corridor. By mid-1969 a new Research Institute had been built about two miles from Seronera, featuring lovely houses for scientists, an administrative building, and extensive laboratory space. Now at least fifteen investigators were working on various projects, too many as far as I was concerned, because size inevitably reduced the spirit of camaraderie. The Institute now attracted a number of biologists who were primarily technicians with little inclination to go into the field. Some viewed the Serengeti as just another nine-to-five job, including the requisite number of coffee breaks. A good field worker must bring a certain sensibility to his task—he must find joy in solitude, he must have the willpower to rise at dawn, and, above all, he must have almost a passion to be out in the forests and on the plains. Research institutes have their Parkinson's laws too and one such might read: the more luxurious the available laboratory facilities the less time the field biologists will spend in the field. But in spite of the many investigators and their wives that lived in an isolated community there was remarkably little friction and most genuinely liked and enjoyed each other. In part this was no doubt due to the relaxed and friendly atmosphere created by Hugh and Ros Lamprey, who presided over the Institute.

I felt that Eric and Mark would enjoy having a pet; at least that was my rationalization for wanting one myself. Disliking animals in cages, it would have to be a pet that could adapt to the freedom of our house and yard. By chance Mr. U. Trappe, who assisted Rüdiger Sachs at Kirawira, mentioned that a baby warthog had been found in a burrow with two dead siblings a few days before and that the animal was at his camp. Did I want it? Pigs have become synonymous with filth and brutality—stupid beasts—and, as is often the case, man has characterized an animal quite erroneously. Pigs actually have many endearing attributes, not the least of which is intelligence, as is recognized in this African fable:

> Once upon a time a warthog took shelter in a cave. A lion suddenly entered the cave. The warthog immediately pretended to support the roof of the cave with its tusks and called plaintively: "Lion, lion, help me hold up the roof for it is falling and we shall both be killed." Thereupon the lion held up the roof with his paws. The warthog then said to him: "You are much stronger than I. Just hold up the roof while I fetch some logs to prop it up." The vain lion was flattered and agreed to stay. And the warthog escaped.

Pigs are also clean and utterly fascinating, and I could wish for no better pet.

The next day, on October 7, 1966, Giri came into our home. We had named her that for the Swahili word "ngiri," meaning "warthog." She was an adorable creature, about three weeks old, dark-gray in color and covered sparsely with coarse hair. A short, stiff mane coursed down her nape. But her outstanding feature was her face, ugly yet curiously attractive. A tiny wart sprouted on each side of her sensitive snout, which tipped jauntily upward at the end, and white muttonchop whiskers flared on her face like fake tusks. Her real tusks were only half an inch long, peeking barely from beneath her upper lips and lifting them slightly to give her an enchanting Mona Lisa smile. Frightened by her surroundings, she hid under the sofa, but when I grunted she came out and suckled milk from a baby bottle. To give her confidence, I took her to bed with us that night. Never had I held a body that was so solidly built and generated so much heat; she seemed to have a perpetual fever. She was also a restless sleeper, rooting around and trying to suckle. After a few nights she was relegated to a box beside our bed. Lying on a hot water bottle and wrapped in a blanket to keep her from shivering, she would watch us with only her snout and beady eyes exposed.

Giri adapted to her new life with alacrity. Within a few days she pattered after me from room to room, grunting softly to herself. If she lost sight of me, she squealed and grunted harshly and her hooves drummed the wooden floors as she raced around in search of me. Happiness to a baby warthog is being in physical contact with someone. When I sat down, Giri leaped into my lap and buried her snout under my arm, grunting with pleasure; when I reclined on the floor she draped herself across my chest in anticipation of being cuddled. To have me stroke her belly sent her into a trance of ecstasy and with closed eyes she would grunt almost imperceptibly. It is amazing how many different emotions can be expressed with a grunt. But Giri was active, too. Playfully she dashed back and forth as if demented, her hackles raised like the keel of a dinosaur's back, yipping excitedly, all the while hooking her head in the typical fighting gesture of adults until her hooves slipped and she slid into a chair or wall with a crash. Young warthogs apparently have a need to root a certain amount each day. Giri nosed my bare legs, snuffling and pushing upward with her damp snout so hard that her hindlegs were at times lifted off the ground. After a few minutes of such rooting a foam of saliva covered me from my ankle to thigh. Then it was my turn to make contact with her and this I often did by rubbing some hand lotion into her dark-gray skin until she glistened like satin. When I returned home in the evening, Giri and I greeted each other with such joy and prolonged affection that Kay complained a little peevishly that it sometimes took me half an hour to notice the rest of the family. Obviously Giri had attached herself to me. The boys were too noisy and unpredictable for her in the beginning and she perhaps sensed in Kay occasional reservations—Kay did not enjoy having her legs smeared with saliva. But an appreciation of warthogs grows with time.

After a few days I took Giri outside on a leash, but she did not like this restriction. She either lay down and refused to budge or she spun around wildly, angrily jerking her head at me. Kay noted somewhat gleefully that Giri and I were perfectly matched except that Giri was even more stubborn. Finally I permitted Giri to roam freely. She amused herself around the house except for one early expedition that resulted in our searching for her frantically until we discovered her asleep on a nearby kopje, and another one when Kay had to chase her for an hour as she ran farther and farther from the house, having panicked at being outside her familiar yard. She rooted in the damp earth beneath an outdoor faucet, sinuously rolling and stretching, and was sometimes quite annoyed when we disturbed her. Her favorite toy was the frayed end of a rope that dangled just within reach from a tree. This she attacked furiously, becoming so excited that she leaped up and twisted nimbly 180° in midair to land at the same spot, now facing away from the object of her porcine passion. She leaped again and again until, exhausted, she dug a furrow with her snout and rested panting in the sun-warmed sand. Giri's leaps had actually an adult function. When pursued, a warthog runs toward its burrow, then leaps around at the entrance and backs in while facing the pursuer. No predator would dare to follow a warthog into a narrow tunnel under such circumstances. However, problems may arise if the burrow is already occupied, as E. Tookey described in the magazine *Wild Life*:

> I remember once watching some hyaenas on the plains and presently, as I got too close, one hyaena went down a hole while the rest loped away. I was going over to examine the hole closer when I saw a Wart Hog coming very fast towards the hole. He, poor thing, did *not* know that just before him his home had given shelter to a temporary lodger. Along he came at full canter, reached the hole, put on his "brakes," reversed smartly and backed, in proper Wart Hog fashion, down the hole, straight on to the hyaena. Next minute a squealing Wart Hog with a lacerated hind quarters was going across the plains again like a scalded cat.

Occasionally we all went for a walk or a picnic, Giri accompanying us and behaving much like a dog. She circled us, dashing along with her tail held stiffly erect in perhaps the most appealing of the warthog's racial idiosyncrasies, and she ran far ahead until our calls brought her zipping back, yipping wildly with delight. Although she foraged some grass for herself, her main food was still milk, including the midnight and dawn feedings required by all babies, supplemented with various exotic items that her whimsical tastes demanded: fresh pineapple, raisins, and lettuce with an oil and vinegar dressing. At the age of six weeks, Giri broadened her menu to include many foods she had disdained even a week earlier, including rice, oatmeal, raw meat, earth, and wildebeest droppings.

She continued to sleep in our room at night until she began to roam around, her hooves clacking like castanets in the silence. We tried to banish her to the living room but she would have none of that. She attacked the intervening door with a combination of such piercing wails and humanlike screams that Kay was afraid the neighbors might accuse us of having a marital squabble of epic proportions. After a couple of weeks Giri regained her old place by our bed.

As the weeks passed Giri settled so fully into the household routine that her needs and wishes were accepted and carried out without conscious effort to accommodate her. At meal times she hovered beneath the table and cleaned up any scrap that fell, and, like a vacuum cleaner, she snuffled along the cracks in the floor, hosing up crumbs, beetles, and other delicacies. Her favorite place, and one that she considered her right to occupy, was along the back of the sofa with me leaning heavily against her. If for some reason I did not wish to have a twenty-pound pig for a cushion, she would stand and look at me with glittering eyes and wrinkled nose, emitting long-drawn grating squeals. Her sounds grew shorter and louder as she grew angrier and she gnashed her teeth. If this still brought no response, she would nip me hard enough to leave no doubt as to her displeasure and then retreat. I was beginning to wonder how I would hold a 120-pound adult warthog comfortably in my lap. But this problem did not arise. On December 22, I noticed that her nose was dry and on Christmas day she had a high fever. With antibiotics having no effect, she was unable to stand up the following day and two days after that her breathing faltered. I think she had brought the seeds of death from her home burrow.

Giri had been a rewarding experience not only because she was sensitive and affectionate but also because she introduced us to warthog nature. Of course by moving into our home, Giri had ceased to be a mere warthog. Like the hero in Matthew Arnold's poem she wandered "between two worlds, one dead, the other powerless to be born." When an animal is taken from its environment, removed from its society and the harsh selection pressures to which it must accede, its character develops to a much greater degree than it would have in the wild. Secure and free, its individuality has a chance to blossom; it can learn and do and express things a normal life would neither have offered nor tolerated. A pet shows the inherent potential for individuality that lies largely dormant in a species. Though we all strive for security, we tend to equate it with conformity and dullness. Perhaps rightly so. But to our precursors even some tenuous security must have been a powerful stimulus for the expression of individuality, and this in turn was one of the factors that made man what he is. From a contemplation of warthogs emerge many thoughts.

In our front yard was a large termite hill, and on July 25, 1966, not long after our arrival, a troop of seventeen banded mongooses moved into it. Banded mongooses are weasel-like creatures, distantly related to cats, with a coarse, gray-brown pelage that is marked with dark, transverse stripes. Fully grown they are some twenty-two inches long and weigh about three pounds. Kay noted that every morning between 7:45 and 8:10, long after sunup, several heads would pop from the holes of the hill and cautiously look around until one or more animals would venture all the way out, sitting bolt upright as they scanned the surroundings for danger. Everything being safe, the others swarmed out of their dark chambers, twittering among themselves, stretching, yawning, or hurrying off to defecate at one of their favorite latrines. After that they moved together into the grass, humping along in a curious gait reminiscent of otters. They returned to the termite hill at dark, between 6:45 and 7:15 p.m., having spent the day foraging for insects and small vertebrates. Being diurnal and highly gregarious, a banded mongoose would make an excellent pet, we thought. Various troops were at that time accompanied by youngsters no larger than small rats, and we hoped that our troop too had a litter. But it did not. And on August 16 it left the hill to take up residence elsewhere. We wondered why a troop would change its home so abruptly. Mark helped to suggest one possible reason. After sitting on the termite hill he told Kay that he itched. And well he might, for he was covered with fleas.

Six months later, on February 14, the troop returned, still consisting of seventeen members. But Kay noted that its daytime routine around the termite hill was now highly irregular, since some animals visited the holes every few hours. We suspected them of having young. Then, on March 5, we saw for the first time six tiny heads peeking forth. Having lost Giri just two months before, we were eager to obtain another pet and debated how best to capture an infant without disturbing the troop too much. Several marabou storks came to our aid. I usually collected the heads of one or more predator kills during my daily rounds, and I threw them on our garage roof, out of the way of hyenas, until they could be cleaned, sometimes several days later. While Kay liked neither the sight nor smell of these heads, to phrase it mildly, vultures and marabou storks had the opposite reaction. They waited in the trees and circled overhead, imparting to our house a somewhat macabre aura. Although marabou storks have joined the vulturine profession, they also capture mice, snakes, and other vertebrates of that size. Probably because they had spotted the infant mongoose, they investigated the termite hill, probing into its holes with their heavy beaks and circling it with deliberate steps.

After a day and a half of this the troop evacuated the hill. We saw them leave just as we sat down to lunch. Though the young could run well by themselves, each was carried by an adult. I raced after the troop and snatched up an infant that an adult had dropped. Fungus, as we later named him, promptly sank his tiny teeth into my finger and breathlessly hissed his displeasure. Yet after a couple of hours in a cozy box he accepted milk and a day later he was absolutely tame, permitting himself to be handled freely by the boys and following us from room to room, all the while emitting his contact call, a strident cheep. I was amazed at the psychic malleability that permitted him to transfer his allegiance and affection from his kind to us so quickly.

Two weeks after we caught him, Kay saw the mongoose troop feeding just outside our yard. To test the reaction of the animals, she put Fungus on the veranda, but stayed indoors herself so that he would emit his usual distress call when finding himself alone. The reaction of the other mongoose was immediate. They moved closer and closer to the house, stopping to stand on their hindlegs, then coming forward again. Three of them started up the veranda steps, though they had never before come this close to the house. Her experiment working beyond her expectations, Kay hastily opened the door and retrieved her pet.

Kay took over the care of Fungus and he attached himself to her in a way that justified his name. She carried him in her apron pocket, where he slept or peered out like a kangaroo from its mother's pouch. At intervals Kay would hold a doll's bottle before him and he would clutch it with his tiny black paws and suckle vigorously. But he also relished other food. We turned on the veranda light in the evening to attract beetles. When one landed on the floor, Fungus would rush at it with a growly shriek, paw it briefly, and crunch it down, licking his lips contentedly afterward. When he wanted something he took it. Should Eric or Mark put down some food, particularly a piece of chocolate or cheese, he promptly ate it. Protests from the owner were to him completely unjustified, and he defended his acquisition with screams of rage and nips at the ankles. Soon the boys learned to eat their food surreptitiously and quickly. Fungus liked to climb into our laps to have his belly stroked before going to bed. To this he responded by stretching himself, purring and giving soft chirps of contentment. Afterward we placed him in his box, where he curled up and slept through the night. When he was a little older, he would on his own accord abruptly leave us around 7:00 p.m., perhaps going first to his sandbox, and then patter to his bed, emitting a musical tu-tu-tu. By that time we felt about Fungus's departure just as we did after having put the boys to bed: relief. He had a remarkably conspicuous personality in spite of or perhaps because of his small size. What he lacked in stature, he made up in the fervor of his expression, so that he was impossible to ignore.

Within a few weeks, Fungus spent much of his day in the yard, either reclining in the sun or grooming himself, busily currying his hair with claws, teeth, and tongue. He also hunted for insects. His sense of smell and perhaps his hearing too were extremely acute. Strolling around, he would suddenly begin to dig with his long claws and finally extract a grub or spider from a depth of one or two inches.

Bruce Kinloch in his book *Sauce for the Mongoose* described well the foraging of his pet mongoose Pipa:

> Choosing a likely piece of ground, Pipa would work across it slowly and carefully, literally leaving no stick or stone unturned. Every hole was searched, every crevice investigated, with lightning-fast movements of his fore-paws, all the time probing, digging, scratching and hooking with his wickedly efficient claws. As he worked he kept up a continuous running commentary to himself; an unceasing flow of quiet, querulous chatter and enquiring squeaks and grunts as if expressing sustained surprise and mild annoyance at the remarkably poor returns for his efforts. In fact, his industrious, methodical hunting and expert professional touch produced a steady yield of assorted beetles, ants, caterpillars, snails and other tasty oddments.

One day Fungus came into the house with the end of his tail almost severed. Knowing of Mark's proclivity to test his scissors on unusual objects, I first accused him of the deed, much to his chagrin, but then assumed that perhaps a white-necked raven had grabbed Fungus. Once I watched a raven land near the mongoose, who humped his back and fluffed out his fur until he was double his usual size. It was difficult to realize that so much mongoose could evolve from so little. Bristling, he charged the raven, which nimbly leaped into the air. This the two repeated several times as if in play. But when Fungus once made a fanatic charge at fifty vultures and marabou storks that sat around our yard, I quickly rescued him. He was also fascinated by the giraffe, George, who came to eat periodically by the house. Fungus would slowly approach big George and when about ten feet distant sit back on his hindfeet and gaze upward.

Fungus had always liked smooth, hard objects, such as quartz pebbles, which he would caress and rub against his belly. When at the age of three months we gave him a chicken egg, something in his mercurial mind clicked with innate comprehension. Picking the egg up in his forepaws and wriggling backwards in a hunched posture until his rump almost touched the nearest wall, he suddenly leaped up slightly and at the same time hurled the egg back between his hindlegs against the wall. The egg cracked and another throw would have broken it. As Tom Eisner and Joseph Davis have noted, this peculiar and fascinating behavior appears to be an adaptation for smashing millipedes, snails, and other hard objects the mongoose cannot crush with its teeth. Once the shells are broken, the contents may be eaten at leisure.

In early October, at the age of about 6½ months, Fungus exchanged his milk canines for his permanent ones, and his coat became handsomer, richer in tone and more conspicuously marked. His querulous temper, never noted for restraint, was even more prominently displayed, not toward us but toward strangers. Sometimes he merely straddled a visitor's shoe or bare foot and rubbed his anus back and forth on it. This deposited a musky fluid. Though it may have been a fine way for him to spread his personal fragrance to the far corners of the park, it was not always appreciated by those whom he had designated as perambulatory scent posts. But when he took umbrage at someone, and those whom he disliked included almost all visiting women and children, he skulked beneath the sofa or other cryptic place until at a propitious moment he suddenly launched his attack in a paroxysm of rage. He bit the person in the ankle, often holding his grip and shaking his head for good measure. This never failed to elicit a response. His disposition grew worse in the ensuing months. Neighbors began to visit us furtively or they wore high boots for protection. We, as members of his troop, were spared his constant wrath, but in the society to which I had so rudely introduced him, unrestrained antipathy toward strangers was not adaptive. We voted for his expulsion from the troop. Just after his first birthday we gave him to one of the research assistants in Banagi. There Fungus continued to thrive until a bird of prey stilled his affectionate but autocratic soul.

Tony and Sue Harthoorn, both veterinarians who during our visits to Nairobi were always wonderfully hospitable and helpful, brought George Adamson to visit us at Seronera. George and his wife, Joy, are famous for having raised and ultimately returned the lioness Elsa to the wild. Later they released Elsa's cubs in the Mbalageti River valley, where after a short time they vanished. In recent years, George had been returning a group of lions to their freedom in Meru National Park of Kenya, an experiment he described in his book *Bwana Game*. George is quiet and unassuming, but even a brief conversation made it apparent that he knew lions as individuals better than anyone I had met. He told me of subtle gestures I had overlooked and barely perceptible sounds that I had not heard. After talking with him, I realized that to enter fully into the lion's world I would have to raise a cub.

To capriciously adopt a lion is easy, to ultimately assure it a pleasant life is not. A four-hundred-pound house pet that may live for twenty years presents certain problems. There are only two acceptable ways of disposing of a lion: give it to a zoo or release it back into the wild. To some a captive lion symbolizes the subjugation of a creature that dreams only of roaming unfettered, the sky for a roof and the grass for a bed. This is romanticism. Having little urge to move as long as they are well fed, lions no doubt chafe less under confinement than do most large mammals. A zoo would be the best home, but lions breed so readily in captivity that most zoos are not interested in accepting someone's pet.

To set a tame lion free requires years of work, as George Adamson has shown, for it has to learn to hunt and kill before it can subsist. And there are other problems. Norman Carr describes in his book *Return to the Wild* how two resident male lions resented the intrusion of his two tame males so much that he had to shoot the former to save his pets. I find it ignoble to kill or evict well-established lions merely to introduce inept outsiders. Lions have in recent years been so often depicted as affectionate and tractable pets that it is sometimes forgotten that grown animals are dangerous and unpredictable. Carr's pets are said to have killed a child, and in recent years one of Adamson's lions both mauled a child and killed a man. So, because of various considerations, I decided not to bring a lion into our home.

I kept this resolve for two years, watching grimly as cubs starved and lost ones vanished. But on the morning of June 20, 1968, some vultures attracted me to a clump of trees, and there, beside the remains of a wildebeest, was a tiny male cub, a starved mound of bones covered with matted, dew-soaked hair. His breathing was feeble and he was so near death that even the inside of his mouth was cold. I noted that his canines were just erupting, making him about three weeks old. He belonged to lioness B, an elderly lioness of the Seronera pride, who had apparently failed to produce enough milk. Finally she had taken her dying offspring to a kill and abandoned him. I was contemplating what to do with the cub when Black Mane and Brown Mane ambled up, also checking on the vultures. When Brown Mane saw the cub he grabbed him by the scruff, as a lioness would do, and carried him five feet before dropping him and continuing on with his friend. I picked up the cub in a moment of compassion and took him home.

We bathed his limp body in warm water, dried him gently, and placed him in a box between hot water bottles and blankets. He remained in a coma most of that day but by evening Kay could drip milk down his throat. We got up several times during the night to feed him and change the hot water bottles. Recuperating rapidly, he could walk wobblingly by the next morning and his eyes had a new luster. To him the previous day had been not only a resurrection but also a reincarnation. He seemed to have forgotten his lion past and accepted his human pride mates unconditionally. Within four days, as soon as he was reasonably steady on his feet, he followed us around the house and yard, and when he met us, he rubbed his head in greeting against our legs. True to his lion heritage, he considered food to be something one fights over, whether or not there was competition for it. Seeing Kay with the milk bottle, he would hurry over with an expression of fierce concentration, and, as she held him, he would growl and claw, all the while suckling so violently that he sometimes pulled the nipple from the bottle. Within two weeks he had fully recovered. His body was rounded and his woolly coat dense and fluffy; his face had lost its gaunt look, becoming rather pensive but with an underlying determination. We named him Rameses for the Egyptian pharaoh Rameses II, who went into battle accompanied by a lion.

Suddenly, at the age of about one month, Rameses feared strangers and he hissed and spit at them when they approached the sofa beneath which he liked to withdraw. But in the security of his family, he was utterly adorable. As I held him, he sometimes emitted indescribably soft purrs. Or he grabbed my arm or face playfully and gently mauled it. Being rather careless of his claws, he occasionally elicited a yelp of pain, and then he would make up for his indiscretion by rubbing himself against me in a veritable orgy of affection. There is something tremendously satisfying about lying in the grass and having a lion exert gentle pressure of his cheek against yours, friendly yet without fawning, without ever losing his dignity or subverting his independence. As he grew older, Rameses added new forms of play to his repertoire. By mid-July he could bound well, and he now enjoyed chasing a plastic bag the boys pulled on a string. Rushing after it and swiping wildly with a paw, he would finally clutch it to his chest and kill it with a bite or two, just as an adult would a gazelle. However, it was not until August 7, when he was about nine weeks old, that he began to stalk his quarry by crouching and creeping slowly closer before attacking. His play also became more aggressive. Sometimes he bowled one of the boys over with a flying tackle. When we prevented him from mauling us by giving him a light cuff on the nose, he would redirect his attacks to his own paw, tearing at it with mock seriousness. Then, exhausted from play, he would lie on some vantage point to survey his domain.

His main concern in life was still food. Every three hours or so he began to dog Kay's steps miaowing harshly, wanting his bottle. Our overtures of affection were then repulsed with snaps and growls, and he remained irascible until fed. I had tried Rameses on raw meat several times after he joined us but he had shown no interest. Then suddenly, at the age of five weeks, he grabbed a gazelle head from me and tore at the meat, a response so new and sudden that a physiological change in his system may have been involved. After that he defended any meat he obtained. Straddling the piece in an attempt to cover as much of it as possible, he growled and blew air through his nose in angry puffs whenever anyone came near.

The hollow rumbling growls of a lion cub can be quite impressive in their own way. Jane Kruuk told Kay of an incident with our Rameses. Once he crawled beneath the Kruuk's house while Kay was next door visiting with Anneke Braun. Jane was busy taking dictation from Chief Park Warden Sandy Field when low rumbling sounds began to obtrude. Jane and Sandy each suspected the other of causing these sounds in eager anticipation of lunch, but as both are very reserved and polite, they continued their work. But courtesy eventually gave way to a reluctant investigation and Rameses was discovered.

I had begun to look for a permanent home for Rameses as soon as he had recovered from his period of starvation, feeling that a change would be less traumatic for him while small than after he had grown more rigid in his outlook on life. Several lions were being collected in Kenya as a gift to the government of Ethiopia, which planned to restock a park with lions. We offered Rameses and he was accepted. On September twelfth Kenya Park Warden Ted Goss flew him out of Seronera. Our last view of Rameses was in his crate, nose pressed against a crack in the slats. We hoped we were giving him a good future as a small repayment for all he had taught us and the pleasure he had given us. Six months later we saw him in Kenya in a pen with two lions of his age. He was a hefty youngster now, with a short mane and sleek hide, about twice the size of a free-living cub of comparable age; he had obviously been living well. Kay, who had loved and cared for the cub more than any of us, went alone to the cage and talked to him. But he gave no definite sign of recognition. The Ethiopia venture collapsed, and Rameses ultimately went to a zoo, no doubt the best place for him, since he had never known the freedom of his kind.

To keep a large wild animal as a pet is a selfish gesture, which I deprecate though I indulge in it. The psychological and physical needs of an animal can seldom be catered to adequately, and in spite of its being secure and contented it is still not complete. Perhaps a genet we knew offered the ideal way to have an animal around the house. A genet is a lithe and sinuous animal, related to the mongoose, with a dark-spotted coat and a long ringed tail, perhaps the most beautiful of the small African carnivores. After we had moved to a new house at the Research Institute for the last six months of our stay in the Serengeti, a genet sometimes came on the veranda in the evening to catch insects that had been attracted to the light. Kay began to put out meat scraps for it, and, when it took those without being unduly disturbed by our presence, she laid a trail of meat from the veranda into our living room. Within a short time the genet bounded into our house, its long tail flowing behind. When we sat still the genet would take bits of meat from our hands, its delicate ears twitching and its huge eyes staring at us a little apprehensively. In the course of an evening it might visit us repeatedly, and each time we felt flattered and grateful that such a lovely creature deigned to grace our abode. Then, with hunger and curiosity satisfied, it vanished into the night, the visit just an interlude in its life.

SCAB-EAR

I HESITATE TO WRITE ABOUT SCAB-EAR BECAUSE I DID NOT know her well. Driving along the Seronera River in search of lions, I sometimes met her, draped with sensuous ease along the branch of an acacia or sausage tree. I would stop to admire her sublime beauty but she seldom acknowledged my presence, and after a few minutes I drove on, feeling as if I had paid homage to an object of art rather than to a leopard. Biting flies attacked her ears so persistently that these were often swollen and encrusted with blood, a feature that caused me to give her such an inelegant name.

Only the most cursory information about the habits of leopards was available when I began my project, and I hoped to study this species in some detail. But I soon discovered that to become familiar with leopards was a whole project in itself. Retiring and elusive, most Serengeti leopards retreated as soon as they heard or saw a car, and I seldom glimpsed more than a flash of dappled hide as the animal was swallowed by a thicket. Only a few leopards, particularly around Seronera, tolerated cars and of these Scab-ear was one.

Scab-ear's range was long and narrow, about nine miles from one end to the other, starting in the vicinity of our house and stretching eastward along the Seronera River and its tributaries that meander onto the plains. The total area covered by her wanderings was on the order of twenty-five square miles. In contrast, leopards in the Wilpattu National Park of Ceylon range over only three to four square miles according to John Eisenberg. Scab-ear and most other Serengeti leopards haunted kopjes and thickets, seldom venturing into the open, but I am not certain that their reticent nature and the ease with which they can hunt in dense vegetation are the sole reasons for this habitat preference. It is also possible that leopards remain near cover to escape lions, for these two cats greatly dislike each other. Scab-ear was prowling along the river one night, intent only on some private endeavor, when Yellow Mane and some lionesses of the Seronera pride sensed her. They stalked her and she barely escaped their rush by clambering up the smooth trunk of a fever tree where the lions could not follow. Another leopardess was not quick enough. Visitors found her dead, bitten through the lower back and throat with eleven members of the Masai pride still pawing at the limp carcass.

Scab-ear shared her range with other leopards. A shy and handsome male used the western end of her range, and two other females, one with a large male cub, resided in the eastern half of it. A fourth female visited the Masai kopjes at intervals, but the main part of her range extended northward into the woodlands. Although these leopards all lived in more or less the same area and they no doubt often saw or smelled one another, each stayed strictly to itself. Adult leopards tend to be asocial in the Serengeti, except of course when courting or when a female has cubs. The tiger, too, was said to be a recluse, but in India I found that two or three adults may meet and share a kill at night before resuming their lone rounds, solitary but not asocial. The Seronera leopards had no such convivial inclinations. I was impressed by the facility with which the cats avoided contact, especially since this seemed to be done mainly by scent-marking in the manner of lions. Leopards also have a call, a repeated, coughing sound that somewhat resembles the rasping of a saw, but I rarely heard it. A female seems to have no territory in the sense of maintaining an exclusive area from which intruders are expelled. However, the fact that only one adult male occupied Seronera suggested that he perhaps did not tolerate others of his sex. Most leopards were sedentary in the woodlands, but a few of them also penetrated the plains, residing there on the kopjes and isolated hills. A total of seven to eight leopards inhabited about seventy-five square miles around Seronera. Their number remained the same over a period of three years even though some died or disappeared, cubs grew up and moved away, and a stranger settled down there. In spite of the various vicissitudes, these leopards managed to keep their population stable. The intricacies of how they did so eluded me, and, as usually happens, I ended the project with far more questions than I had asked at the beginning.

Three adults, including Scab-ear, were at Seronera throughout my period of study. Scattered through my notebooks are brief entries about them, giving a fragmentary picture of their life. To read these is rather like looking through an album of family photographs re-creating the past in brief and static glimpses. I usually met Scab-ear resting alone in a tree. She had a cold and detached look, none of the carefree indolence of a lion or the aristocratic reserve of a cheetah; she conveyed visions of a nocturnal hunter, stealthy and implacable, and this rather deterred one from seeking empathy. At times the remains of a gazelle or reedbuck were wedged among the branches of her tree. Leopards often store large kills in trees to keep them out of the jaws of other predators. Hyenas are poor climbers. Lions climb fairly well, but they find it difficult to recognize prey animals hanging in a distorted fashion above them and they may thus pass up some easy meals. Once The Young Female of the Masai pride limped along the river, lean and hungry because a leg injury prevented her from hunting. Scab-ear had stored a reedbuck in an acacia while she attended to some other matters. The Young Female smelled the buck. She circled the tree, sniffing the trunk and the air, and she stared directly at the carcass hanging only thirteen feet away and in clear view. Yet she did not "see" it. Finally she hobbled away. However, on a few occasions a lion spotted a leopard with its kill in a tree 'and promptly climbed up and appropriated the carcass.

A tree not only helps to keep the kill away from predators, vultures, and ants, but it is also a convenient larder to which the leopard can return at any time for a snack. Scab-ear once had three gazelle tucked into the branches of the same tree. I have almost no information as to how often leopards kill. On one occasion, Scab-ear had a gazelle that lasted her for three days, during which time she ate everything except the bones, some skin, and the stomach contents, and then on the fourth day she killed a reedbuck. Prey was not always this bountiful and she probably averaged slightly more than one such animal per week when gazelle were available. At other times she no doubt captured hares, guinea fowl, and similar small prey that are not stored in trees.

Leopards are catholic in their tastes, catching anything available up to animals weighing as much as 150 pounds. Once I came upon a male leopard who had killed a female topi weighing perhaps 250 pounds. In addition to various antelope, warthog, zebra foals, and the like, the Serengeti leopards included such exotic items in their fare as a python, several European storks, and jackals. One day Scab-ear rushed from the high grass and killed two bat-eared foxes on the airfield beside a bus filled with visitors. Though generally unobtrusive, Scab-ear and her kin occasionally made their presence known by hunting at Seronera. Here is an excerpt from the monthly park report:

> During the Chief Warden's absence on safari, his staff were roused at night by an appalling clatter coming from the kitchen roof. They ran to the scene with torches and discovered that a leopard had torn off a large section of guttering in an attempt to reach some hyrax which were hiding between the roof and the kitchen ceiling. The leopard made off on being disturbed, but the nerves of the hyrax were so shattered that they spent the whole of the next day in self-imposed confinement, afraid to issue forth and regain their rocks.

Myles Turner had two pet serval cats and he described the fate of one in a letter to me:

> Last night our two serval cats were lying on our bed at 9 p.m. and we were in the sitting room when one of the cats came flying down the passage looking very scared. Turned out a leopard had come into the bedroom through the window, breaking the mosquito gauze and taken the bigger serval. Never saw him again, not a trace of hide nor hair.

While leopards would seem to have ample food available everywhere, they too may have shortages. During the prolonged rains of 1968 one cub out of a litter of two starved to death near the Masai kopjes because its mother was unable to support both.

Only rarely did I observe a leopard in pursuit of prey and on these occasions it usually failed to live up to its reputation of being a consummate hunter. Of the nine stalks I witnessed in daytime only one culminated in a rush, a successful one. The following hunt was typical. One young male had settled for awhile on a sparsely wooded knoll that guarded the entrance to the Mukoma plain. Gazelle migrated past this knoll through patches of high grass, giving him the opportunity to capture an occasional unwary animal. But he had no success the morning Kay and I watched him. He had been sitting around, waiting for gazelle to wander by, when finally he saw a small group wending its way toward him. He crouched in what he hoped was their line of approach. The animals passed him at some thirty feet, but he then followed them, stealthily, gliding along so smoothly that he seemed stiller than when he had not moved at all. The gazelle halted. He crept closer until only twenty feet separated them and he was visibly tensing for a charge. Suddenly the gazelle herd exploded, living fragments bursting in several directions. The foiled leopard trudged back to his knoll to await another chance.

Scab-ear had a litter in January 1967. I do not know how many cubs she had, perhaps two or three as is often the case among leopards, but only a female cub survived. She kept it hidden in the hollow bole of a sausage tree for awhile, and after that it usually remained in some thicket. Occasionally I saw the two tracing the edge of a riverine thicket, the mother in the lead. At such times she always had her tail raised in a graceful loop to expose the strikingly white underside of it. It seemed almost as if she were lighting the way for her daughter by holding high a torch. Leopards develop faster than lions, and by the age of thirteen months Scab-ear's daughter began to travel by herself at times. The rainy season came and the grasses grew high and I did not often meet the pair in the ensuing months. But I knew that they continued to associate even though their social bonds gradually weakened. On August 18, 1968, mother and offspring were about three hundred feet apart, each with a gazelle in a tree. The cub could now take care of itself. Their fleeting contacts continued into November but then ceased. At the age of twenty-two months the youngster was wholly on its own and she now roamed so widely that

I seldom saw her. But Scab-ear remained at Seronera. Sometime in February, just over two years since the birth of her previous litter, she had a secret tryst with a male. I met her in early June, walking along, her breasts heavy with milk. She led me to a kopje in whose recesses her young were hidden, and, later that summer, Alan Root told me that he had seen two cubs playing among the rocks.

The family history of another cub was similar to that of the young female. This one, a male, was born in September 1967, to a small, trim leopardess who was usually found along one wooded tributary to the Seronera River. He remained with his mother at least until December 1968. I met them in the middle of that month as they played, golden flashes racing through green grass, pouncing and wrestling while lightly clasped in each other's arms. Finally she growled and bared her teeth and they broke apart. The cub became quite solitary early the next year and by May he was essentially independent. Yet mother and son, too, retained their social ties until the latter was at least twenty-two months old. At times they had ardent reunions, rubbing their cheeks and bodies sinuously and licking each other's face, obviously excited and delighted with the meeting. Witnessing such tenderness, I realized that these leopards merely masked their warm temperament and emotional depth beneath a cold exterior.

I wish that leopards would reveal this side of their nature more often, for it would evoke friendliness in man. And leopards need all the friends they can find if they are to survive. There may be five hundred to six hundred leopards in the Serengeti park and these are reasonably safe for the moment, as are those in some other parks. But throughout their vast range, which stretches from Manchuria through India to the Middle East as well as over much of Africa, leopards are being relentlessly persecuted for their lovely hides. Catering to the vanity of wealthy women, the fur industry has created such a demand for leopard-skin coats and other such nonessential items that the existence of this cat may soon be endangered if present trends continue. Norman Myers queried a number of governments and conservation organizations about the extent of the leopard slaughter, and I can do no better than to present two excerpts from his 1971 report on the matter:

ETHIOPIA. Thousands are shot or trapped illegally throughout the country . . . As a source of leopard skins, Ethiopia . . . runs to possibly 6000–8000 a year, perhaps more . . . It being a very lucrative business, the dealers can afford to pay generous bribes to Government officials, including members of the Wildlife Conservation Department. As a result, not only is a blind eye turned to their activities but they receive valuable assistance and protection from those whose job it is to protect wildlife. Game Guards know that to interfere with the "recognised" dealers will result in their dismissal if not worse, whereas cooperation will be rewarded by generous "bonuses" over and above their meagre salaries. Similarly a little judicious bribery among more senior officials enables the dealers to have their skins stamped with the official Wild Life Conservation Department stamp, thus rendering them "legal" . . . Leopard are undoubtedly on the road to extinction in Ethiopia as things are at present. As skins become more difficult to obtain their value increases and provides a bigger incentive to the local poachers to hunt down every last leopard . . . The 300 Ethiopian dollars (U.S. $120) for which a poacher can sell a good skin is equivalent to nearly a year's wages for an unskilled laborer.
J. H. Blower, *Chief Game Warden, 1968*

KENYA. In parts of the Northern Frontier District of Kenya . . . large gangs of ex-Shifta (terrorists) are hunting in parties numbering from 20 to 80 persons . . . one party of 68 persons were equipped with 42 firearms, which included 2 Bren

guns and 4 Sten guns . . .These gangs are, primarily, interested in obtaining leopard and cheetah
skins . . . Leopards five years ago were common but
now have been systematically exterminated . . . A
recently captured prisoner divulged . . . a gang had
killed more than 300 leopards over a period of 3
months . . . In the Matthews Range Hunting Block
. . . there are no leopard at all as they have been
poached out of existence, whereas formerly they
were well represented. In South Turkana, nearly
every waterhole has its leopard trap.

East African Wildlife Society
Report on Poaching, 1970

In 1968 a total of 9,556 leopard skins were imported
into the United States alone, and the figure for 1969 was
7,934, most of them from Ethiopia, Kenya, and India. In
1970 only 996 skins were brought in, mainly because New
York had passed the Mason Act, which prohibits the manufacture and sale of leopard products within the state. Concerned about the plight of leopards, several African and
Asian countries have banned the export of skins and the
International Fur Trade Federation has asked its members
to agree to a three-year moratorium on the use of this cat.*
These worthy measures may slow the precipitous decline of
leopards but they will not halt it. In the final analysis, it
is a question of morality. The fate of leopards now depends
on the charity of man. The species represents a test of his
good intentions, a test to see whether or not he can overcome his avarice and vanity simply to preserve something
that is beautiful. For the sake of both leopard and man I
hope that he can.

---

* Several other conservation measures have been taken since
this manuscript was completed. For example, on February 3, 1972,
the U.S. government announced a ban on import of leopard skins.

AN ENIGMATIC CAT

HAVING ONCE STUDIED WILDLIFE IN INDIA, I TENDED TO think of cheetah mainly as companions to royalty. Families of the maharajahs still talk of using trained cheetah for hunting blackbuck antelope and some Moghul paintings show an emperor with his retinue taking these cats on a chase. Casually, like that of a farmer going to work in the fields, a bullock cart would draw near a blackbuck herd. On the cart sat a cheetah, its eyes hooded, waiting to be released. When the cart was about three hundred feet from the antelope, the keeper would remove the hood and turn the head of the cheetah toward the quarry. Slipping off the cart, the cheetah would begin its stalk, selecting a buck with shiny, black coat and long, spiralling horns, as it was trained to do. Finally it sprinted after the animal with that phenomenal, that glorious burst of speed that has made it the fastest of all land mammals. If the cheetah captured its quarry, the keeper would cut the throat and give the cat a cup of blood in reward and sometimes also a little meat. If the prey escaped, the keeper would approach chanting, "Oh,

Great King, do not be angry, you will kill the next one," as the hood was again placed over the cat's eyes.

Today both the sport and the cheetah are extinct in India. The ruler of a small princely state in central India was cruising around in his jeep one night in 1948. On the road he met three cheetah. His private secretary proudly sent their obituary to the Bombay Natural History Society: "All these cheetah were shot by the Durbar of our State. He was driving at night and they were all seen sitting close to each other. They were all males . . ." The year 1952 marks the last definite record of cheetah in India. A few still survive in Iran and possibly in the Turkmenistan province of the USSR, but their main stronghold is now Africa, the open woodlands and plains stretching from Chad and the Sudan through East Africa and Rhodesia to southwest Africa.

Although cheetah have been closely associated with man for nearly three thousand years, little was known of their habits when I began work in the Serengeti. No study had been made of them in the wild and for mysterious reasons they generally refused to breed in captivity. Jahangir, Moghul emperor from 1605 to 1627, wrote: "It is a fact that the hunting leopards [cheetah] do not pair in places other than their habitats. So that, my revered father once collected together 1000 leopards. He was very eager that they should pair, but this in no way came off." Later these cheetah did produce one litter of three cubs, but with a thousand animals this was a poor record indeed. Between then and 1967 only eight litters were born in zoos. Intrigued by this enigmatic cat and attracted by its elegant beauty, I began to take detailed notes, beginning with the first animal I saw striding lithely across the plains. But during that first year I failed to establish a close rapport with cheetah. In part their self-contained mien stifled a ready intimacy and perhaps, too, the strong personality of the lion pervaded my consciousness to such an extent that the gentle character of the cheetah was unable to infringe. Kay was attracted to cheetah more than to any other species. The combination of hauteur and timidity, of long-limbed grace and contained vitality perhaps appeals particularly to women, for Anneke Braun and Dorothy Baldwin also sought every opportunity to watch these cats. I benefitted from their enthusiasm in that they passed many interesting observations on to me.

During the first dry season I occasionally met cheetah around Seronera, some of them often enough for me to recognize them as acquaintances. With the onset of the heavy rains in March 1967, all of them disappeared at the same time as the Thomson's gazelle. Not until early July did I again find cheetah at Seronera, and their arrival coincided with that of the gazelle returning from the plains. The following year, when the rains lasted a long time, both cheetah and gazelle abandoned Seronera for six months. Gazelle were the principal prey of cheetah in that part of the park, and the cats obviously migrated with their food source in a rather one-sided partnership. While such movements were interesting, they also frustrated my attempts to study specific animals because these were so difficult to find once they had dispersed over the plains.

Cheetah were surprisingly scarce in the park. I would guess that no more than 250 of these cats inhabited the whole ecological unit, or about one animal per forty square miles. In Kruger National Park there is also a low density, with about one animal per twenty-seven square miles. Only a few of the Serengeti cheetah were approachable, the others trotting away or hiding as soon as they perceived a car.

In July 1967, I met a female cheetah, a large raw-boned and blunt-featured animal. In the ensuing two years she and her offspring provided me with some of my most memorable wildlife experiences. I never named her. At first her look of arrogance seemed to forbid such familiarity and later it was redundant to do so—she was simply "The Cheetah" to all of us. At the time of our meeting she had cubs hidden among the boulders and shrubs of the Masai kopjes. I did not observe her when she first led her cubs to kills but some people told me that she had six offspring, others that she had four. Either figure is possible, but by mid-September she had only three and then one of these disappeared, leaving her with two female cubs. A high death rate between the ages of 1½ and 4 months is usual among cheetah, yet I have little information about what happens to such missing youngsters. Some were ill, judging by the way they lagged behind their families, others were no doubt taken by birds of prey such as the martial eagle, and by hyenas. Visitors once saw two lionesses first attack a cheetah who was carrying a cub and then kill the infant while the mother escaped.

Kay and I often visited the family. Usually it rested in the sparse shade of an acacia tree. The mother would lie on her side with her legs stretched out stiffly and her round head raised. Her deep-amber eyes roamed the horizon with that inscrutable gaze which seems even more pronounced in cheetah than in other cats. The cubs huddled against her, frail and wistful replicas of their mother even to the two dark lines running like tear stains from the eyes to the corners of the mouth. But unlike their mother their fur was almost black with faint dark spots, and a mantle of silky blue-gray hair covered them from crown to rump. When the sun touched this mantle, it radiated like a silver halo, turning the cub into a shining ikon of exquisite beauty. No other cat has such a distinctive natal coat. For years I have pondered about the possible selective advantage that such a coat may have, but I remain perplexed. It makes the cubs conspicuous and hence vulnerable to predation. Someone suggested that the coat resembles that of the ratel, or honey badger, and this is true. The ratel is strong and short-tempered—one attacked the tires of my car when I halted near it—and predators would supposedly shy away from such an irascible beast. When the cubs are hidden in a thicket, the coat would seem to be of little advantage, and, afterwards, when they follow their mother no predator would be fooled. And by the age of three months, the mantle begins to fall out. Perhaps the prominent light and dark pattern helps a mother to keep her cubs in view when they are still small and slow on their feet.

The family stayed by itself, disdaining even to acknowledge the other cheetah that occasionally wandered by. Adult females are solitary, at least in the Serengeti, except when courting or when accompanied by cubs. Males also tend to lead a lone existence, although two or three of them may at times become companions in the manner of lions. The small groups of males and females that are occasionally seen consist of grown youngsters who have separated from their mother but have not yet split up among themselves. Watching the cheetah family, I always had the feeling that their social contacts were constrained. Although they sometimes rested with bodies touching, they had none of the intense desire to touch, to feel, that is so typical of lions. A cub may nuzzle its mother's face, or two cubs may lick each other, purring loudly, but there was none of the sinuous rubbing of heads and bodies so typical of most cats. They mainly gave an impression of being alone together. Even in play the two cubs usually retained some restraint. When one dashed away, the other chased it, the two sprites flitting in and out of the grass, around a termite hill, through a gulley, until one tagged the other with a touch of its paw. But they seldom wrestled like lions and their body contact was usually brief, a quick slap or two, a mock bite, before they separated perhaps to pursue each other once more.

The female moved her cubs from the Masai kopjes after they were fully mobile, taking them across the Seronera River onto the gentle slope that stretches toward Mukoma Hill. There they remained for two months on about five square miles of grassland broken by several dry river courses, roaming from kill to kill, from rest site to rest site. Scattered herds of Thomson's gazelle grazed on the sparse stubble, and these were the cheetah's main food source. Since it was not known how often cheetah make a kill, I decided to spend several weeks with the family. Although cheetah may move around at night, sometimes, for example, wandering to a river to drink or even making a kill in moonlight, they generally rest, and dawn finds them at the same place as on the previous evening. This saved me the trouble of spending every night with the family. Kay, Anneke, and others helped me in these vigils, which we made almost daily from October 13 to November 5 and from November 14 to 19. Dust hung motionless over the plains at that season, and around noon the air was heavy with silence and charged with heat. We waited. The cheetah hunted not by searching for prey but by remaining in one place for hours until some prey animals drifted into the vicinity. Time dragged, but we stayed, seduced by the expectation of that one brief moment when her indolence would explode into violence.

One morning, shortly after eight o'clock, the female saw several gazelle about eight hundred feet away, and by the intensity of her stare I knew that she was evaluating the possibility of catching one. Then, followed by her cubs, she trotted toward them. She held her head low, her muzzle strained ahead, giving her a determined, even ominous look as she flowed through scattered patches of grass to within three hundred feet of the gazelle. There she halted briefly and surveyed her quarry, which, unmindful of her deadly stare, continued to graze. She advanced sixty feet, crouched, and moved closer once more, her cubs still trailing and making no attempt to conceal themselves. A large fawn was grazing closest to her, somewhat separated from the other gazelle. She waited tensely, one minute, two minutes, until the foraging gazelle faced completely away from her. Suddenly she sprinted. Her supple back coiling and uncoiling like a spring as she raced faster and faster, gaining on the fleeing gazelle. With death imminent, the gazelle zigzagged once, then again, but the cheetah followed each turn, her feet kicking up dust as she abruptly reversed direction. Then, with a light flick of her paw she touched the gazelle's thigh and it crashed on its side. Lunging in, she grabbed its throat, holding the struggling animal down with the weight of her chest. The cubs, who had eagerly watched the 750-foot chase, now bounded up and tugged impatiently at the carcass. But first the female dragged it three hundred feet to the shade of a bush. Dropping the body, she noted that the gazelle still kicked feebly. She held its throat once more until all movement ceased. Nine minutes had elapsed since the beginning of the hunt. Cheetah may be built like grey-hounds, but, like all cats, they lack stamina: their stored energy is expended in one brief burst. A fast run of several hundred feet exhausts them, and the female now panted for eighteen minutes while her cubs tried unsuccessfully to chew a hole in the carcass. Finally she did this for them, exposing the muscles of a thigh. While they tore at the meat, she rested another ten minutes before joining her youngsters in the feast.

Everything about the cheetah is built for speed, the slender legs and slim waist, the deep chest and small head. The flexible spine is alternately shortened and extended as the cat moves along with huge galloping bounds, and this suppleness is said to add nearly two miles an hour to its running speed. The movable shoulder blades enable it to lengthen its stride by about four inches, another means of increasing velocity, according to Milton Hildebrand, who has studied locomotion in cheetah. The top speed of a cheetah raced on a greyhound track in England is said to have been sixty miles per hour, and measurements taken from film footage gave one speed of fifty-six miles per hour. These figures may not represent the maximum of which the cat is capable. Cheetah in captivity are usually not in their best condition and those in the wild run only as fast as necessary to catch up with and then stay close to their prey until they can trip it. During the lower Pleistocene a lion-sized cheetah lived in Europe and it must have been truly impressive to see this large cat in pursuit of its prey.

At some moment between spotting a herd of prey and chasing it, a cheetah must select one individual, and I was particularly interested to find out what determined that choice. I described this selection process in an article that was published in a 1970 issue of *Natural History* magazine:

Size of prey was obviously one factor. In the parts of the Serengeti where I observed cheetahs, Thomson's gazelle was the preferred prey (91 percent), followed by Grant's gazelle, wildebeest, impala, and hare in that order. A Thomson's gazelle weighs some 35 to 40 pounds, just one large meal for a cheetah weighing 110 to 130 pounds. Adult Grant's gazelle, impala, and reedbuck were also killed, but of the wildebeest only the calves were captured. Similarly, some 68 percent of the cheetah kills reported from Kruger National Park consisted of impala, and most of the other prey was relatively small too. A cheetah hunting alone seldom preys on anything weighing much more than itself and this limits it to the small antelopes and the young of the large ones. But several cheetah together may attack a large animal, as in Nairobi National Park where four males killed kongoni and zebra.

Prey selection can operate in two ways. In one, the predator chooses a particular animal out of a herd—a sick one, a newborn one—and pursues it, ignoring all others. In the other, the prey selects against itself, so to speak, by becoming vulnerable in some way. Leopards, for example, catch nearly twice as many adult male Thomson's gazelles as would be expected from their number in the population. These seem to be mostly non-territorial males that roam through high grass and along river courses where leopards hunt, in contrast to females and territorial males that remain in areas of short grass where they are not so vulnerable to leopards.

Cheetahs hunt mainly in the open plains. There they catch about 25 percent fewer adult males than expected, possibly because cheetahs prefer to select prey that is fleeing rather than standing around alertly as territorial males do. I collected and aged the jaws of 163 gazelle kills. The cheetahs had captured many fawns less than six months old, whereas yearlings, some 9 to 24 months old, were almost immune to predation. The cheetahs took many adults but no age class was particularly selected. Most of the adult prey taken were presumably healthy, although the cats may have been able to detect slight disabilities, which I could not. Gazelles sometimes suffer from heavy infestations of lungworm or sarcoptic mange and such animals possibly respond less briskly to the cheetah. However, when the ages of gazelles killed by cheetahs are compared with those killed by lions, it is obvious that the two cats select very similarly. A lion captures its prey by surprise in a short fast rush, during which there is little or no time to test for weakness in an individual. In contrast, the cheetah may take its prey with a long run. Despite their different hunting techniques the adult gazelles killed by these two cats had a similar age structure, except that lions kill fewer small young and more yearlings. Possibly cheetahs catch the sick, and lions, the healthy, but I am inclined to think that most prey selected by both species was in reasonably good condition.

When observing a cheetah hunt, the selection for fawns is obvious—any fawn in a herd is immediately pursued. This is not surprising when hunting success is considered. Although cheetahs can attain tremendous speed, they are unable to keep it up for more than about 900 feet. If the gazelle dodges several times, the cheetah, exhausted, may have to give up the chase, and 23 out of 26 unsuccessful hunts that I observed failed for that reason. A fawn can run neither fast nor far, and in 31 chases after them, the cheetah was successful every time after an average run of 600 feet. On the other hand, of 56 pursuits after large young and adults only 54 percent resulted in a kill after a chase up to some 900 feet. Cheetahs are pragmatists: better a small meal than none at all.

Cheetahs prefer to hunt a solitary individual or one in a small herd, because they have difficulty selecting a gazelle and keeping it in sight in a large milling herd. Individuals that enter tall grass, graze behind some bushes, or otherwise enable the cheetah to stalk undetected are chosen. With endless patience the cat may wait for a gazelle to lower its head and graze while briefly facing away from the danger, thus giving the cheetah an undetected second during the rush—often the difference between success and failure. The selection process is not always an easy one. Cheetahs sometimes bound toward a herd, then give up for no obvious reason, probably because they are unable to find a suitable quarry. Or they first pursue a herd at moderate speed before suddenly making a selection.

During the twenty-six days that we watched the female and her two cubs she killed a total of twenty-four Thomson's gazelle and one hare. She failed to catch something on three of the days, even though she tried, but then captured two gazelle each on two days. Andrew Laurie, a research assistant who helped observe cheetah with the same enthusiasm that he had shown in observing lions with me, watched another female with cubs for a week and found that this family, too, killed at the rate of almost once a day. I was surprised that the female could do so well because visitors harassed her almost daily. When she stalked, they sometimes blocked her view while taking photographs or chased away the prey; when she rested, they thumped the sides of their cars to make her look up. She ignored such overtures but did not forgive them. Occasionally she saw a car in the distance and promptly crouched or lay flat on her side, later peering over the grass to make certain it had gone before continuing with her daily routine. To help her remain concealed I often parked some distance from her, for in wildlife reserves a stationary car attracts other cars as a carcass draws vultures.

The insensitivity that many visitors exhibit toward animals continually amazed me. It says much for the adaptability of the predators that they will tolerate the packs of clattering monsters that roar at and encircle them, while heads of strange creatures pop out all over and make noise. Watching tourists almost daily, I concluded that, on the average, the French and then the Indians were the most tactless in their dealings with animals. Germans tended to comment loudly on every trivial action but were fairly well-behaved, and Americans were either silently bored or just loud. By traveling in convoys and massing around some object of interest, usually a predator, visitors completely lose the quality of their wilderness experience. Parks should limit the number of vehicles that are allowed at one place at one time and make an effort to teach tour guides and visitors to show animals the same courtesy they expect from one another.

Ronald McLaughlin, a Canadian zoologist, conducted a study of cheetah in Nairobi National Park, and his findings, published in the *East African Wildlife Journal,* supplement mine in several interesting details. Cheetah in that park are sedentary, as is most of their prey, and they confine themselves to definite home ranges that overlap considerably. One female with cubs used about twenty-nine square miles of terrain, and a pair of males about thirty-nine square miles. The cats traveled an average of 3.7 hours a day, covering a distance of a little over 2½ miles. About three quarters of their prey consisted of impala, Grant's gazelle, and Thomson's gazelle. "Of all kills, 54% were juveniles in contrast to their presence of approximately 20% in the living population. Adult females of species which occur in breeding herds are relatively safe from attack if juveniles are present, be-

cause, if given a choice, cheetah invariably select the latter."
About thirty-seven percent of the pursuits Ron observed were
successful. As in the Serengeti, female cheetah with cubs
killed on the average of once a day. However, single cheetah
captured prey only once every two to three days. Given
these killing rates, the Serengeti cheetah accounted for about
thirty thousand animals a year, one half to two thirds of
which were young ones.

A kill does not necessarily imply a meal, because
cheetah are timid creatures who readily relinquish a carcass
to another predator. Of the twenty-five kills that were made
by the female and her two cubs during the period of inten-
sive observation, she lost three, one to a hyena and two to
lions. When attacked by a lion, the youngsters scatter and
flee and the mother, too, retreats and then often circles the
site, moaning loudly in anger. I shall never forget the sad
hunting tale of one young female. She saw several gazelle
some six hundred feet away, among them a small fawn
that she caught after a brief chase. A hyena loped up. Dropping her prize, the cheetah backed off and merely hissed as
the hyena settled down to devour the whole carcass in ten
minutes. The cheetah had drifted off, but the hyena, recognizing a meal ticket, casually followed. Soon the cheetah
killed another fawn—and the hyena had another snack.
On two occasions many white-backed vultures lined up
shoulder to shoulder and advanced on a feeding cheetah,
who then ignominiously retreated. A total of twelve percent
of cheetah kills ended in someone else's stomach. No wonder
these cats are nervous eaters, always glancing around as
they bolt their food.

Cheetah usually consume the meat off one thigh first
and then chew it off the abdomen and chest before starting
on the other thigh and forelegs. Blood that collects in the
body cavity may be lapped up, useful behavior in an animal
that often lives in areas where water is scarce. All that remains of a gazelle after an hour or so is an untidy heap

consisting of the digestive tract, the skeleton, and some skin. Carcasses are abandoned after one meal, even if much meat remains. In spite of being parasitized by other predators, the Serengeti cheetah live quite well. The female we watched killed at the rate of twenty-two pounds of food per day. Subtracting the kills that were stolen and those parts of the carcass that were not eaten, she still had some 11½ pounds of meat left. This she had to share with her cubs, but even so she ate considerably more than she needed. It always rather pleased me that in the Serengeti the meek reaped such a bounty.

Cheetah cubs must learn to hunt well before reaching independence, because, unlike lions, they cannot depend on a group for food. At first the two youngsters tended to play unconcernedly while their mother stalked. Then, at the age of about three months, they began to watch hunts alertly, usually remaining discreetly in the background. At that age a mother may begin to train her young to hunt by placing them in a situation where they can learn to do so. One day Dorothy Baldwin and Kay were with the cheetah family. The mother caught a gazelle fawn, but instead of killing it, she carried it to her four-month-old cubs. Dropping the fawn in front of them, she stood idly by while it fled, clumsily pursued by her cubs. They managed to knock it down once but were unable to kill it. Finally the mother did it for them. However, Ron McLaughlin once observed five-month-old cubs killing a Thomson's gazelle fawn.

The family vanished in early December with the onset of the rains. I searched for them on the plains, checking each group with high expectations but in vain. Whenever acquaintances disappeared, we conjured up tragic fates, but we need not have worried. In July all three reappeared in their old haunts. The cubs were now a year old, gangly adolescents about two thirds the size of their mother. Although they now stalked prey and chased after it on occasion, their efforts were surprisingly inept. For instance, in August one of the cubs bounded after a gazelle fawn and knocked it over. The fawn jumped up and raced away, only to be struck down again and again. Finally the mother dispatched it expertly. And on the next three hunts she took the initiative. On October 1, when almost fifteen months old, the same cub bungled yet another hunt.

Kay was with the family one day when a male cheetah approached, an unusual event, for adults are careful to stay out of each other's way. He came to within twenty-five feet of the mother and cubs, moving a step at a time as he sniffed the ground, once walking closer on his elbows, a most peculiar posture. One cub lunged at him, and when it did so again he charged in return. After circling the family cautiously, he reclined ten feet from them. It was dark now and Kay departed. By next morning the male had gone. Ron McLaughlin watched six such encounters in Nairobi Park and on four of these the male attacked the family, once trying to bite a female in the flank. Perhaps it was just as well that our cub tried to repulse the advances of the strange male.

On the afternoon of October 17, Kay was again with the family. As usual all were together, a closely knit group that never fought, even small gazelle fawns being shared so amicably that growls were rare. Yet the following afternoon the two cubs had separated from their mother—completely, permanently. Their sudden break at the age of fifteen months was dramatic. We had no intimation that it would occur. Unlike lion and leopard cubs, these youngsters did not sever the social bonds gradually by first taking tentative, solitary excursions; they even left their mother before they could hunt well. Ron confirmed such behavior in Nairobi Park, where he watched two litters separating suddenly from their mothers, one at the age of sixteen months, the other at seventeen.

The two sisters lost weight, their hip bones protruding more and more. Once again we worried about their welfare.

One day the two cheetahs rested near our house, both so terribly gaunt that when Kay and Anneke found a dead gazelle fawn they carried it to where the cats had been lying in order to give them this small offering. But they had vanished. Later Hans told them that the cheetah had killed a gazelle for themselves near his house. In December, as in the previous year, they left Seronera.

Two months later, on February 14, I was hiking near the Barafu kopjes some twenty-five miles east of Seronera, when I saw a cheetah at rest along one of the many erosion terraces in that part of the plains. Slowly moving closer, I finally reclined a hundred feet from her. Casually, as if such meetings were routine, we looked at each other. Suddenly I recognized her: she was one of the sisters. She had severed her ties with her sibling and was now leading a solitary existence typical of her species. We remained there quietly. After some fifteen minutes she jerked to attention and then I too heard the bleat of a gazelle fawn. Four adult gazelle and a fawn swept over a nearby rise closely pursued by two jackals. The cheetah sprinted past me and after a brief chase slapped the fawn and grabbed its neck. She was now an adept huntress. The jackals, deprived of their meal, trotted up to the kill, hoping at least for the scraps. But they saw me and bolted, looking back in a harried manner as if this corner of the plains was becoming rather overcrowded with predators.

The cheetah carried her unexpected kill 250 feet to a small waterhole and there began to eat. Crawling closer on my hands and knees, I was soon within fifteen feet of her. She paused occasionally, glancing at me with guileless eyes, then resumed her meal. I was quite astonished at her acceptance of me. While she had learned to tolerate vehicles, even to the extent of jumping on their hoods and using such vantage points to look around, she must have had few encounters with persons on foot. Thirty-five minutes after making the kill, she finished eating and sat down, scanning the limitless expanse with the wind whipping into her face. Ambling to the pool, she crouched down and lapped some water only ten feet from me. I purred but she ignored this blatant overture. Abruptly she walked up the slope a hundred feet, then returned, drank again, and checked over the remnants of the kill. After that she reclined fifteen feet away, her back to me. Never had I been treated with such studied indifference and it almost rankled. Over 1½ hours had now elapsed since the appearance of the fawn. A hooded vulture wheeled over us, its eyes fixed on scraps of skin and bone. Slowly the cheetah walked away, past the pool, up a slope, and out of sight, leaving me alone to exult over the fleeting embrace of our spirits.

Such meetings are immensely satisfying as token returns to a world from which man has long been an outcast. I remember my elation when one day a curious gorilla and I sat together on the same branch in the wilds of the Congo. Animals are obviously amenable to taming and that is what some biologists have done with their study subjects. Groups of Japanese macaques were tamed by providing them with food so that now these animals climb up your legs and search for tidbits in your pockets; by using salt as bait, Valerius Geist was able to get Canadian mountain sheep so used to him that he could readily touch them. The results these studies produced were remarkable. How much more could I learn about lions as an accepted pride member! However, unless the animals are strictly protected, as was the case with the monkeys and sheep, the temptation to become too friendly with one's study subjects should be resisted, for such intimacy may be their death warrant. All projects come to an end. What happens to the animals then? Unafraid of man, they are easily killed by poachers, when they raid crops, and in other situations. An overly tame animal is not even desirable in a reserve. One elephant in an African national park became so used to a biologist that it accepted oranges from him. Should that elephant decide to raid tourist cars for such delicacies, the fruits of its labor would be a bullet in the head from the gun of a warden.

My cheetah friend from the plains arrived back at Seronera in April, her sister in May, and her mother a month later. All three roamed over essentially the same area, none laying claim to a particular plot of land. One would never have guessed that they were related to each other, for they never associated. Every species' virtues and vices are uniquely its own, yet in my world of reason I could not help wondering why cheetah dealt in absolutes, why they should avoid contact so completely. When two of them saw each other they veered apart or merely watched until one moved from sight. The mother had a new family, three cubs, which must have been conceived some seventeen months after she had given birth to her previous litter. One of the cubs was ill. It trailed the others listlessly and was unsteady on its feet. Kay and I longed to raise one of these enchanting creatures and debated whether or not to take it home. But we hesitated, knowing of the responsibility such a pet engenders, and realizing that we would be leaving the Serengeti in a few months. In the meantime it disappeared.

One morning the mother left her remaining two cubs along a sparsely wooded gulley while she pursued and captured a gazelle. Standing by the kill, she chirped loudly. It is such a strange and ephemeral sound from so large a cat that I looked around the trees for some exotic bird the first time I heard it. Low chirrs were interspersed with the chirps, both calls signifying "come here" to the cubs. The cubs came —and so did another female with two cubs from a different direction. The two litters were of similar age. The new female approached with her head lowered in threat, but the other merely chirped and chirped. The newcomer suddenly fled, her cubs at heel. Becoming bold, a cub chased the retreating family and attacked another cub, hissing and cuffing. Both mothers rushed up, intent on defending their young, and once again the new one retreated, followed by her cubs—and also by a cub from the other litter. The families separated. The one mother ate, rested, seemingly quite unaware of the fact that she had lost half her litter. However, the other female knew that she had one cub too many. Yet she could not distinguish the changeling from her own. Consequently she repulsed them all. Every time a cub came near she narrowed her eyes to slits of gold, bared her teeth, and furiously slapped at them so hard that her paws hit the ground with a loud plop when she missed. After being clouted several times, all cubs cringed and abjectly crawled around just out of her reach. Finally she retreated from them. The cubs had no trouble in recognizing the stranger in their midst, for they exchanged blows with it several times. The mother was in a torment all day, vacillating between leaving the cubs and returning to them, with the result that she ended up by circling them. Several times she gave loud, ringing chirps, and the cubs ran to her exuberantly only to be hit again. I left the cheetah at dusk, fearing that all three cubs would be abandoned, but somehow the two families sorted out their litters during the night.

On May 19 one of the sisters was being courted by a male not known to me. She was about twenty-two months old at the time and probably in her first period of heat. Both cheetah were excited, chirring and chirping constantly. She walked off, closely followed by her suitor, then swatted him gently in the face before coyly rolling over and squirming on her back. The two had unfortunately chosen the airfield for their courtship, a location that hardly assured them peace. When several workmen rolled a barrel past them, the male retreated, but she, quite perversely, remained in the shade of an airplane wing. Her allure proved stronger than his fear, and he joined her again. During the next disturbance he sought refuge in a patch of tall grass nearby. I could see him there most of the day, waiting, only the top of his head visible. At dusk the airfield finally grew silent. He came forth, only to have her amble into a hangar. After some hesitation he entered too. She teased him mercilessly, flopping before him with wild abandon, then leaping ahead as soon as he came close to her. This she repeated often, at times varying the routine by raking him across the face with her claws. Yet he merely chirped. Having courted beneath a plane and in a hangar, she searched for further novelty—and found it on the top of my car. She leaped on the hood and sat there as if daring the male to join her. But his ardor was tempered with restraint and once more he just waited. A few minutes later she joined him and they walked off into the darkness. Having made an appointment to meet someone, I left the pair, confident that I would find them the following morning. I searched for them at dawn, spending several hours at the task without success, much to my annoyance, for I had never observed a cheetah courtship in detail before. On two previous occasions when I had seen courting males with a female, the animals fled as soon as they perceived me.

My findings that adult females are solitary and have contact with one or more males only when in heat suggest one reason why captives have so rarely bred. Zoos usually keep all their cheetah in one enclosure, forcing the animals into a continuous contact quite contrary to their way of life. Perhaps females need the stimulation of strange males before becoming sexually aroused. In this context it is interesting that a private zoo in Italy has had exceptional success in twice breeding a female by borrowing a male from a neighboring zoo when she came into heat.

Our attention that dry season was focused on the other sister because she had mated soon after I had met her on the plains. In early July, as she reached the age of two years, her breasts enlarged and we knew that birth was imminent. On July 12, as I was cruising around with a visiting friend, Bob Krear, we saw two cars parked on the plains, the people obviously intent on something in the grass. With curiosity overcoming my reluctance to join a crowd, we investigated.

There, in a bower of grass stems, were three cheetah cubs a day or two old. The mother was just carrying a fourth cub away, heading straight across the plains toward a thicket nine hundred feet away. When the other cars departed, I knelt down by the cubs and cupped one of the tiny bodies in my hands. It weighed little more than half a pound, and its eyes were closed, giving its face a puckered look as if it were squinting into the sun. It was so frail, yet it already rebelled against the new sensation of being held by squirming and chirring softly. I tucked it back into the grass and soon its mother came at a trot. She carried them all away, one at a time, and then she returned once more and sniffed intently around the lair as if to make certain that none had been forgotten. Finally she departed, but, just to make absolutely sure, she checked the site again.

The cubs remained hidden in their thicket for over a month. I was tempted to spend much time with these youngsters, to watch them grow, to observe how their mother cared for them, but I was afraid to disturb them. Cheetah are subtle and deliberate creatures. They may seem to ignore an intrusion, but they might subsequently move the cubs to another and less suitable site or even abandon them. I did not want to burden my conscience with their deaths and, besides, some information on young cheetah had already been collected by others. Joy Adamson, whose tame but free-living cheetah had several litters, found that cubs can stand up by the age of nine days, that their eyes remain closed for as long as eleven days, and that they can walk quite well at twenty-one days. P. Florio and L. Spinelli published a report on a litter of captive cheetah that was raised by the mother. In it they wrote that "at the age of 18 days the cubs started to eat donkey meat regurgitated by the female . . ." I never saw such regurgitation in the wild, perhaps because only very small cubs are fed like that. Various members of the dog family feed pups by regurgitation but cats had not been reliably reported to do so before.

Simon and Laila Trevor, who were photographing the cheetah and other animals in the Serengeti at the time, saw the mother lead her four cubs from the thicket on August 15. During the next four days she somehow lost a cub, for Simon and Laila saw her take only three youngsters to a kill on August 19. This may have been their first visit to a carcass. The gazelle was not quite dead and the cubs were frightened when it kicked. For them the long task of becoming hunters had begun. In mid-September another cub vanished. The fate of the others remained unknown to me, for I left the Serengeti, my project finished.

The cheetah had taught me much of their life, but I was not satisfied. Having reached a peak of evolutionary perfection, why were these cats so scarce? Food was plentiful and readily caught; females reached maturity earlier, reproduced faster, and had larger litters than other big cats; and the death rate of young was not excessive. The reason for the cheetah's rarity must be discovered, for without help from man this enigmatic cat may well continue its retreat into extinction.

Kay had returned to America the previous month with Eric and Mark, terribly sad at this final parting from the Serengeti. The three generations of cheetah had held a special place in her heart. Knowing such animals individually, one begins to view an area with a new intimacy and with a caring that turns into a special enchantment; and then, as life renews itself, there is a feeling that things will continue unchanged for ever and ever. All this heightens the pain of leaving, yet at the same time makes it more bearable.

HUNTING DOGS

I HAD READ A NUMBER OF ACCOUNTS ABOUT HUNTING DOGS before beginning my project in the Serengeti and few had anything good to say about these animals. A vignette from Carl and Mary Akeley's book *Lions, Gorillas and Their Neighbors* is rather typical:

> Carl reached for my little .275 Hoffman and the moment I put the brake on the car he began to shoot. There was no need to stalk these beasts from the ground. Sportsmanship did not demand it . . . In a few seconds three shots told off three dogs and scattered the rest of the pack . . .
> "Go on, follow them!" Carl commanded. My rickety car lurched ahead in hot pursuit. Three more shots! Down went three more dogs . . .
> "Go on!" he shouted, "I want them all."

After shooting all nine dogs Akeley declared with satisfaction: "That's the first shooting on this whole trip that I've enjoyed."

The purported reason for such antipathy is that dogs are said to annihilate wildlife populations or at least drive them out of an area, and that they may attack livestock. But I suspect that a less tangible reason is involved too. Hunting dogs chase and attack their quarry in daytime and finally kill it untidily by disemboweling. This has given them the reputation of being ferocious, lustful killers. The noble lion, the king of beasts, usually does his deeds under the cover of darkness, strangling the victim neatly but slowly. Some moral could be drawn from this. Physical appearance also affects man's judgment of animals, and hunting dogs are not particularly prepossessing. They are small animals, weighing about forty pounds, with a scruffy brownish coat that is splotched with white, black, and yellow. Although they are not closely related to domestic dogs, judging by their dentition and the fact that they have only four toes on each foot, they vaguely resemble the rheumy-eyed mongrels in the African villages. But they do have a kind of beauty— speed, and strength and a natural grace of movement—an image forged and tested by evolution to create a perfection all its own.

Little was known about the behavior of hunting dogs until in 1964 the German ethologist Wolfdietrich Kühme studied a pack for several months in the Serengeti. I had read his intriguing scientific report, in which, for example, he described how after a pack had killed and eaten, the dogs headed back to the den: "After 5 minutes they returned to the burrow and disgorged the meat in front of the begging pups and the guards who had stayed behind." It is an unadorned statement, but one that evokes a deep responsiveness, for these simple words create a vision of a society that amicably shares its food and takes special care of its young, traits man numbers among his ideals. It is not familiarity with a species but the lack of it that breeds contempt. Those who would persecute the hunting dog might hestitate to do so after observing its family life.

I arrived in the Serengeti most eager to observe hunting dogs. They were so rare, however, that five months passed before I even found a pack. Cruising around Seronera one morning, I suddenly saw the heads of several dogs peering above the grass, their parabolic ears cocked in my direction. Slowly I drove closer, but I need not have worried about disturbing them. Hunting dogs have little fear of cars, nor it seems of anything else, for their world consists primarily of creatures that are either eaten or ignored. I parked about a hundred feet from them and waited. There were twelve dogs, nine adults and three pups about seven months old, at rest in the shade of an acacia. Three hyenas rested at the periphery of the pack. Nearby was a sloping granite boulder with a small depression filled with water. When several dogs trotted over to drink, one hyena followed and all lapped up water together, their heads only a foot or two apart. Having observed the constantly strained relations between various kinds of big cats, such mutual tolerance between hunting dogs and hyenas was a revelation. Afterward a dog trotted to the car, inspecting it. He stood beneath the window and looked up at me, his alert brown eyes taking my measure, and then returned to the shade of the tree. On other occasions dogs sometimes reared up on the bumper or chewed on a tire.

All pack members rested until 4:30 p.m. At that time two dogs rose and decided that the others must get up too. Running from dog to dog, their white-tipped tails raised in excitement, they nipped the laggards in the flank or rump, they nudged them, pulled their ears, tried to burrow their noses beneath them, and jabbed them with their forelegs in a show of friendly aggression. Their lips were retracted in a gleaming grin of white teeth, and all the while they emitted a twittering sound, like a flock of agitated birds, interspersed with whines. Soon all dogs bounded around exuberantly, tails wagging, chasing each other and leaping up against and over each other. Occasionally two dogs walked parallel, their heads lowered while one nuzzled the lips of the other, or one grinned and bowed with forequarters lowered in appeasement before nuzzling another animal. In either case, the gesture was a form of greeting, analogous to head-rubbing in lions. Hunting dogs, both adults and pups, also beg for food by pushing their noses against the lips of another animal. It seems likely that such food-begging behavior has become ritualized in evolution, taking on a new meaning, that of a greeting. The whole scene was one of chaotic, cheerful abandon, a pep rally that helped all to reach a proper pitch of excitement before they set off together on the evening hunt.

At first the pack members played a little while traveling, but soon they settled into a relentless trot. Moving in single file, with the male Notch, who had a deep cut in his left ear, in the lead, the animals dipped into a shallow valley and angled up the far slope. All frivolity was forgotten as they jogged along at some five miles per hour, their tense dark forms conveying an atmosphere of impending doom for some prey. Two of the three hyenas who had spent the day with the pack loped behind, seemingly aware that soon their patience would be rewarded. The pack topped a rise, and there, less than half a mile ahead, was a herd of Thomson's gazelle. The dogs swept ahead on a broad front, racing now at thirty miles per hour, but still undecided about a specific quarry. The gazelle streaked away. Some bounded in that curious gait called spronking, in which all feet hit the ground together. Suddenly a female gazelle broke away from the herd and fled at right angles to it. A dog on the right flank pursued her immediately, and a second dog then did so too. They raced after her, remaining within thirty feet of her, traveling at thirty-five, then forty, and finally at forty-three miles per hour. Perhaps they ran a little faster than that, but by then I was afraid that even a glance at the speedometer while traveling so fast across the uneven terrain might distract me long enough to hurl the car into a termite hill or other obstruction. I concentrated on keeping up with the trio, but the other dogs knew better than to waste their efforts in this fashion. They lagged far behind, running just fast enough to monitor the chase. Soon the gazelle began to veer to the right in a large arc, still closely pursued by the two dogs. Two other dogs noted this maneuver on the part of the gazelle, and, picking up speed, they took a short-cut, bearing down on their quarry from the side. Intercepted, the gazelle swerved, a tactic that slowed her down. As she turned to head in a new direction, there was the rest of the pack barring her way. Her capitulation was sudden and complete: she slowed to an aimless walk and a dog grabbed her thigh and pulled her down.

The three pups had fallen far behind the pack, but now they hurried up as fast as their short legs would carry them. When the pups arrived at the kill the adults had just gulped their first bite or two of meat. As if on signal all adults stepped back from the carcass and permitted the pups to eat by themselves; even though the adults were hungry, the youngsters had exclusive rights to the kill until they were satiated. As the pups gorged themselves, the adults surrounded the kill, forming a protective circle past which no hyena dared venture. Within minutes eight hyenas and three jackals hovered nearby. A few sidled closer until sharp nips from the dogs drove them back. Finally replete, the pups stepped away from the kill and the adults took over the spoils. Once Robert Ardrey watched a similar hunt with me, and the violence of the kill followed by selfless sharing obviously had an impact on him, for he later wrote: "I find it a subject for meditation that within my limited career of animal-watching the two images most horrid and sublime were separated by little over sixty seconds." Morality is not just confined to the beliefs of man; there is also a racial morality, or habitual behavior, which in hunting dogs assures that the pups receive a major share of the food and are guarded from marauding hyenas. Certainly the fascination of hunting dogs stems in part from the fact that they are psychologically close to us.

Notch and his pack remained around Seronera for a few days but then vanished, drawn on by a compulsive force to move that has no equal among other African predators. Hunting dogs have been seen on the barren summit glaciers of 19,340 foot Mt. Kilimanjaro. What possessed them to make this ascent? Packs do not confine themselves to a relatively small area as do lion prides but roam over vast distances. They sweep through an area like a storm, always staking their future on a distant hunting ground, regardless of the amount of prey available to them. Some packs trailed the migratory herds to the plains and then retreated to the woodlands for the dry season. I do not know how many square miles of terrain a pack uses in the course of a year. The travels of one pack encompassed some 275 square miles as it moved between Naabi Hill and Seronera, but its total range was probably at least three times that figure. Notch's pack moved to the Simba kopjes soon after it left Seronera, and then, three months later, I met it at Olduvai Gorge, about forty-five miles east of Seronera.

A pack settles down at a den just before a female is due to give birth and it stays at the site for about three months until the pups are big enough to accompany the adults on their endless treks. Only by finding a den would I be able to watch the family life of the dogs in detail. Hans Kruuk, who shared my enthusiasm for dogs, and I located a total of four dens on the plains between 1967 and 1969. But having found the dens, I did not study the animals with the intensity they deserved; I failed the dogs and myself because of a personal idiosyncrasy. The mere academic search for facts becomes hollow to me unless the situation also has an aesthetic appeal. To observe a pack returning from a chase, the dogs bounding exuberantly toward home, mere black specks skimming across the immensity of the plain, while at the den, having spotted the successful hunters, the guards wag their tails and give joyful little leaps of anticipation, makes the whole scene alive and intensely beautiful. The charm is lost when other cars disrupt the mood by their presence day after day. The occasional visitor was welcome, even though I might be momentarily annoyed at the intrusion. The dogs could not help but captivate any sympathetic observer and in that lies their best hope for survival. But often several cars encircled a pack, and I particularly resented one photographer who every year rushed to the scene as soon as we discovered a den and simply usurped the site for weeks.

I found my first den in late March of 1967 southeast of Naabi Hill. Driving across the featureless plain one day, I spotted several inquisitive heads looking from the multiple entrances of a burrow. The pack had been spending the hot midday hours underground in an abandoned hyena warren and the approach of my car had alerted them. There were eleven pack members—four adult males, six yearling males, and an adult female. As I discovered later, many packs contain more males than females, and in the population as a whole the ratio is six to four in favor of the former. This uneven sex ratio is already evident in small pups. A preponderance of males is unusual in a population and I do not know the reasons for it. The sole female was obviously lactating; in fact her fourteen teats were so pendulous and engorged that she was little more than an ambulatory milk bar.

During April and May, I spent many days with this pack and so did Alan and Joan Root, who had then just begun to film my project for the National Geographic Society. In the process of making wildlife films, Alan and Joan have become far more knowledgeable about animals than many professional zoologists. Alan's impulsive and uninhibited nature is nicely balanced by Joan's serene competence, and together they produced a fine film entitled *The Serengeti Lion*. With typical generosity they told me each day what they had observed, and their accounts greatly enriched my notes on hunting dogs, cheetah, lions, and other animals. Aside from that, they were delightful companions, whose intermittent stays in the Serengeti we always anticipated with pleasure.

I saw the pups for the first time on April 6. The female went to one of the den entrances shortly after dawn and whined softly. And suddenly the pups came tumbling out, an avalanche of small yipping bodies, fourteen of them. They were two to three weeks old, still somewhat unsteady on their feet, floppy-eared, pug-faced, with dark-gray woolly coats; they also had white tail tips and white spots on each side of the anus. A yearling male ran over excitedly and regurgitated a chunk of meat among the pups with a convulsive heave. But the female grabbed and bolted it. Then she ducked into the den, followed by her swarm of offspring. When that evening the pups ventured out once more, the adults were ecstatic to see them. They nuzzled and nibbled them, they turned them over and leaped around them, all the while chittering in a frenzy of affection. Three males disgorged meat. Apparently the mother thought the pups were still too small for such friendly pandemonium. Picking up a youngster by the head, she carried it into the den. Ever helpful, a male grabbed a struggling pup by the tail and dropped him into the burrow. Hunting dogs obviously do not use the precise neck grip that cats employ for transporting young.

Two weeks later, Alan told me that the pack had killed a zebra that morning. Not having anything urgent to do, I decided to observe the den all night. The animals spent the afternoon lazing around, their abdomens taut with meat. At 5:25 p.m. three yearling males peered into the den, then hurriedly backed off as the pups tumbled out. Their mother ambled over to them, and they squatted in a crowded line on each side of her and suckled. After a few minutes her resigned look changed to one of temper and she drew back her lips and snapped at the scrambling youngsters until they dispersed. At dusk a heard of zebra passed the den at a distance of three hundred feet. The pack decided on an impromptu hunt. Blacky, a male who often took the initiative in such matters, led six other males after the zebra. But instead of fleeing, the zebra merely crowded together and faced their puny adversaries. When two dogs ventured closer, a stallion charged them, head lowered as if to bite, and the dogs leaped nimbly aside. Suddenly the pack charged and the startled zebra fled, braying. After a chase of only three hundred feet, the dogs halted, having failed to find a vulnerable individual, neither a foal nor a sick adult. Another zebra herd was nearby, and the pack chased it for half a mile, their hard bodies racing lightly along the flanks of the thundering animals. Then, abruptly, they called off the hunt and returned to the den. By chasing herd after herd until they find a vulnerable animal, dogs serve an important function in weeding out those that are physically below par.

It was dark now, and the dogs settled themselves for the night, the adults huddling in several tight clusters near the den, the pups underground. At 10:00 p.m. a violent squall lashed the plains. My world became a void of abysmal darkness filled with a metallic roar as the elements hammered against the unyielding sides of the car. Peering into the raging night, the beam of my flashlight cut through the shafts of water to reveal the ghostly form of the female frantically rushing in and out of the flooded den, with each trip rescuing a pup. She left the pups by the entrance, which, because of some excavated earth, was a little higher than the surrounding terrain. The males, too, had found refuge on bits of high ground. Once the female picked up a pup as if to evacuate the site entirely, but the gale buffeted her so much that she abandoned the attempt. For two hours the night howled and then the storm passed abruptly. The angry clouds thinned, and moonlight suffused the plains. Before me stretched not land but a sea, glistening like obsidian, and then, as the clouds parted, like an arctic waste. It was silent except for the whimpering of the pups, who remained soggy and shivering by their den throughout the dismal night.

At 6:10 a.m. the males rose stiffly. Padding about across the muddy ground, they greeted each other, and left together on the morning hunt. The female remained with her pups. I followed the departing dogs. But every hollow was still filled with water and my car almost immediately slipped into a flooded warthog burrow, the wheels churning futily. I stepped out of the car to inspect the situation and the dogs promptly surrounded the car to inspect me. They stood forty feet away, heads cocked alertly, as I dug around the wheels. Their curiosity satisfied, they continued their tireless search for breakfast. Not wanting to miss the hunt, I followed on foot. But my trot was not tireless. Although at first I was a scant three hundred feet behind the pack, the distance between us widened gradually after the dogs speeded up on sighting wildebeest. They scattered the herds, but, finding nothing to their liking, harried some zebra instead. The plain sloped away to the east at this point, and I could see the dogs surround a lagging zebra mare, pulling at her flanks, biting at her abdomen and nose, and yanking at her tail, until she sank to the ground after nine minutes. Standing there, deprived of my culture's armor, I was just one predator among many. The dogs and I were once again wanderers on a prehistoric earth. So easily could I have rushed in and taken their kill to feed my primal group, the fierce ghosts of my past urging me to do so but more rational impulses prevailing otherwise. The sound of a car abruptly brought me back to the present. Alan and Joan drove up. Having discovered my abandoned vehicle, they had gone in search of me.

The pups had reoccupied their old burrow but all was not well there. Alan saw the female haul out a dead pup and eat part of it. The following morning she was in the process of moving her litter to another den two hundred feet away when I arrived. Trotting back and forth, she carried the pups one at a time to their new home. She also retrieved three dead pups from the burrow and partially devoured them. Nine pups had survived the storm, six males and three females.

I watched the pack off and on during the following weeks, never ceasing to marvel at the amity of the animals. Hunting dogs and lions both have the same basic goals—to eat and to raise young. Each is obviously successful in these tasks, yet selective forces have shaped their societies in a drastically different manner to achieve the same ends. Whereas the lion obtains his food by force and threat, the hunting dog depends on equitable sharing. Hunting dogs seldom even growl in disputes over a kill. When one animal wants a bone from another, it may lower its forequarters and chitter. This appeasement gesture may stimulate the other to behave likewise, and with both animals acting submissively a fight is unlikely to erupt. There is one report of two dogs fighting almost to the death, but the fact that neither Kühme, Hans, nor I ever observed serious disputes shows that these are rare indeed. One published account claims that the males in a pack have a dominance hierarchy and that the females have one too, a pattern similar to that found among wolves. Although some individuals may displace others around a kill or at a den, it was my impression that in the packs I observed such interactions were often based on occasional antipathies between certain individuals rather than on a rigid hierarchy. However, packs probably differ in their social structure, depending on size and the age composition of the members. Packs need to be studied in far greater detail than they have been to date.

Sharing meat is anathema to lions but it is a basic way of life to hunting dogs. Pack members obviously derive pleasure from feeding the pups and guards at a den. One dog in a pack had a shriveled hindleg. He dropped far behind during a chase, and when he finally reached the kill site no meat remained on the carcass. As soon as he begged

Wildlife concentrates near a waterhole in the Northern Extension.

A giraffe keeps a wary eye on a nearby lioness.

Stiffly alert and poised for flight, a reedbuck watches several lionesses.

Crowded around a waterhole, wildebeest become vulnerable to predation.

A pack of hunting dogs scans the plains for prey.

Hunting dogs pursue a zebra herd.

A zebra foal has been overtaken and pulled to a halt.

Hunting dogs crowd around the kill.

Hunting dog pups play with a grass tuft.

A blackbacked jackal tries to chase vultures from the remains of a kill.

A hyena carries off a gazelle.

A stalking leopard.

A leopardess licks her large son.

George captures a sick zebra foal while simulating the life of an early hominid.

Myles Turner directs the destruction of a poacher's camp.

Cheetah family at rest.

A cheetah female with her three cubs.

A cheetah drags her gazelle kill.

A giraffe feeds in our front yard.

Blowing out the contents of an ostrich egg.

A picnic in the Moru Kopjes.

*George feeds Giri, our pet
warthog.*

*Fungus, our banded
mongoose.*

Eric and Rameses, our lion cub.

Mark wrestles with Rameses.

from the others, some meat was regurgitated for him. It is probably important that all pack members remain at about the same physiological state of hunger. If some were gorged and others lean, the former would have little interest in contributing to the communal hunts. Hungry members might find it difficult to locate the pack again should they decide to search for prey on their own. Thus, food sharing is probably essential if packs are to retain their cohesiveness. Sharing pervades dog society and in no context is it more evident than in the care of pups. Lion cubs often survive in spite of rather than because of parental attention, but the dogs' existence revolves around their young. Males feed, guard, and fondle the pups almost as much as do the females. Richard Estes and John Goddard reported a fascinating incident from Ngorongoro Crater in which the only female in a pack died, yet the males successfully raised her litter, surely the ultimate test of their ability and devotion.

Although both dogs and lions live in groups, there are some major differences in their social systems. All dogs belong to packs in which most spend their whole life, in contrast to all male lions and some lionesses, which lead part of their existence outside of a pride. Whereas members of a lion pride may be widely scattered, dog packs usually remain together. Individuals may become separated during a chase after prey but their bell-like rallying call—hoo-hoo-hoo—soon brings them back together again. All pups stay with the pack for at least awhile after they grow up with the result that large packs consist of extended families comprising several generations of both sexes. Yearlings occasionally split off on their own, judging by the composition of some packs. Large packs, too, divide, for it would be difficult to find enough food for all members. Packs with some forty individuals have been seen in the Serengeti, but the average there as well as in other parts of Africa is about ten. Possibly packs retain some social ties after splitting, for individual dogs have been reported to switch from one pack to another. It seems unlikely that a pack would readily accept a total stranger.

With the major emphasis of my project being the relationship of predators to their prey, I was interested to find out precisely what the dogs killed and how much of it. Some hunts began leisurely with the pack first exploring its surroundings. One morning the dogs set off with determination, but soon various other matters drew their attention. One dog nosed an abandoned burrow. Another rolled on his back by a stunted shrub, possibly impregnating the site with his powerful body odor, before spraying several squirts of urine. A male may lift not only one hindleg when squirting but also both of them in a perfect handstand. Meanwhile the other pack members had trotted ahead and stopped on a small rise to scan the horizon. Gazelle often graze in the vicinity of a den—prey does not vacate a locality merely because dogs are there—but as soon as they see a pack on the move most flee fast and far. They are so apprehensive of dark forms on the horizon that even a family of warthog may panic them. The dogs ignored the gazelle but not a hyena. It had probably just settled down after a night of prowling when the dogs bounded up full of mischief. Dogs do not like hyenas near their pups and, besides, they seem to enjoy tormenting them. Dancing around the hapless animal, one dog or another darted in to nip it in the rump. The hyena whirled around in a tight circle with its hindquarters tucked in while growling most ferociously. It finally broke through the cordon and raced into a nearby pool. There it sat while its tormentors patrolled the shoreline. But the dogs soon lost interest in the hyena, and, after lapping some water, they departed.

The Hunter led the pack straight across the plains. No tempting prey was in sight but he had apparently made up his mind and the others followed. He or Blacky usually led the pack, determining where to go, what to hunt, and often what animal to select. Other adults also took the initiative at times, but more often than not one of these two leaders decided things. Some packs had a leadership core of several adults, never yearlings, and Richard Estes observed a pack that had only one leader. Leadership does not, however, imply priority in other matters such as obtaining part of the kill. Brown Dog was the epitome of a follower, yet he had just as much right to a carcass as a leader. I particularly remember one morning when The Hunter wanted zebra for breakfast. None were near the den. So he headed north with his retinue, passing through thousands of gazelle with no more than cursory interest. The other males made a couple of half-hearted pursuits, but he forged relentlessly ahead, drawn on by his private vision. And the others followed unquestioningly. Miles later the pack finally came across some zebra and killed a foal. After bolting as much meat as they could hold, all returned to the den. This quixotic whim of The Hunter had entailed five hours of arduous treking over a distance of twenty-five miles!

But that morning the pack simply looked for anything it could catch. Moving along in a ragged front, they now settled into that inexorable trot, which in its determination has an almost sinister force. Black clouds roiled ahead and the hounds bounded toward them as if their play in the Elysian fields was ended and they were now returning to a Stygian world. A herd of wildebeest appeared, a dark mass moving ponderously under the glowering sky. The dogs halted, scrutinizing the herd intently. I knew that they were looking for a small wildebeest calf. They spotted one, less than two months old and still in its light-brown natal coat. Blacky took the lead as the pack moved closer at a steady lope. Then, when the dogs were about four hundred feet from the herd, they bunched up and stealthily walked closer, their ears retracted, their heads lowered but with muzzles pointing forward, while the wildebeest stood looking at them. The dogs reminded me of a gang of toughs just before a fight. The formation has an important function. A slowly moving, bunched pack can approach prey more closely than a scattered one. Suddenly the tails of the dogs whipped up and the pack dashed at the herd, which wheeled and fled in a compact mass. The wildebeest ran slowly, at about twenty-five miles per hour, the calves crowding the flanks of their mothers toward the middle of the herd. Dogs must scatter the herd to reach a calf, and they now raced behind and beside it, yipping with excitement, each animal an integral part in this cooperative effort. When the herd circled, two dogs met it from the front. This was enough to split the herd and a fragment of it with a calf veered to one side. The pack immediately concentrated on that calf. At first its mother tried to place herself between the dogs and her offspring, but soon she just ran along, trailed by her doomed young. While two dogs nipped her legs, one of the others bit the calf in the thigh and pulled it to a standstill. Within seconds the others tore at its rump and abdomen. The chase had lasted only half a mile. The female wildebeest ran on. She stopped briefly to look back when her calf bleated, but then hurried after the departing herd. Ten minutes later, the first dog set off for home, his belly full, and five minutes after that the last dog abandoned the untidy remains to a hyena. And at the den the pups and their mother awaited their share. The morning's hunt had required only six miles of travel. At that season food is plentiful on the plains, which is probably one reason why packs tend to have pups there between January and May.

Hunting dogs killed whatever they could, but Thomson's gazelle and wildebeest were their main food on the plains and around Seronera. Some fifty-seven percent of their kills consisted of wildebeest, most of them calves, from January to June, and twenty-four percent of Thomson's gazelle, in addition to such items as warthog, zebra, and Grant's gazelle. When available, small wildebeest calves were favored, not only because they provided much meat but also because they were easy to catch. Dogs generally do not like to run far, and if a chase lasts for more than two miles they may abandon it. Pursuits after wildebeest calves were over after an average of only .7 mile and they were successful three quarters of the time after the dogs had selected a specific quarry. A large gazelle, on the other hand, required a chase of one mile, on the average, and only half of the attempts ended in a kill. But from July to December, when small wildebeest calves were unavailable, hunting dogs had to live mainly on gazelle and seventy-nine percent of their kills consisted of this species during those months. In addition to their cooperative effort, dogs used two other techniques to approach the fleet gazelle. At times a pack would run full speed over the crest of a rise, both surprise and momentum carrying them close to the prey. At other times a pack would loiter near a gazelle herd, waiting, it seemed, for that brief period at dusk when it is too dark to see well yet still light enough to distinguish individuals. At that time the dogs launched their attack.

Hunting dogs may also pursue adult wildebeest and zebra on occasion. Being too small to kill such large animals efficiently, they may have to tear and bite at their quarry for fifteen or more minutes before it sinks to the ground. Usually an animal did nothing to defend itself. Sometimes it stared mutely into space, probably in shock, at others it lunged futilely ahead. In every instance such animals had been selected because they had lagged behind the fleeing herd, obviously sick. I realized that if dogs did not remove them, they would die a lingering death, yet I could not develop an indifference to the final agony of such beasts.

On two occasions a wildebeest sought the protection of my car after having been attacked by dogs. That animals facing death, whether from illness or when pursued by predators, may overcome their aversion to man has been reported a number of times, but no one knows the reasons for such mysterious behavior. An account in the monthly park reports from the Serengeti gives another instance of it:

> On 3rd October, death, as it must to all creatures, came to one of the fine old buffalo bulls who live near the Wogakuria Guard Post. At 3 p.m. this old buffalo walked right into the Guard Post and lay down within 6 feet of the Ranger uniport door. After their initial surprise, the Rangers, seeing he could not rise, attempted to get him on his feet, but all efforts to move him failed. The buffalo died that night, and the Rangers had to dismember the corpse and cart it away on a wheelbarrow. This is the second incident of a buffalo coming right into this camp to die. One can only surmise that, feeling death close, they feel safer near human beings than in the bush, where hyaena and lion would tear them to pieces.

Once a stalwart animal defended itself vigorously against a pack of dogs—not a warthog hooking with curved tusks nor a zebra slashing with sharp hooves, but a mouse. Several dogs met the mouse away from its burrow. When one snapped at it, the rodent turned, squatted on its haunches, and, with tiny forepaws raised and mouth agape, faced its enemies. Startled, the dog leaped back. Another dog poked stiffly at the mouse with one foot and was promptly bitten in the pad. Two more dogs joined the fray only to be attacked by this furry fury, one being nipped in the nose. Finally, after five minutes, longer than it usually took to subdue a wildebeest, a dog grabbed the mouse and shook it.

The hunting dogs are by far the most efficient of the larger predators in the Serengeti: when a pack sets out on a hunt the chances are nine out of ten that it will kill something, or at least scavenge a bit of meat from hyenas. Wondering how much prey The Hunter, Blacky, and other members of that pack actually captured over a long period, Alan and Joan Root and various members of the Research Institute helped me to tally all kills over a sixteen-day period in April. Thirteen wildebeest, five zebra, three Thomson's gazelle, two warthog, and one Grant's gazelle fell prey, a total of twenty-four animals, or 1.5 per day. With wildebeest calves so vulnerable, the dogs killed at the rate of twenty pounds per dog per day, which leaves each dog with twelve pounds of food after the inedible portions are subtracted. Some of this meat went to the pups. Still the pack killed considerably more than it could eat. Since dogs generally do not return to a carcass for a second meal, the excess went to hyenas and jackals.

All predators kill more than they need if they have the opportunity to do so. Hunger is not always a prerequisite for hunting and killing. An incident with hyenas showed this dramatically. It had been a violent night, with clouds scudding low over the Mukoma plain lashed on by rain and wind. Thomson's gazelle had massed on that plain and several hyenas had raced among them, blindly biting and ripping at the animals as they blundered around in the darkness. At dawn I went to the area in search of lions. As the golden rays crept over the low curtain of drifting clouds, the grass glistened with hoary splendor. But there were also strange white mounds. Driving closer, I saw they were the bellies of dead gazelle. Puzzled, I examined some and found deep bite wounds, often around the heads. A few survivors hobbled on the battlefield, skin torn off their flanks, legs dangling uselessly. And lying here and there, happily bloated, were the perpetrators of the carnage. Seeing Hans's car stopped in the distance, I knew that he, too, had found the bodies. Together we collected thirty-three uneaten ones for autopsy. Over a hundred had been killed or maimed.

Periods when a predator can catch its meals with ease are uncommon, and such occasional wanton sprees have little effect on the prey populations. And, besides, meat is never wasted. What one predator cannot eat simply benefits another. Later that year, I tracked a dog pack for several days near Seronera at a time when prey was not abundant. Each dog then killed only three pounds per day. A dog captures about fifty to sixty animals a year, over half of them young and many others sick. This, together with the fact that hunting dogs are rare, points to the obvious conclusion that the impact of these predators on the Serengeti prey community is small. Man is always quick to condemn but slow to gather facts, and, if some are available, even slower to accept them. If the reverse were true, the hunting dog's future in Africa would be somewhat brighter.

With meat plentiful and care devoted, the nine pups at the den thrived. The female moved her young again on April 22, carrying them to a new den nearly half a mile away. Perhaps she did this because several lions had recently stopped at the den and sniffed around. The adults had stood at a respectful distance and barked without attempting to attack, as they are sometimes said to do. The pups now spent more and more time around the den entrance, wandering up to fifteen feet from it. They tumbled around in play, wrestling and having tugs-of-war with tufts of grass, they bumbled about exploring, and they begged for meat from whichever adult came near. By early May, when they were about seven weeks old, they had turned from puppies into miniature dogs. Their muzzles and legs had lengthened and their huge ears were now erect; their coats were splotched in the adult pattern. With this physical change came a mental one too. Their interests were now directed away from the den. Although they still slept underground and dived unhesitatingly toward the entrance when an adult barked in alarm, they tried to become members of the pack. When the males set out on a hunt, the pups gamboled behind them, yipping with exuberance. After some three hundred feet the males would stop, then patiently lead the pups back to the den before departing once more. On May 12, at 4:00 p.m., the female suddenly decided to vacate the den and she led her excited brood to a new one nearby. This den remained their base for about a month. On June 9 all were still there, fine, husky youngsters almost three months old. At last able to keep up with the pack, their time to begin a nomadic life had arrived. When I checked the den six days later it was empty.

As one delves into the life of an animal, more and more questions obtrude for which no ready answers exist. One obvious question is: "Why are hunting dogs so rare?" Perhaps no more than three hundred dogs, excluding pups in the den, inhabit the ecological unit. Here are unsurpassed hunters, which, by virtue of their nomadic existence, are usually near ample prey. A female may have as many as sixteen pups in a litter and young are coddled, as if to assure that many survive. Various factors usually prevent a species from realizing its reproductive potential. For unknown reasons fewer than half of the adult females had young in any one year, and many packs failed to raise their litters, although I had no inkling of what happened to the pups. Yet a third of the dog population consisted of large youngsters, showing that its reproductive success was greater than that of any species of large cat. Myles Turner told me that the dogs had maintained their low numbers since at least 1956. To keep the population stable like that, one third of the adults would either have to emigrate or die each year to make room for the new crop of pups that had grown up. Only disease, I reasoned, could account for such a loss, but I looked in vain for seriously ill animals. Once, however, I saw a sick pup that could not keep up with the pack. It lay down, and the adults turned back and nudged it, urging it to rise. Here was a clue to the fate of dogs, but at the time I did not comprehend the significance of the event.

Late in March 1968, Hans told me that a pack had once again settled at a den near Naabi Hill. The pack consisted of seven males and three females, one of which had sixteen pups. My visits to the den were intermittent and all were still there on May 12. Being preoccupied with lions and chee-tah, I gave little thought to this pack in the ensuing months. Then, on August 16, it suddenly arrived at Seronera. I was delighted to meet the animals again but concerned because all was not well. Two pups had disappeared and several others had weak hindquarters, as if they had been starving. The pack vanished for a week and my hours of searching for it were futile. But on August 23 it reappeared with only twelve pups. A week later, in the evening, the animals swept through Seronera once more, and this time there was no doubt that a disease was raging among them. One male and seven pups had disappeared in the past week and another adult and two pups were sick. A second adult had a spastic tick in its hindleg. The animals staggered along, terribly thin, and a gray mucus clogged the corners of their eyes and mouths. It was important for me to find out what disease afflicted them. Leaving the car, I ran after one of the sick pups, and, after a brief chase, it suddenly rolled on its back in utter submission. The adults either just watched or ig-nored me. I picked the pup up by the scruff and carried it to the car, hoping to deliver it alive the next morning to Bernt Schiemann, a veterinarian who at the time worked in the Corridor on wildlife diseases. The pup reclined unpro-testingly in the back of the car and whimpered quietly to itself. Two hours later it died. Part of Schiemann's autopsy report read: "a typical picture of the gastro-intestinal form of distemper." Only twelve dogs were left by September 8. And when I met the pack once more on November 4 there were only ten out of the original twenty-six dogs—five adults and five pups.

The survivors were back on the plains early in 1969. Since one female was heavily pregnant, I was most eager to find the den site and gather another season of informa-tion. However, I could not find the pack and even an air search failed to reveal it. Somewhere on the eastern plains it raised a litter in privacy, for once not disturbed by cars.

On August 10, almost a year after the onset of the epidemic, the pack returned to Seronera, bringing seven healthy male pups with it.

The discovery that distemper has such a brutal effect on packs provides only a partial answer as to why hunting dogs are so rare. Some other factors must also be operating on the population to keep it stable. A mild case of distemper probably makes the survivors immune, and, given the reproductive potential of the dogs, I would expect the population to fluctuate with the erratic incidence of the disease. But it has apparently not been doing so. I met the pack for the last time in September, just before leaving the Serengeti. The animals trotted along the crest of a ridge with the plains rolling away to the east. They were monuments against the sky, monuments to a land that once was. In it they could move, move toward the retreating horizon as if possessed by an instinctive force to know what lies beyond. But few parks are large enough to hold their elusive spirits, and when they leave the protecting borders they come into conflict with man. Therein may well lie their ultimate demise.

THE MOST
DANGEROUS PREDATOR

Scientists usually come to East Africa for a year or
two, study their chosen subject intensively, and then vanish
like the migratory wildebeest. They are then no doubt ex-
perts in their limited specialty, but they have not had time to
acquire the broad knowledge held by many park wardens.
Some wardens have spent their lives in the wilds, often on
foot, witnessing the rare incidents that can place a species'
behavior into a new perspective and seeing the land with the
historical depth necessary before one can understand it.
Much of what is known about wildlife was until recently
based on their observations. But these wardens are a vanish-
ing breed, political vicissitudes taking a continuous toll because most are British citizens.* With their passing an era
will end, for the new African wardens are desk-bound, concerned with administration rather than with natural history.

* By 1973, Sandy Field and John Owen had left the Tanzanian
park service, as had most other Europeans; Myles Turner had been
transferred to Arusha.

They lack a personal involvement with the parks, they lack the possessiveness that is the basis of dedication. And dedication is surely needed to maintain the wildlife against the constant pressure of poachers and other threats.

Myles Turner has been in charge of protecting the Serengeti for a long time. Raised in Kenya, where he was once a professional hunter, he came to the Serengeti with his wife Kay in 1956 and he has been there ever since. I enjoyed talking to Myles, for one senses his deep commitment to his work and besides he is an excellent observer, who over the years has carefully recorded incidents of interest. He always made an extra effort to report predator kills, to locate lions for me by air, and to help in other ways in spite of being busy leading antipoaching patrols with his staff of about sixty-five rangers. The results of his efforts were evident from the monthly park reports:

August, 1967. On 2nd August, while on patrol in the Ikoma area, the Field Force were in pursuit of a gang of poachers. One of the poachers while trying to escape fell in long grass onto one of his poisoned arrows, which pierced his leg. This man died in 40 minutes in spite of all possible assistance given, a warning to users of this deadly acocanthera poison, the only function of which is killing animals.

September, 1967. September was yet another extremely heavy anti-poaching month with no sign as yet of any lessening of the pressure both inside and outside our boundaries. In the Kira Wira section a strong sweep was carried out between 5th–10th September resulting in the capture of 25 poachers, 23 bows, 71 poisoned arrows, 50 steel wire snares and 4 wheel traps. Two large camps on the Mbalageti were razed to the ground. The Ikoma area, north of the Park, was heavily poached throughout September. Three separate sweeps were made in this area resulting in the

244 · *Golden Shadows, Flying Hooves*

capture of 21 prisoners, 124 steel wire snares, 165 poisoned arrows and 27 bows. The horrors of un- limited poaching were well illustrated by the sight of a) a cow eland caught in a snare by the back leg which was cut to the bone, b) several zebra cut to pieces but still alive in snares, and finally c) a rhino, still walking along with a foot-wide "collar" of red and suppurating flesh around its neck with a broken snare still firmly embedded, dying by inches.

August, 1968. On the lower Ruwana, on the 14th August, our patrol intercepted a man on a bicycle heavily laden with game meat. When asked where he had obtained it, he showed the patrol a full scale game meat butchery in action near the settle- ment. In the butchery, being sold for cash were the meat of 2 eland, 3 wildebeest, 1 topi and a cheetah skin. 5 arrests were made.

April, 1969. The increase in motorised poaching in the Western areas of the Park gives cause for grave concern. On 13th April at about 7 p.m. our Field Force patrol intercepted and captured a jeep vehicle containing two senior Government offi- cials, an Italian contractor and two local people all hunting in the Park. When captured they had already shot: 1 cow eland, 2 wildebeest, 1 topi, 3 warthog, 2 Thomson's gazelle, 1 kori bustard, 1 zebra, 1 hyaena.

The effects of man, the most dangerous predator of all, must also be considered in a study of predator-prey relations. Though I did not have time to study poachers, I wanted to at least become familiar with their techniques, and I was eager to join Myles on an antipoaching patrol. Like many persons who choose to dwell in the earth's lonely places, Myles often shunned social contact, and the patrols with his African staff gave him a means to withdraw and to shake off the heavy moods that sometimes beset him. My request to accompany him was rather ambivalently received and not until many months later did he consent to let me intrude on his private quest.

It was the midafternoon of August 30, 1969, when Myles and I rose in the single-engined Cessna from the landing strip at Seronera and headed southwest. Once in a while I enjoyed flying. I saw the land as a vulture would, the tree-fringed course of the Mbalageti River, the rugged Nyaraboro Hills, and I caught glimpses of secluded valleys that no Land Rover tracks had ever marred. The airplane has become a most useful tool in the Serengeti and other parks, enabling wardens to search for poachers and scientists to census wildlife. It has also become somewhat of a toy. Seduced by the glamour, speed, and ease of flying, some biologists have deluded themselves into thinking that one can learn to understand animals merely by flying over them at sixty miles an hour and at an altitude of six hundred feet. Over a hundred years ago Thoreau warned against men becoming "the tools of their tools." This applies to science as well as to other endeavors.

The Duma River marks the southwestern boundary between the park and the Maswa Game Reserve. The Mamarehe guard post along the Duma was our destination. Two Land Rovers with several rangers and our equipment had already arrived from Seronera by the time we landed. At the river's edge, in the shade of huge fig trees, was a hut Myles used during his periodic visits to the area.

It was still dark the next morning when a servant called "Chai" (tea). With the first light we left camp. Myles headed east into the park, and I accompanied several rangers west into the game reserve. My notes describe the day:

> We head cross-country toward some rocky hills. The terrain is open, broken by occasional acacia thickets and wooded ridges. Next to me in the front seat is the head ranger Okech Onduta, a powerfully built Luo tribesman. Like all rangers he wears dark-green shorts and shirt, but his

mark of distinction is an Australian bush hat. In the back are four more rangers, all armed with rifles. There is little wildlife, only an occasional impala, kongoni, or giraffe. In contrast to the animals within the park, these are extremely shy. Topping a rise, Okech suddenly stiffens. A mile ahead is a flash of white. Binoculars reveal a poacher, wrapped in a white sheet against the morning chill, moving across a tongue of grassland with his friend. The Land Rover bears down on them and they crouch, surreptitiously pushing several wire snares and their bows and arrows beneath some brush. The rangers surround them. Few words are exchanged as the rangers handcuff the two together. The poachers watch the proceedings indifferently, probably used to the procedure from previous encounters with rangers. Two minutes of searching reveal the hidden weapons. I examine some arrows. The points consist of flattened nails heavily smeared with a sticky black poison. This poison is made from the tree *Acocanthera friesiorum* whose wood is cut into small pieces, placed into a clay vessel filled with water, and boiled for about seven hours. The extract is then concentrated by evaporation. The arrows are fletched with vulture feathers, and distinctively carved notches at the end of the shaft identify the owner. The two poachers are taken into the Land Rover and we move on.

At 7:40 a.m., as we drive toward a dry streambed, a poacher breaks cover ahead. Since the car cannot pursue across the rough terrain, the rangers do so on foot. I follow. But after a chase of nearly a mile my breath comes in gasps. The poacher escaped among some kopjes. All of us return to the creek. There in the shade of the embankment is a snared zebra, its viscera piled neatly to one side and the hindquarters sectioned into loads manageable for carrying. The rangers split up, some going upstream, some down. Game trails cross the creek at frequent intervals—and along each trail hangs a snare. These snares are simple but deadly devices. One end of the wire is tied to a tree and the other end, consisting of a large loop, is suspended upright in the trail, tied lightly into place with thin strips of bark. Any animal from a gazelle to an eland that comes along slips its head into the loop. Feeling the wire tighten, it lunges ahead—a fatal response. We smell something dead. Following the odor we come to a mound of grass beneath some shrubs. Pushing the grass aside, I find a male lion, a prime animal. He has been skinned. His feet have also been cut off, for the claws find a ready market as trinkets in the form of necklaces, brooches, and so forth. Poachers hide such carcasses to keep vultures from congregating and advertising the presence of snares. Our lengthy search fails to reveal the poachers' camp and we drive on.

At noon we reach a couple of huts roofed with grass. A few small fields are nearby and beyond is still wilderness. But cultivation is spreading inexorably, and in a few years all land along the western borders of the park will probably be under crops. The rangers barge into the dark interiors of the huts and poke around, looking under blankets, into cooking pots. In a corner they find a rotting eland hide, full of maggots, and outside, hidden beneath some straw, they uncover several impala hooves. A reedy man, wrapped in a dirty loincloth, has been watching silently. Now the rangers add him to the other prisoners. I feel sorry for him. But then I look at his two small children staring at us. Their legs are bent and spindly, and their bellies are grotesquely swollen, signs that they are suffering from Kwashiorkor, a disease indicating protein deficiency. They certainly have not been receiving the poached meat to eat. Last night, when I sympathized with the farmers who supplement their meager diet of maize and sorghum with a bit of meat, Myles replied:

"Sure, I feel sorry for the poor devils. But most poaching is done for the market. It's a big commercial enterprise. These chaps are well organized. Some set the snares, others butcher the meat, and porters carry the dried meat off at night in forty to fifty pound loads. A snare costs anywhere from four to eight shillings* Dried meat brings two shillings a pound; a wildebeest tail sells for ten shillings. So the returns are great. We catch these fellows and have to take them all the way to the magistrate in Musoma. They get two to four weeks in jail or a fifty shilling fine, and then they're at it again!"

We returned at 4:00 p.m. and soon afterward Myles did too, his Land Rover piled high with dried meat that he had confiscated at a poacher's camp. After washing off sweat and dust in a canvas tub, we had dinner in the gathering darkness. Clouds had balled up and distant lightning sundered the sky. A leopard moved slowly upriver, his progress marked by rasping coughs. Our talk was desultory, broken by lengthy silences. I commented on the sparseness of wildlife in the Maswa area, and Myles said, "There are lots of animals here now compared to a few years ago. Poaching was really bad then. Once, in 1956, I collected 1011 snares in a single day. Game was so scarce that when I saw a kongoni I raised my hat to him in admiration. I really did. Any animal that had managed to survive was something special."

Another dawn and we departed from camp in search of more snares and poachers' camps:

The Land Rover bumps along the edge of a dry streambed. At a place where the grass has escaped the dry-season fires, Okech signals a halt. He examines first the dusty soil, then the sandy bottom of the creek. A human footprint is there. Silently the rangers spread out, two advancing down one side of the stream, two down the other. After about fifteen minutes of stealthy walking, we see three men flush ahead. They bound through the high grass, only their heads and shoulders visible. The rangers pursue grinning happily, ob-

* About 7.5 shillings then equaled $1.00.

viously delighted with the chase. A flurry and one poacher is caught, but I am too far behind to see the details. The remaining poachers angle across the creek, but the rangers there cut them off, a hunting technique much like that used by lions. Lunging forward, a ranger grasps the shoulder of one poacher and throws him down. And the third poacher crouches like a frightened hare, clasping his hands over the back of his head when he hears the pounding feet of his pursuers. Then he rolls on his back, whimpering. The ranger raises the rifle as if to butt him, then desists when he sees me. All three poachers are handcuffed and taken to their camp nearby. Each had carried a bow, a quiver of arrows, and a knife, and the rangers collect these for later evidence in court. The camp is hidden well beneath the drooping boughs of a shrub. It is a simple camp. Three bags of millet, three pots, and four water gourds are stored in one corner, and slabs of drying eland meat are draped over the branches. A search along the creek nets us eight snares.

We find another small camp an hour later, but its occupants have vanished, leaving behind two butchered eland calves, a bushbuck, and four onions. Since their campfire is still burning, we impale some eland meat on sharpened sticks and roast it. Waiting for lunch, I lie on my back and close my eyes. It is cool in this arbor. The meat sizzles and the murmur of the low-talking rangers seems far away. I have almost drifted off to sleep when Okech nudges me and hands me a share of the meat. I feel a little guilty for enjoying the poachers' spoils as I eagerly devour them.

Myles had discovered a number of snares in an acacia thicket, as well as a partially butchered giraffe, which had been caught in a special snare set some eight feet above ground. After a long search, he had found the poachers' camp, a large one, but the owners had escaped when they heard the car. Wanting me to see this camp, Myles left four rangers there to guard it for the night while he returned home. That evening he talked with longing of his youth on a ranch in Nanyuki in Kenya, of riding horseback over the range, and of trapping marauding leopards. I realized then, too, that soon my Serengeti years would only be part of my dreams of long ago. This was actually my last night in camp before leaving the Serengeti, and I listened to the scops owls calling and watched the fireflies blinking with the heightened consciousness that comes before a final parting.

In the morning we went to the poachers' camp. It was indeed a fascinating place, a charnel house hidden beneath a huge *Grewia* bush. Dark meat was draped everywhere from the boughs and crude rafters like obscene decorations. Several poles had chunks of fresh meat tied to each end, having been carried in this manner from the snare line to camp. Hides of gazelle and kongoni were spread on the ground and there was the skin of a lioness too. Myles told me that to sleep on a lion skin is said to increase virility and that the owner of a skin may rent it out for several shillings a night. I examined several pouches that lay scattered among gourds and pots. One contained rock salt, another tobacco, and two of them marijuana; a fourth had in it an assortment of gazelle horns and warthog tusks, used for making medicine. About a hundred feet from the camp was a simple but effective leopard and hyena trap: a piece of meat suspended over a sharpened stake. While jumping up and down to reach the morsel, a predator may impale itself. The previous evening one of the poachers had returned to fetch a bow and arrows he had forgotten in his rush to escape. He was promptly apprehended, and he now sat there despondently, a superpredator in his larder. The fresh kills in that one camp included: 12 Thomson's gazelle, 6 warthog, 6 zebra, 5 impala, 5 giraffe, 3 wildebeest, 2 buffalo, 2 kongoni, 1 roan, 5 eland, 1 reedbuck, 1 topi, 1 lion, and 1 white-backed vulture. And three charred piles of bones attested to many other animals that had passed through this camp on their way to market.

While the rangers destroyed the camp, Myles and I had breakfast before returning to Seronera.

I added up the results of this brief antipoaching campaign: 7 poachers arrested and 85 snares collected. Some 65 freshly dead animals were in the various camps, a small percentage of the many thousands that are captured every year. Myles's efforts in 1969 had yielded 364 arrested poachers and 2,715 snares. I saw only one shy lion in 125 miles of driving cross-country, and the poachers' camps showed me why I had not met more. For comparison, a month earlier I had driven seventy miles in two days around the Ndoha Plain and Mbalageti River deep within the park and seen thirty-seven lions.

While poaching menaces the wildlife, the activity is being contained and could be almost stopped at a relatively small cost. Being resilient, most species would increase to their former abundance within a few years—if their habitat survived. With the human population burgeoning, the agriculturalists and pastoralists are taking over more and more of the remaining wilderness. The woodlands to the north and west and southwest of the park are being converted into fields, and in a few years the wild animals will not be able to live there anymore. The people need the land, but so do the wildebeest, zebra, and others. In such a situation the claims of man will be upheld. Inevitably the migratory species will have to change their age-old routes and the resident animals will have to retreat into the park or die.

To the east of the park is the Masai tribe, Nilo-Hamitic pastoralists who lived near Lake Rudolf some four hundred years ago but then advanced south, conquering all tribes in their way until by the early 1800's they had penetrated far into Tanzania. One section of the tribe pushed out some pastoralists who inhabited the plains west of the Crater highlands and then settled down there. The Serenget, as the group called itself, lived in what is now the park until in 1890 a rinderpest epidemic swept down Africa. The loss of most of their cattle created a famine among the Serenget, for blood and milk from these animals were their principal food, and a smallpox epidemic, too, decimated them. As if this were not enough, intratribal war broke out. Within ten years the Serenget were either dead or had dispersed, leaving the land empty. Not until after World War I was the area resettled. Their tenure came to an end in 1959, when the last Masai were moved out of the park.

An American rancher once came to the Serengeti, and, seeing the sea of grass rippling gently in the breeze, noted that with a borehole every ten square miles the area could support so-and-so many cattle. In his view God made grass to feed cattle. The Masai have the same limited perspective. With the assistance of veterinary services, the number of cattle among the Masai has increased tremendously and the tribe needs ever more land and water. The eastern plains, desolate and windblown, are suitable only for grazing by livestock and wildlife, not for agriculture. Most wild animals are better adapted to living in this harsh environment than cattle, needing less water, growing faster, and permitting a greater density. Wildebeest and other grazers compete with livestock for food when they move to the eastern plains and spend several months there each year. In the early 1960's a fence was built across a valley in the Gol mountains to deflect the wildebeest on their annual trek, but the black horde simply swept around and through the obstacle.

The Masai will probably remain and any management policy must satisfy both their needs and that of the wildlife. There may have to be a limit on the number of cattle and wild animals that are allowed to use the plains, a limit based on the long-term carrying capacity of the range. Some wildebeest may some day have to be cropped. More water sources for the Masai may have to be provided, for at present the livestock clusters within a ten-mile radius of the few pools at which the animals must drink every other day. This causes overgrazing and severe trampling of the fragile soil.

Whatever is done, the unique spectacle of the migrating herds must be preserved. At present economic arguments are sufficiently potent to convince the East African countries to save their parks, for tourism provides a greater monetary return per square mile of park than could any other form of land use. There is, too, the moral obligation for every country to preserve a small part of its natural heritage for future generations to enjoy. Yet, while preserving the Serengeti and other parks we must be aware of and beware of a paradox, expressed well by Aldo Leopold: "But all conservation of wilderness is self-defeating, for to cherish we must see and fondle, and when enough have seen and fondled, there is no wilderness left to cherish." I have my memories of the Serengeti, and I fervently hope that others will also be able to gather theirs until the end of time.

FOOTSTEPS INTO THE PAST

I WAS MORE AWARE OF A SENSE OF TIME IN THE SERENGETI
than in any other area in which I have been. Walking across
the plains I would find obsidian flakes in wind-eroded depressions, carried there from far hills by some early hunter
in search of prey. As I looked across the undulating grasslands with their endless herds, I felt a unity with it all, a
unity so intense that memories of the past seemed to pervade
the air. The wildebeest and zebra were ghosts trekking
through the millennia and the volcanoes of the Crater highlands still stood there, as they have done since the dawn of
man, their internal fires now largely damped. Looking
toward this rampart in the midday heat, I saw the distant
plains dissolve into a glistening lake, a mirage that re-
created an ancient reality. Olduvai Lake once more lapped
against the base of these mountains as it had two million
years ago. But the lake is gone, and a river has cut through
the layers of sediment, lava, and volcanic ash to reveal
its primal shores. This is now Olduvai Gorge, sometimes
called the Grand Canyon of Evolution. At various depths in

its eroded walls Louis and Mary Leakey have found a remarkable succession of near-men and men, indicating that the Serengeti has been continuously occupied by hominids of one kind or another since the dawn of our species.

In the lowest layer at Olduvai, near the bottom of Bed I, were found the remains of two types of hominids. One of them, *Australopithecus robustus*, was about 5 feet tall and weighed some 130 pounds, a powerful, heavy-set being. The other was a wiry little creature, about 4 to 4½ feet tall and weighing perhaps 75 pounds. Leakey named it *Homo habilis*, thus demonstrating his contention that it was, to date, the earliest known member of the genus that includes man. But other anthropologists consider it to be a subspecies of *Australopithecus africanus*, a widely distributed hominid who lived south of the Sahara several million years ago. In fact, there are some who think that there were not two kinds of hominid but only one, the larger representing the male of a species, and the smaller the female. A marked sexual dichotomy in size is, for example, present in baboons and gorillas. Leaving aside morphological arguments, I doubt that this interpretation is correct, my doubt being based on what I learned about social carnivores. With the lion and other species in which the sexes are very different in size, the males are little involved in caring for young, sharing food, and other familial matters; on the other hand, the males of both the wolf and hunting dog, which are only as large as or slightly larger than females, are intimately involved in all group activities. A division of labor in most tasks and complete food sharing may be difficult when the sexes are widely disparate in size. And it seems likely that the full cooperation of the male was essential to the survival of hominid society, as I will describe later. It is not surprising to have two different hominids existing side by side. The closely related chimpanzee and gorilla inhabit the same area, as do the lion and leopard. *A. africanus* could walk or at least trot and run upright, judging by its limb bones, which resemble those of man; *A. robustus*, too, could walk bipedally but there is some evidence that it might also have needed to partially support itself with its hands. The brain size of these two species was only on the order of 400 to 700 cc., i.e., no larger than that of apes. *A. robustus*, the larger of the two, seems to have become extinct about three quarters of a million years ago or somewhat later, but the other is thought to have evolved into *Homo erectus*, a true man with a brain capacity of 800 to 1300 cc., who appeared more than a million years ago. *Homo erectus* used fire. And he roamed far about the world, spreading from his place of genesis through Africa, Europe, Java, and China, among other places. From this man evolved *Homo sapiens*, who in various forms has held sway for the past 200,000 to 300,000 years.

Successive groups of *Australopithecus* camped along the shore of Olduvai Lake, and, like other later hominids, they had the proclivity to litter. Various crude tools—scrapers, choppers, cutting tools, and others—were left behind, as were unworked stones that had been transported to the site from somewhere else, perhaps to be converted into specific tools or merely used for pounding. Tools may be employed for fighting and for obtaining food, from digging up a root to bashing a gazelle over the head and then cutting up the carcass. The debris of bone around the camp sites indicated that at least a fair proportion of *Australopithecus'* diet consisted of meat and that the tools had been used to capture and prepare it. Frog, bird, lizard, and rodent remains were preserved, as were the bones of pig, various antelope, and even giraffe. Near one camp were the bones of *Dinotherium*, a type of elephant whose tusks in the lower jaw arch downward. Mingled with these remains were various tools, indicating that the animal had been butchered. Also found by the Leakeys was an arc of stones, possibly a windbreak; if it was, then it is man's earliest known structure.

These tools have been ascribed to *A. africanus*, for it has been stated that, being a vegetarian, *A. robustus* was unlikely to have made cutting tools of a form that could have been used as hunting weapons. The supposition that *A. robustus* was a vegetarian is based on the fact that its teeth are heavily worn and abraded, as if it had chewed plant food with much grit. I doubt that *A. robustus* ate only plants, but the amount of meat in its diet may have been less than that of *A. africanus* and it may not have made easily recognizable tools. The environment contains an assortment of tools in the form of naturally broken rocks, which can be used once and then discarded. Richard Gould describes such casual use of tools among Australian aborigines in a *Natural History* article:

> Once my wife went out to collect honey ants with some Ngatatjara women from the Laverton Reserve. While they were out, one of the women's dogs chased and killed a kangaroo. One woman picked up a natural flake of rough quartzite from the ground and used it to slit the animal's belly and cut the intestines. Then the stone was thrown away. On another occasion, I was traveling . . . in the company of two Ngatatjara men from that region. These men had caught several goannas early in the day. In camp late that afternoon they roasted these lizards and ate the fleshy parts. Then they placed the backbone, head, shoulders, and tail on top of a small rock, which they used as a kind of anvil. With hand-held stones, they pounded the cartilaginous bone and scraps of meat together into a pulpy mass, which they then ate.

Perishable tools such as sticks are not likely to be preserved, and casually used bones and stones can be recognized as possible tools only if they have accumulated at a site where otherwise they would not be. I think that man's precursors have been tool users and perhaps tool makers for many millions of years, whenever they lived under ecological conditions that made it advantageous for them to use such implements. *Australopithecus* was in existence at least 5½ million years ago, judging by the finds of Brian Patterson near Lake Rudolf in northern Kenya. *Ramapithecus*, a Miocene creature which lived about fourteen million years ago in Africa and India and which is believed by some to represent a possible ancestor of *Australopithecus*, probably made tools, and so did its ancestors back to and beyond the point where man began his lineage from some primal ape.

Sherwood Washburn, whose ideas concerning the selective forces that shaped man have been both highly imaginative and logical, rightly suggests that tool use was intimately involved in the evolution of the upright posture in man. Increased tool use helped to bring about changes in body structure, such as an upright stance, and this freed the hands for the development of greater manipulative skills, one reinforcing the other until cause and effect became difficult to distinguish. A gorilla may stand up and look around, but in its day to day existence there would be no advantage in foraging bipedally. However, a creature that found it advantageous to incorporate tools into its behavioral repertoire —to brandish sticks at enemies and to club prey—would benefit from having its hands freed for such tasks. It must have been a powerful benefit, for by standing up man also lost one of the main attributes of a large four-footed animal —speed to flee and speed to run down prey. Almost every large mammal in East Africa can run faster than man. But habitual tool use provided the promise and the power that led to our existence.

For awhile some anthropologists resisted the idea that a creature with a brain capacity only as large as or a little larger than that of an ape made tools and used them for hunting; that, in fact, it had a culture which at its basic subsistence level was in many respects like that of today's hunters and gatherers. However, even chimpanzees show the rudiments of tool making, as A. Suzuki, Jane van Lawick-Goodall, Clyde Jones, and others have noted in East and West Africa. These apes may break off twigs or grass stalks, shorten them to a desired length, trim off the leaves, and then insert them into a termite hill. After leaving this probe there for awhile, they withdraw it carefully and eat the termites that cling to it.

I became fascinated by A. *africanus*, and, when walking across the plains, the past so palpably around me, I would try to view my surroundings as one of these near-men might have done. I remained alert for a possible meal, a future shelter, an enemy. Of course, the landscape has changed somewhat from what it was two million years ago. At that time the climate was a little more moist than at present. Acacia woodlands, swamps, and a lake covered what are now the Serengeti plains. Ngorongoro was about fifteen thousand feet high, some three thousand feet higher than any peak in the area today, before collapsing inward to form a huge caldera. But it was in the animal life that differences were most striking. There are about seventy-four species of antelope in Africa today, yet the fauna is impoverished. Only around two thirds of the genera of large mammals in Africa a million or so years ago survived to the present. We are witnessing the twilight of the great beasts, whereas *Australopithecus* lived when these animals were at their most diverse, an age when giants roamed the earth. A long-tusked pig, *Afrochoerus*, as large as a rhinoceros, rooted in the swamps, and the gorilla-size *Simopithecus* baboon traveled over the savannas; *Libytherium*, a relative of the giraffe, browsed on trees, its head adorned with palmate horns; and ponderous chalicothere, related to horses and tapirs, lumbered among gazelle, zebra, and other familiar creatures. Just as the herbivores were more diverse than at present, so were the carnivores. About eight species of hyenas inhabited Africa then as compared to three today. And there were saber-toothed cats, an ancient and successful line that vanished while such relatives as the lion and leopard persisted. No one knows why these species became extinct. Some may have been so specialized in their foraging habits or mineral requirements that when the environment in some way placed a heavy strain on them they were unable to adapt. A few species may have been so uncommon, slow-moving, and vulnerable to cooperative assault that groups of hominids were able to hasten their demise. R. Ewer suggested that some hyena species were so dependent on scavenging from saber-toothed cats that the extinction of the latter also affected the former. But why did the saber-tooth die out? The idea has been advanced that these cats were specialized for killing pachyderms and that the extinction of various elephant resulted in their extinction too. Perhaps. Yet none of the surviving predators have specialized completely on a particular species of prey; meat is meat, whether killed or scavenged. Food would still seem to be plentiful enough to support other predatory animals.

It was in the open woodlands and plains, areas rich in wildlife, that man the hunter evolved. Dense, tall forests, such as those found in the Congo basin today, contain few grasses and herbs on which a variety of herbivores can subsist. Large animals are notoriously sparse in forests of that type. It has been suggested that man's precursors were forced to seek a life on the ground when the forests in which they lived retreated during some dry climatic era. With forests destroyed or fragmented, they had to exploit their new environment or die. But rather than viewing my ancestors as refugees stranded away from their arboreal homes, I prefer to think of them as highly adaptable and widespread. Just as baboons and chimpanzees have exploited several habitats, so did a species of ancient ape occupy the available niches, not from necessity but because they were available. Man's precursors no doubt lived in the forest, along the forest's edge, in open woodlands, and on the plains, being at home in trees as well as on the ground, wherever they could fulfill their needs. Populations in open terrain were in a sense preadapted to a situation in which tool using and meat eating could develop. And develop they did, perhaps because it was more economical to capture prey than to compete with the many herbivores for the limited forage. And, once discovered, the advantages of these traits were so obvious that through social learning the traits were then incorporated into the creatures' basic mode of life. The populations that adapted to the new methods evolved into hominids, but those that continued their old existence in the forest, free from want and free from problems, died out, possibly when the climate changed.

The social life of *Australopithecus* has a special relevance to man today. How was its society organized? Was it territorial or not? Did it scavenge or hunt for its meat? How did groups interact? Man is almost obsessed with a need to answer questions about himself, to define himself and his place in nature. By understanding *Australopithecus* we may help to define ourselves, our unique qualities as well as those traits we share with the animal world. And we need this knowledge. We need to know where we came from, who we are. "Man is a rope tied between beast and Superman . . ." according to Nietzsche. We left the beast behind when we acquired symbolic language and self-awareness. Now, instead of adapting to various selective forces, we change them, we conceive our destiny and try to achieve it, not always with great success. We attempt to be Supermen but with a mind and body still rooted in the wilderness. Although we can grasp the complexity of the universe, we are unable to understand ourselves, the basis of our aggressiveness and intolerance, our propensity to kill, all those factors that not only prevent us from fulfilling our dreams but also endanger our existence. Man is now a threatened species in spite of or, more accurately, because of his numbers. And I think he is worth preserving, if only as a unique product of biological and cultural evolution.

In trying to gain an insight into the life of early hominids, anthropologists and zoologists have looked for clues in several places. From the archeological record it is possible to deduce the physical characteristics of hominids as well as certain behavioral traits, including the facts that they used tools, hunted prey, and had a home base. Another source of information is the hunting and gathering peoples who still survive in isolated parts of the world. These people are, of course, not primitive, except in their method of subsisting, and even their material culture, encompassing such items as bows and arrows and cooking vessels, is far more complex than that once characteristic of *Australopithecus*. But by becoming familiar with the problem of survival that hunters and gatherers face it is possible to view the past in the right perspective.

Many field studies of monkeys and apes have been made in recent years, including my own two-year project on mountain gorillas. Although I was greatly interested in gorillas themselves, I also hoped that knowledge about them might contribute to an understanding of the social life of hominids. Gorillas are amiable giants who live in cohesive groups numbering from some five to twenty-five individuals. They spend much of the day munching leaves, bark, vines, and other vegetation, and at dusk, having traveled a mile or two during the day, they build themselves nests and go to sleep. A group confines its leisurely existence to an area of about ten to fifteen square miles, a large area for a primate, many of whom may spend their life within a few acres. Gorillas showed me that it is possible for a group of apes to subsist peacefully, seldom asserting rank in competition over food and mates, but they taught me little that could be applied to early man. Instead of being a sedentary vegetarian, *Australopithecus* ate much meat, a means of subsistence different from any monkey or ape. Although baboons and chimpanzees occasionally kill and eat a gazelle fawn or hare, such items are incidental additions to their diet rather than an important part of it. A hunter requires space, as much as several hundred square miles in areas where food is scarce, and this alone changes his basic habits, indeed his entire world view.

Soon after I finished my gorilla study, various investigators observed the chimpanzee and found a social organization differing strikingly from that of the gorilla even though the two apes are closely related. The members of a chimpanzee group, which may number as many as eighty individuals, are often widely scattered over their range in small units of varying size, each searching for scattered food resources such as isolated trees in fruit. If a good feeding site is found, loud hoots may bring chimpanzees together, but afterward the animals again split up. Thus social systems of species are poor indicators of phylogenetic relationship, as the different group patterns of gorilla and chimpanzee well show. In fact, populations of the same species may behave differently from area to area. Baboon males in a group living under the harsh conditions of a savanna may have a strong rank order, whereas those that lead a comfortable existence in a forest may not have one, or at least they seldom assert themselves. Since the social system of each nonhuman primate species is strongly influenced by its own unique heritage and ecology, one might question the usefulness of emphasizing studies of monkeys and apes to learn about man's society. It would also be profitable to observe animals that are phylogenetically unrelated but ecologically similar to the way in which early man probably lived. Such animals are the social carnivores, the lion, hunting dog, and others. They, too, are hunters that roam widely over large areas in search of prey. This is not to imply that the social systems of these species were necessarily similar to those of early hominids. However, some of the same evolutionary processes and environmental forces that shaped, for example, hunting dog society probably also influenced *Australopithecus*, and by understanding one we can deepen our knowledge of the other.

Man is a unique creature, a primate by inheritance but a carnivore by profession, and we cannot hope to understand him without considering this dual past. Some of his attributes, such as some of the communicatory patterns, are not influenced strongly by environmental forces, and the nonhuman primates offer a logical choice for deducing the various gestures an early hominid may have used. When a monkey or ape wants to repel an intruder, it may jump up and down, screech and hoot, shake branches, and throw things. When presented with a stuffed leopard, free-living chimpanzees may even pick up sticks and club the animal, as Adrian Kortlandt has shown. Man, too, behaves like that when he meets an enemy, waving his arms and hurling rocks. Thus, it seems likely that *Australopithecus* would have used a similar intimidation display to put a lion to flight. Another example is the greeting gesture. For example, lions rub heads after a separation and hyenas stand head-to-tail and lick each other's genitalia. Most primates lack a greeting ceremony, largely because group members are usually together and don't need it, but chimpanzees have one, as described by Jane van Lawick-Goodall:

> The most common greeting occurs when one chimpanzee goes up to another and reaches out to touch it with the flat of the hand or with the back of the slightly flexed fingers. The top of the head, the shoulder, groin, thigh, or genital area may be touched in greeting . . . Another form of greeting occurs when a male stands upright, one arm above his head, while another runs toward him. The two then fling their arms around each other.

Nonhuman primates often show their teeth in a grin as a sign of appeasement in a threatening situation. In man, too, the grin may denote anxiety, but the gesture has become ritualized, conveying now also friendly intent. An *Australopithecus* may well have grinned as it approached a friend after a separation and then hugged him.

Many patterns of behavior, such as the food quest, land tenure, group movements, and so forth, are influenced by ecological conditions, and in these aspects the social carnivores can contribute importantly to an understanding of early man. Here I present only a few findings and ideas that intrigued me, without trying to treat all the many complex factors that helped to shape *Australopithecus* society. Gordon Lowther, an anthropologist then at Nairobi University, and I discussed some of this information in a paper published in 1969 by the *Southwestern Journal of Anthropology*. A good general introduction to the whole topic is John Pfeiffer's *The Emergence of Man*.

Although it is clear that *Australopithecus africanus* ate meat, there are several ways of obtaining it. Animals often die of disease or old age or they may drown when crossing a river or be killed in a fight, to become ready sources of food for a scavenger. It is also possible to drive lions off their kills or steal carcasses that have been stored in trees by leopards. Sick individuals and young ones may be caught at times, and small animals, such as insects, frogs, mice and nestling birds may be a source of food during certain seasons. And, finally, healthy adult prey may be hunted. The large predators obtain their food by all these methods, with the exception of cheetah, which are usually too timid to scavenge. It is interesting to speculate how *Australopithecus* may have obtained its ration. It could have scavenged and chased other predators off their kills, but this would seem to be a haphazard way of making a living aside from being dangerous. It could have been a hunter either of small creatures or of large ones or of both. The fossil record only reveals bones, not how they were obtained. Some anthropologists believe that hominids evolved in three stages, from vegetarians through scavengers to hunters. Not a single carnivore in today's predator community in the Serengeti has become adapted to a complete scavenging existence in spite of there being so much prey. There seems to be no empty niche for a large mammalian scavenger at present nor perhaps was there one in the past. *Australopithecus* was no doubt a typical predator in that he obtained meat in any way possible.

Once Gordon Lowther and I speculated about the ways in which hominids might have obtained their food, and we decided to test a couple of our ideas with simple experiments. We wondered, for instance, if a hominid could kill enough crouched gazelle fawns to make an exclusive search for them worthwhile. Gazelle crouch only during the first week or so of life and after that age they can easily outrun a person. It was late January. Thousands of gazelle had congregated and were fawning around the Simba, Gol, and Barafu kopjes. I walked many miles in that area, sometimes alone, at others with Gordon, Kay, or other helpers, looking for newborn fawns crouched motionless, often in the shadow of low shrubs. Walking like that, dependent only on my own senses and muscles, I was tensely alert. Though scanning ahead for fawns, I also took note of the many small happenings around me, particularly those that might mean food or danger—the low purposeful flight of a vulture, a loping hyena. Even though we only simulated kills, any approach to within twenty feet or less of a fawn counting as one, we unconsciously reverted to our primordial actions and emotions during these searches, showing to what depth the hunting way of life has permeated our psyche. Once, when Kay saw a fawn, she immediately tensed and slightly crouched with raised arm, ready to pounce, and then glanced self-consciously around to check if I had seen her do it. On another occasion Peter Matthiessen and I had had a long and fruitless search. Then, in the grass ahead, I spotted a gazelle that had died of disease. I bounded toward it, elated beyond measure, as if our next meal did indeed depend on this find. During the experiment we walked thirty-three man hours, or about a hundred miles, finding only eight fawns, or one fawn per four man hours of walking, a small reward for so much work. But we also discovered other items as described in our report:

> While walking we also could have killed a hare. In addition, we discovered a female Thomson's gazelle dead from disease and a male gazelle from which only the viscera had been eaten. The meat from these 2 animals would undoubtedly have disappeared before our arrival had not most of the vultures normally in the area moved to a wildebeest concentration several kilometers* away. We also found a gazelle skeleton from which we could have obtained 1.5 to 2 kg. of meat and skin, and a gazelle head from which the brains could have been extracted. We watched a cheetah in the distance hunt and kill a gazelle fawn and could have taken the carcass. Adding up the approximate weights of the killed and scavenged animals, and subtracting inedible parts such as bones and rumen contents we obtained some 35 kg. of meat, viscera, and skin.

In early July, at the height of the dry season, Gordon and I established a camp along the Mbalageti River. Our tents were surrounded by borassus palms and overlooked a pool in the rocky streambed. On the opposite bank the slope was gentle, giving us a view of the parched woodlands, some of them burned, but other sections covered with tall, dry grass. We sat before our tents in the gathering dusk. A bull elephant strolled by, and later, on the other side of the river, a young male lion. We had come to find out how much meat we could catch and scavenge at a time of year when thousands of animals were concentrated near the rivers. A group of hominids could never have had it better.

That night the lions visited us, roaring nearby and stumbling over the guy ropes as they circled the tents. I wondered how *Australopithecus* reacted to predators in the

* 1 km = .6 mile; 1 kg = 2.2 lbs.

darkness and how they spent the night. Perhaps they huddled together on the ground or on a kopje hoping to remain undiscovered, or perhaps they built crude sleeping platforms in trees, as do today's apes. The roars were a good reminder that this was one corner of the world where the wilderness persisted unchanged.

We rose at dawn and set off together along the riverbank, where kills are most likely to be found. The terrain was broken by numerous brush-fringed ravines and small thickets. These we skirted carefully so as not to startle a dozing buffalo or lion. Yet our apprehension was somehow seducing, and we thoroughly enjoyed the first hour or so in spite of the fact that the personality of the lion pervaded the area. As it warmed up, the tsetse flies became murderous. Gordon was the perfect companion in this situation: the flies preferred him to me. He wore a most disreputable cap, shaped like a flaccid, reddish-brown pancake, to which the tsetses were immensely attracted. As many as twenty-five flies would sit on it even though Gordon remonstrated vehemently. Later I read that tsetse prefer livestock of that color. Clouds of tiny flies hovered around our faces, crawling into our ears and sticking to our eyes. Being more preoccupied with our insect adherents than with our surroundings, we bumbled onto eleven lions. They growled with annoyance as they fled.

A little later we spotted a couple of hooded vultures sitting low in a tree with the kind of determined interest that indicates a lion kill. The grass was high and the tree stood at the edge of a thicket, a situation which dictated a rather cautious approach. We carried no firearms. The security of a gun leads to carelessness and provocation. An animal may, of course, charge but it is less likely to do so if one fails to display the unconscious aggressiveness that a gun imparts. A so-called attack may be simply a bluff, but a person with a gun is unlikely to give the animal the benefit of the doubt. To carry a gun reveals also a certain attitude toward life that I find alien. A gun would certainly have dulled our atavistic pleasure in being hominids. However, as we inched toward the kill, listening, craning our necks, that pleasure had given way to slight fear. But the lions were gone—and so was all the meat. The cats had killed a zebra near the riverbank. Only the skeleton and a patch of skin remained. Gordon descended to the riverbed and searched among the pebbles until he found one that had been crudely chipped by natural forces to leave a rough edge. With it he whacked a leg bone until the bloody marrow was exposed. And with the same tool I bashed in the back of the skull, exposing the brain, potentially a nice snack.

By 8:30 the sun seared the valley and even the slight breeze failed to bring relief. Many zebra and a few impala and wildebeest trudged to water. At our approach the zebra and other herds wheeled and fled, their hooves throwing up clumps of sod and churning up the soil, so that they almost disappeared in clouds of dust. Then they stopped safely a few hundred feet away and looked back. Being slow of foot and lacking projectile weapons, hominids would have found it difficult to attack such herds. But when the animals were near water, especially if they had to descend some narrow defile to reach a pool, it would be possible to get near them. I tried to do so later that day. A number of wildebeest were drinking. The animals fled when they sensed us, running singly and in twos along a narrow path up the riverbank. Sprinting toward them partly hidden by the dust, I was within twenty feet of a wildebeest bull before he saw me. He swung around and threateningly lowered his horns while cantering sideways. I halted abruptly, having decided that I was not hungry after all. But a group of hominids could have surrounded such an animal and pulled and clubbed it down. Or they could have encircled a suitable waterhole, waiting there in ambush until they were able to corner some animal in the riverbed or the water itself. The fact that lions are able to learn and execute some quite sophisticated cooperative hunts suggests that *Australopithecus* must also have been able to use such techniques as driving prey toward members in ambush, encircling animals, chasing herds into a cul-de-sac, and so forth.

Recently, in the journal *Oceania,* Richard Gould published some observations on Australian Aborigine hunting and these corroborate some of our ideas:

> Hunting is mainly by stealth rather than pursuit. The favourite method is to construct blinds of brush or rocks within easy spear-throwing distance of a water source, generally near a defile or gorge which will restrict the movements of game in trying to escape. Night-time hunting from blinds is sometimes practiced (particularly on moonlit nights) to take advantage of the nocturnal habits of the larger game.

It is doubtful that *Australopithecus* would have exposed itself to predation by hunting at night. However, *Homo erectus,* who knew the use of fire, may have done so. In Kenya, Glynn Isaac excavated Olorgesailie, a site dating from the Middle Pleistocene. He found that the hunters had killed primarily giant baboons, which must have been formidable adversaries. As Isaac points out, baboons are most easily captured at night when they are clustered in their sleeping trees. In fact, the Hadza, a tribe presently living near the Serengeti, have been reported to capture baboons in that manner.

No doubt *Australopithecus* also hunted alone for gazelle and other small prey. Stealth again must have been important. Once more the observations of Gould on Aborigines are pertinent:

> In stalking an animal, natural cover is used as much as possible for concealment. However, I have often watched a hunter approaching a kangaroo browsing in an open spinifex-plain, where

no natural cover is available. The favored technique in such a case is to get downwind of the
animal and then walk upright directly toward it.
Windy days are best for this, for the wind covers the
noise of approach . . . The hunter fixes his eyes on
the kangaroo's head and ears, for he must freeze
in place instantly at the slightest movement or
sign that the animal hears him coming. He may
remain frozen for several minutes until the animal
returns to its browsing; then the approach is resumed. I have seen hunters approach kangaroos
out in the open like this on windless days from
distances of over one thousand feet to within
seventy-five feet . . .

The similarity of the Aborigines' hunting method to that used
by lions is striking except that the latter do not heed wind
direction.

We found two more lion kills that morning, a zebra
foal and a wildebeest bull, but only the bones were left. This
was not surprising because in the week of our study we
saw at least sixty-six different lions within an area of seventy-
five square miles. The average size of lion groups was six,
enough animals to strip a carcass within a few hours. Having
walked almost five miles we decided to swing back toward
camp. We reached it just before noon, very desiccated, for
the alkali pools in the river are not very palatable, and happy
to be able to relax in the shade. It was still during these
hours. Not even flies buzzed. Occasionally a dove cooed,
intensifying the silence by its contrast. Around 4:00 p.m.
life quickened again and we went on another food quest,
this time upriver. Not far from camp two lionesses lumbered
off and we became noticeably more alert after that encounter.
I checked several grass nests of the social weaver bird for
young but all were empty; it was not their breeding season.
We arrived home at dusk, without having found food, but at
least no expectant women and children were there to note
our failure. It had been a hard day though we had worked

for only five hours. Gordon's legs were stiff and swollen with tsetse bites. He counted the bites on his left leg, and then ruefully but somewhat proudly announced that there were fifty-two of them.

We were back along the thickets and creeks shortly after sunrise. At one place a game trail descended into a deep ravine and out the other side. Filled with joie de vivre, I dashed down one side and up the other and almost into a group of nine or more lions. Without stopping, I raced back the way I had come, going considerably faster and passing Gordon near the bottom of the ravine. He had not seen the lions but asked calmly and with prescience: "Are you looking for a tree?" We halted on the opposite bank and briefly watched the lions, who still sat there, somewhat puzzled. It is often said that one should never run from a lion. This is nonsense. One's response must be based on the situation. A lion that charges from a distance might be bluffed to a halt if one stands and faces it. But in an inadvertant meeting at close range it may be best to retreat quickly, for each species has a critical distance past which it does not tolerate an intrusion without attacking. To stand one's ground in such a situation simply invites a charge. We had ample opportunity to observe the responses of lions to us those first two days: we met seven different groups. To avoid face-to-face encounters we decided to carry an alarm system with us on subsequent days. Gordon had a hoard of six cans of beer, one of which he quaffed every evening. Being British, he did not mind the beer being warm. Into one of these cans we dropped some pebbles and used it as a rattle whenever we came near a thicket or any other potentially dangerous place.

Lions and hyenas are far less aggressive during the day than at night, and this fact was no doubt of great benefit to early hominids. In fact, *Australopithecus* had the capacity to, and likely did, fit well into the ecological community as a diurnal social hunter of large prey. The only other large carnivore with these characteristics is the hunting dog, which is active mainly at dawn and dusk. Competition existed between hominids and other predators, just as it does now between lion and leopard, but by hunting in groups during the day, *Australopithecus* and later hominids reduced their chances of a dangerous encounter.

That second day we found no meat to eat in our circuits from camp. By having a home base we were definitely limited in the amount of terrain we could traverse. Richard Lee found that the Kung Bushmen in the Kalahari desert considered it uneconomical to exploit their resources beyond a distance of six miles from camp, and this was certainly true of us too. A home base, even for only a few days at a time, was probably a necessity in *Australopithecus* society. Monkeys and ape groups carry their infants with them on their leisurely foraging trips, the youngsters clinging to the backs of their mothers. More often than not a group sleeps at a place different from the one used the previous night. *Australopithecus* infants lacked the prehensile foot with which to cling to their mothers. And for a mother to carry her infant during a hunt would be such a burden that her efficiency, as well as that of the whole group, would be markedly reduced. The death rate of *Australopithecus* young from one cause or another was probably high, on the order of at least fifty percent, judging by some of today's social carnivores and primates. Of twenty-two *Homo erectus* found at Choukoutien in China, fifteen had died when they were less than fourteen years old and only one had passed the age of fifty. No doubt most *Australopithecus* females were either pregnant or had small youngsters underfoot. Childhood was fairly long, as it usually is when survival is to a large extent dependent on learning. Taking all these problems into account, the obvious solution is a home base at or near which the females and young can wait for the return of the hunters. Once a hominid took up the hunting way of life, a division of labor based on sex was a logical development, an adaptive response also shown to at least some degree by hunting dogs. We still retain in our body and mind some remnants of this sexually based differentiation of making a living by hunting: males throw better and are more interested in hunting than are females. Food sharing is essential in a society in which a division of labor is prominent. Hunting dogs readily divide their spoils, and *Australopithecus* must have done likewise, either bringing meat home or leading the group to a carcass. In contrast, monkeys and apes have no division of labor with respect to gathering food, nor do they share freely.

We camped for eight days along the Mbalageti River and on six of these we walked in search of food, covering a total of about sixty miles. To simulate several groups spreading in different directions from home base, we drove by car about sixty miles in two days, the equivalent of about three groups searching each day. Our success at finding lion kills the first day had led us to expect that we might locate many. We discovered a total of only four kills, none with meat, even though we watched the flight of wheeling vultures and investigated the most likely ambush places. But one of our hunting days would have gladdened the heart of the most morose hominid. A zebra foal stood alone on a tongue of grassland, apparently abandoned by its family. I walked toward it slowly, waiting to see what its reaction would be. Once on the plains a sleeping foal had wakened at my approach, and, instead of running to its family nearby, had trotted up and stood by my side. However, this foal fled. Its slightly stumbling gait showed that it was sick. I sprinted after it, while Gordon tried to intercept it. Stumbling on the uneven ground, the foal collapsed. I grabbed it by the mane and tail, then released it. Later that day we saw a giraffe followed by a large young that behaved peculiarly in some indefinable way. As I stalked closer the mother saw me and walked away, but her offspring continued to stand, alert yet undecided about what to do. Placing each foot cautiously, I sneaked to within twenty feet of it, then ten feet, and finally I stood before it, looking up at its face. It was blind, both eyes being covered with a white film. To simulate capture, I circled quietly and grabbed its tail. With that the giraffe exploded, jerking me violently forward as it crashed through the thorny branches of a fallen tree. But when I released my hold, it calmed down and joined its mother nearby a few minutes later.

Excluding bones and other waste, the zebra and giraffe would have provided us with about three hundred pounds of food, a heavy load to carry back to camp. In such a situation, one out of a group of hominid hunters might have returned home to fetch the women to help transport the spoils. But with so much meat in camp, how could *Australopithecus* guard it from other predators during the night? Having many times seen how a hyena pack will chase lions off their kill, I doubt that those predators would have hesitated to treat early hominids in similar fashion. I cannot believe that *Australopithecus* simply slept beside its meat. Neither lion, hunting dog, nor hyena keep meat at their lair, where it would attract other predators and thereby endanger their young. Possibly the remains were hung somewhere in a tree, as is done by leopards, or perhaps they were submerged in water, as hyenas sometimes do, a useful method if there are no crocodiles. Or maybe the meat was simply covered with stones and branches and left a short distance from camp with the hope that something might be left in the morning. To us, sitting in the security of a home, such primal ponderings might seem trivial but to *Australopithecus* food storage was a matter of life or death.

The following day we were attracted by some vultures and came to a tree along whose branches these scavengers sat shoulder to shoulder. Occasionally one leaped into a thicket below. The behavior of the vultures indicated that no predator was near the hidden carcass, but still we approached cautiously. It was a buffalo bull who had died of either disease or old age. Although hyenas and vultures had eaten the viscera and much of the rump, a great deal of meat remained, rather putrid but nevertheless edible. It was our last find. Our conclusion from this week of trying to obtain meat was that under similar conditions of prey abundance a group of *Australopithecus* could have subsisted by a combination of scavenging or killing sick animals and whatever small prey was available. However, in areas where wildlife was less abundant than along the Mbalageti River at that season, they would have to kill healthy adult animals in order to survive as hunters. Being adaptable, hominids obviously did whatever the situation demanded.

We had not worked hard at our task, spending only some three to five hours a day searching for food. Lions, hyenas, and other predators satisfy their needs in the Serengeti in a similar amount of time. Interestingly, Bushmen and Australian Aborigines also spend only about two to five hours in their subsistence effort even though much of their food is derived from vegetal matter. Richard Gould timed the activities of four Australian Aborigine women and found that it took them an average of about 4½ hours to collect enough food for a day, principally two kinds of fruit. Another 2½ hours were spent in grinding, husking, and otherwise preparing the meals. The men added a few lizards they had caught. Considering the fact that man has managed to survive quite well by working a five-hour day for at least ninety-nine percent of his history, it puzzles me what induced him to become an agriculturalist, to trade his combination of freedom and easy life for constant toil lasting daily from sunup to sundown. And in the past agriculturalists still had famines as severe as those experienced by the hunters and gatherers who seldom bothered to store food. Only now, after ten thousand or more years of a settled life, is man once more creating an affluent society in which a five-hour work day may become possible.

Today's hunters and gatherers subsist more on berries

roots, leaves, and other such food than on meat. Richard Lee, for instance, calculated that the diet of a Bushman group over a four-week period comprised sixty-three percent vegetable matter and thirty-seven percent meat. The women in these societies provide most of the subsistence, not the men. On the basis of such evidence it has been suggested that *Australopithecus* also ate mostly vegetable foods with meat being of secondary importance. The Aborigines and Bushmen live today in marginal habitats, barren wastelands where prey is sparse, and to survive they must use all the available resources. On the other hand, *Australopithecus* in East Africa was surrounded by one of the most bountiful supplies of wildlife the world has seen. The archeological evidence shows that it ate meat, although the record is biased because bones are remarkably durable whereas vegetal matter is seldom preserved. *Australopithecus* in the Serengeti must certainly have eaten fruits, such as *Tamarindus* and *Sclerocarya*, which both jackal and man favor, and they probably collected roots and leaves, too, as availability made possible and necessity dictated. But man is essentially a hunter and we can only hope to understand him if we heed the words of Sherwood Washburn and Jane Lancaster, who wrote: "In a very real sense our intellect, interests, emotions, and basic social life—all are evolutionary products of the success of the hunting adaptation."

Hunting peoples and nonhuman primates have superficially similar societies. Most monkeys and apes live in groups of anywhere from about four to two hundred individuals. Members of a group tend to be related to each other and all are intimately acquainted. Such societies are often relatively closed in that strangers may be repulsed, although an occasional animal may switch from one group to another. Members of a chimpanzee group may be widely scattered, yet they seem to retain their identity as a social unit. Turning to hunting peoples, such as the Mbuti pygmies and Aborigines, we find that groups change in size and composition. With respect to Bushmen, Philip Tobias noted that "the band structure is extremely flexible. It is at its maximum in times of plenty. During scarcity, a single band may break up into several hunting and gathering bands, then re-unite when food is once more in good supply." However, changes are primarily within a social unit of fairly small size, a system similar to that suggested for chimpanzees. The extent of cohesion in primate groups, whether in monkey or man, is related to ecological conditions. The early hominids must have had a flexible system too, one that permitted them to adapt to the vagaries of the food supply. To note the similarity between chimpanzees and men may be instructive, but it reveals little about the selective forces that shaped and maintained their societies. The environmental pressures certainly affected vegetarians and meat eaters differently.

Group life confers certain benefits on all societies, among them the chance for youngsters to learn certain traditions and the possibility for members to warn and protect one another from danger. But the social carnivores derive certain advantages from living in groups that have no relevance to a nonhuman primate society. When several lions and hyenas hunt together, they are at least twice as successful in capturing animals as when they pursue prey alone. Both of these predators also increase their food resources by hunting in groups. A solitary lion hesitates to tangle with a buffalo, but a group may attack it. The fact that early hominids would have been able to capture and kill more and larger prey in a cooperative effort than when hunting alone was no doubt a potent force shaping the whole structure of their society. Hunting the occasional small animal neither necessitates a group effort nor confers much advantage by its practice, the yield being small yet still having to be shared, and hominids who subsisted on such prey may well have been divided into nuclear families—one man, one woman, and their offspring—at least for part of the time. In fact, jackals, foxes, and some other carnivores have such a social system. But to hunt large prey probably required at least two to five able men, which in turn indicated a group size of up to twenty or more, including women, children, and those adult males who were unable to hunt well. For instance, Ralph Solecki found a Neanderthal man in the Shanidar Cave of Iraq whose right shoulder and upper arm had been underdeveloped since birth and whose left eye was missing. Yet he survived with the help of his group until at the age of about forty years he died in a rock fall. In addition to providing life insurance, group life benefitted hominids in other ways. The more members a group contains, the more likely these will win in a competitive situation. One hyena fears a lion but many hyenas chase a lion off its kill. By traveling in groups, *Australopithecus* increased its chances of being able to chase predators from a kill or simply from its path and defend its meat supply against lions, hyenas, and others.

A hominid group that splits and reunites at irregular intervals and that also maintains a division of labor based on sex will tend to organize itself around small family units. The size and composition of the unit will depend on ecological necessities, personal preferences, and familial relationships. The genetic basis of social life has been overemphasized in the past as scientists searched for universals in human behavior. Just as marriage today remains largely an economic transaction, so the social unit in the past was dictated to a great extent by environmental pressures of making a living. Man has been and still is highly adaptable in his social system, but it is now imperative to find out the limits to this plasticity. Deep personal bonds probably developed among members of hominid family units, just as they do among many carnivore species, and these resulted in lasting relationships within a large group. If, as was most likely the case, copulation was used to reinforce social bonds between male and female, particularly after a separation, then it would seem unlikely that a male had close ties with more than two or three females for logistic reasons alone. The females of all mammalian species except man go through brief periods of estrus during which they are sexually receptive. The loss of estrus and continuous receptivity in humans was probably related to the fact that copulation also functioned as a form of social contact not related to reproduction *per se*.

In trying to deduce what kind of land tenure system was practiced by *Australopithecus*, today's hunters and gatherers and social carnivores provide a spectrum of possibilities. The Ona of Tierra del Fuego are said to have had territories that they defended against intruders. The Mbuti pygmies also have well-defined territories, but the Australian Aborigines do not. Many peoples, such as the Bushmen, Central Eskimo, and Dogrib Indians, change their hunting areas seasonally. Turning to social carnivores, we note a similar variability. There is the territorial lion and nomadic hunting dog. The hyena may be territorial during some periods of the year but not during others and it may also leave its home to commute to distant prey concentrations. The early hominids obviously had a choice of systems open to them, and I believe that they used them all, depending on local circumstances. Early man may have had the proclivity to be territorial, but under certain economic and social pressures he readily accepted alternatives.

On the basis of what is known about some nonhuman primates and social carnivores, hominid groups were relatively closed, strangers usually not being welcome. The outcome of meetings between groups probably depended on the nature of previous interactions, including possible familial ties, but, on the whole, I suspect that contacts were often not amicable, and occasionally degenerated into fights. The fossil record includes ample evidence that hominids sometimes died violently, and *Homo erectus* in China was apparently a cannibal. *A. africanus* may have been intolerant of *A. robustus,* and vice versa, if the reactions of lions and leopards to each other provide valid clues. It is probably not coincidental that as one line of hominids evolved into man the other died out. Possibly *A. robustus* could not compete against its aggressive and well-armed relative. This does not imply that all *A. robustus* were directly annihilated but that as *A. africanus* and its successors increased in number and held sway over more and more terrain, the other species managed to survive mainly in isolated marginal habitats, where over the millennia it quietly retreated into oblivion.

While there is no question that man is an aggressive species, this trait should not be uncritically correlated with a hunting way of life. Hunting dogs are gentle and amiable whereas lions are volatile; rhesus macaque are irascible whereas langur monkeys tend to be restrained in their social contacts. Levels of aggressiveness can obviously not be correlated with a carnivorous or vegetarian subsistence. Aggression within hominid groups was probably muted, for food had to be shared and mates were for the most part tied to specific individuals by social bonds. Nor was a drive for power and leadership necessarily cause for strife. In hunting groups, whether man or carnivore, the individual or individuals who on the basis of age and experience are most adept at a particular task assume leadership during that activity. But overt aggression may have been prominent when repelling other groups at territorial boundaries. Instead of avoiding contact, hominids might purposely have indulged in vocal and physical jousts with other groups to show their strength or simply to break the monotony of life, behavior also known in other primates from monkeys to modern man. In addition, aggression was essential when dealing with competitors, including other species of hominids and other predators. The combination of aggressiveness and the unemotional acceptance of killing as a result of a hunting way of life lies at the root of one of man's problems today.

While aggression is a prominent trait of man, another trait mitigates its effect somewhat, as John Pfeiffer noted:

Man has unique capacities for cooperation as well as conflict, one reason why inference from the behavior of other species may be dangerous. Non-human primates may be highly organized, but the organization is in the main internal, within the troop; social systems are generally closed, all matings taking place among troop members. Their foreign affairs, however, are rather less well ordered than their domestic affairs. Troops tend to ignore one another, or fight. Man alone attempts to form organizations of organizations, tribal unions, and confederations.

However, such an extensive network of social relations may to a large extent be based on language, which man did not have in the early stages of his development, for increased communication, essentially of ideas, tends to make a society more open.

Interactions within an early hominid group were probably quite peaceful, regulated by grunts, screeches, and other vocalizations as well as by various gestures and postures, just as is the case in other mammal societies. A rigid rank order did not exist within a group, although males, because of their superior strength and perhaps size, were dominant over females. Males asserted their rank by strutting, the hair on their shoulders and nape erect, in the manner of apes today, and they threatened an opponent by drawing back their lips to expose the teeth, by staring, and perhaps by waving a stick or other object over their heads. They probably used their penises as a threat symbol too, for this structure is not only conspicuously large in man but is also made prominent by his upright posture, as pointed out by R. Guthrie. Some monkeys use penile presentation as threat, having in addition brilliantly colored genitals, and some

New Guinea tribesmen wear long penis sheaths to enhance the effectiveness of the display. A threatened hominid would then look aside, lower his head, or even crouch, all gestures of submission among primates.

Probably *Australopithecus* existed wholly in a biological dimension at first, living and dying as natural forces dictated. It had, of course, a culture in which each individual learned from his elders how to hunt, how to select pebbles and make tools from them, what to fear, and the many other important and trivial bits of information that enable a social creature to exist as an integrated member of the group. While some tasks, such as the manufacture of tools, were quite complex, all could be learned by observing an elder at work. A deep mental chasm separated the earliest hominids from later ones, for these early hominids probably had no self-awareness and were unable to use learned symbols to communicate abstract ideas. Although tool use and other kinds of behavior initiated a basic change in the hominids' life, removing them somewhat from the constraints of the environment, freeing them to evolve through social learning, they still could not anticipate the future or discourse about matters contrary to fact. As Teilhard de Chardin noted: "The animal knows, of course, but certainly it does not know that it knows."

Self-awareness, so basic to our human existence, is virtually absent from the rest of the animal kingdom. On several occasions I watched lions approach a waterhole to drink. As their muzzles came near the water, they apparently saw their reflection staring at them. They retreated, hissing, as if they had met a stranger. Chimpanzees, however, can be taught the rudiments of self-awareness. G. Gallop reported that chimpanzees whose faces had been marked with a spot of red dye and who were then exposed to their images in mirrors seemed to be able to learn to recognize their own reflection. Only through self-awareness was man able to make the world intelligible to himself. As Theodosius Dobzhansky wrote in his book *Mankind Evolving:*

> Through self-awareness man attained the status of a person in the existential sense: he became conscious of himself and his environment. He is able to form mental images of things and situations which do not yet exist but which may be found, brought about, or constructed by his efforts. Man can create in his imagination worlds different from the actual one and can visualize himself in these imaginary worlds . . . The adaptive value of forethought or foresight is too evident to need demonstration. It has raised man to the status of the lord of creation.

Self-awareness is to a considerable extent related to language. Just when, how, and why language emerged is one of the most fascinating mysteries in evolution. *Australopithecus* did not need language. Gestures were sufficient to coordinate hunts, observational learning adequate for passing on traditions of tool making. Early hominids naturally vocalized, but their sounds conveyed primarily emotional states. A particular incident, such as the sight of a stalking predator, may elicit a particular intensity of response, with the result that the rest of the group learns to associate the two. The gap between such communication and the ability to converse by means of symbols is enormous. Chimpanzees seem to be able to form rudimentary symbolic conceptions as the well-known experiment by the Gardners has shown. Washoe, a young female chimpanzee, was taught hand signals based on human sign language, and after considerable practice she was able to distinguish the names of different objects. For instance, she readily transferred the proper sign for "dog" to pictures of dogs and to hearing dogs bark, and she combined signs, such as "sweet" and "drink" to signify soda pop. However, her sentences consisted simply of several discrete signals without structure. Man, however, possesses not only an inborn capacity that enables him to learn structured language but also the ability to communicate abstractions by vocal means. The emotional utterances of animals are mediated by a phylogenetically ancient part of the brain, the limbic area, whereas language is under intellectual control in the cortex. The two systems evolved quite independently. L. Carini noted in the journal *Current Anthropology:* "The thinking of which a human being is capable differs qualitatively, not just quantitatively, from the thinking of other animals. Even if the chimpanzee were taught a few words, he would never disclose his view of the world to us, because he would be totally restricted to the meanings we give him. Without metaphor, he cannot turn a phrase to describe a new experience."

The genesis of language is obscure, and a number of linguists believe it did not originate for purposes of communicating. Such a purpose would in itself require a language in order that the idea be conceived and conveyed to others. Carini speculated that the propensity of babies to babble and for the mother to babble back resulted in specific sounds becoming associated with specific actions and objects. Be that as it may, once symbols began to be used for communication in the daily life of a hominid, the advantages to the group were obvious. A new means of interpreting the world opened up. The members could plan for the future. Instead of moving together, the group could split up and agree to meet at a certain time and place. They could retain the past, accumulating the social experience of generations. Language permitted members of the group to interact with a finesse and complexity unknown to other animals; it dampened and subordinated violent emotions, replacing these to some extent with compromises based on mutual agreement.

It is not known when man reached this momentous plateau of his existence. The development of language was most likely associated intimately with the growth of the brain. An ape has an inborn potential for symbolism that is

286 · *Golden Shadows, Flying Hooves*

neither needed nor developed in free-living animals. The *Australopithecus* brain, too, must have harbored an unrealized potential that was not drawn upon during several million years of tool making and cooperative hunting. But certainly at some stage the social life and means of subsistence of *Australopithecus* encouraged, so to speak, the mind to play at the fringes of its possibilities. Finally the rudiments of language gave this creature a fuller awareness of itself and its environment. With an increased sensory input, evolution favored the development of more neural connections in the neocortex, which in turn enabled the brain to assimilate more information, a mechanism that became mutually reinforcing. If this was so, language must have evolved during the transition from *Australopithecus* to *Homo erectus*. The early hominids had a tool-making culture for an incredibly long period without changing their obviously successful pattern. I wonder if environmental forces triggered the fundamental change to self-awareness and language or if it was generated from within the society itself. Even after man became man, the rate of cultural evolution, as exemplified by tools, continued at a surprisingly slow rate. Man was conservative for most of his history. Within his grasp he had the awesome power to transform his habits within a generation, rather than blindly waiting for the slow changes brought about by natural selection, yet he plodded down the centuries, putting his dreams into practice with almost unbearable deliberation. But on this firm base rests our humanity in all its splendor and with all its weaknesses.

A basic problem is that man does not yet understand the animal within himself. As Robert Ardrey wrote in his book *The Social Contract*:

> The new brain speaks in a language that the old brain does not understand . . . Through moods and emotions the old brain can communicate with the new. But only with the greatest difficulty can we talk back, for it is precisely the

equivalent of talking to animals . . . For those who persist in denying the evolutionary influences of human behavior there is truly little hope. The animal within us, whose existence is denied, whose ways are ignored, or whose presence if suspected is secretely hated or feared, remains a wild animal. But the animal who is accepted, whose ways become known to us, to whom we speak in his language rather than ours, may become a tame animal.

The ability to hold a dialogue with ourselves and with others will someday enable us to discover fully and then come to terms with the persistent savage that lurks in our depths.

The Serengeti years taught me many things, but above all they made me aware of man's uniqueness. It makes me feel more distinctly human to realize that both the frailty of the ape and the power of the carnivore shaped my mind and body. This ambivalent past has been our source of strength and creative energy. Now, in our unheeding rush to conquer our environment, we are in danger of destroying the roots of our nature, the wilderness that saw the whole of our evolutionary history. Perhaps as we transcend our past, adapting to new patterns of culture and becoming less human by today's standards, the wilderness will become superfluous. But for the present the salvation of our humanity lies in the spirit of such areas as the Serengeti, where man can renew his ancient ties and ponder his uncertain destiny.